SACRED SUMMITS

SACRED SUMMITS

KANGCHENJUNGA, THE CARSTENSZ PYRAMID AND GAURI SANKAR

PETER BOARDMAN

Vertebrate Publishing, Sheffield
www.v-publishing.co.uk

SACRED SUMMITS

Peter Boardman

 Vertebrate Publishing
Omega Court, 352 Cemetery Road, Sheffield S11 8FT, United Kingdom
www.v-publishing.co.uk

First published in Great Britain in 1982 by Hodder and Stoughton (London).
This edition first published in 2021 by Vertebrate Publishing.

This book is a work of non-fiction based on the life, experiences and recollections of Peter Boardman. In some limited cases the names of people, places, dates and sequences or the detail of events have been changed solely to protect the privacy of others.

A CIP catalogue record for this book is available from the British Library.

ISBN 978-1-83981-060-2 (Paperback)
ISBN 978-1-906148-77-5 (Ebook)

10 9 8 7 6 5 4 3 2 1

Cover design and production by Rosie Edwards, Vertebrate Publishing.
www.v-publishing.co.uk

Vertebrate Publishing is committed to printing on paper from sustainable sources.

Printed and bound in Great Britain by Clays Ltd, Elcograf S.p.A.

CONTENTS

FOREWORD: A GREAT PARTNERSHIP

by Chris Bonington

It was 15 May 1982 at Advance Base on the north side of Everest. It's a bleak place. The tents were pitched on a moraine, the debris of an expedition in its end stage scattered over the rocks. Pete and Joe fussed around with final preparations, packing their rucksacks and putting in a few last-minute luxuries. Then suddenly they were ready, crampons on, rope tied, set to go. I think we were all trying to underplay the moment.

'See you in a few days.'

'We'll call you tonight at six.'

They set off, plodding up the ice slope beyond the camp through flurries of wind-driven snow. Two days later, in the fading light of a cold dusk, Adrian Gordon and I were watching their progress high on the North East Ridge through our telescope. Two tiny figures on the crest outlined against the golden sky of the late evening, moving painfully slowly, one at a time. Was it because of the difficulty or the extreme altitude, for they must have been at approximately, 27,000 feet (8,230 metres)?

Gradually they disappeared from sight behind the jagged tooth of the Second Pinnacle. They never appeared again, although Peter's body was discovered by members of a Russian/Japanese expedition in the spring of 1992, just beyond where we had last seen them. It was as if he had lain down in the snow, gone to sleep and never woken. We shall probably never know just what happened in those days around 17 May, but in that final push to complete the unclimbed section of the North East Ridge of Everest, we lost two very special friends and a unique climbing partnership whose breadth of talent went far beyond mountaineering. Their ability as writers is amply demonstrated in their books.

My initial encounter with Peter was in 1975 when I was recruiting for the expedition to the South West Face of Everest. I was impressed by his maturity at the age of twenty-three, yet this was combined with a real sense of fun and a touch of 'the little boy lost' manner, which he could use with devastating effect to get his own way. In addition, he was both physically and intellectually talented. He was a very strong natural climber and behind that diffident, easy-going manner had a personal drive and unwavering sense of purpose. He also had a love of the mountains and the ability to express it in writing. He was the youngest member of the Everest team and went to the top with our Sherpa sirdar, Pertemba, making the second complete ascent of the previously unclimbed South West Face.

As National Officer of the BMC, he proved a diplomat and a good committee man. After Dougal Haston's death in an avalanche in Switzerland, he took over Dougal's International School of Mountaineering in Leysin. He went on to climb the sheer West Face of Changabang with Joe Tasker, which was the start of their climbing partnership. It was a remarkable achievement, in stark contrast to the huge expedition we had had on Everest. On Changabang there had just been Pete and Joe. They had planned to climb it alpine style, bivouacking in hammocks on the face, but it had been too cold, too great a strain at altitude, and they had resorted to siege tactics. Yet even this demanded huge reserves of determination and endurance. The climb, in 1976, was probably technically the hardest that had been completed in the Himalaya at that time, and Pete describes their struggles in his first book, *The Shining Mountain*, which won the John Llewelyn Rhys Prize in 1979.

Pete packed a wealth of varied climbing into the next few years. In 1978 both he and Joe joined me on K2. We attempted the West Ridge but abandoned it comparatively low down after Nick Estcourt was killed in an avalanche. In early 1979 Pete reached the summit of the Carstensz Pyramid, in New Guinea, with his future wife, Hilary, just before going to Kangchenjunga (the world's third-highest mountain) with Joe, and Doug Scott and Georges Bettembourg. That same autumn he led another comparatively small team on a very bold ascent of the South Summit of Gauri Sankar.

The following year he returned to K2 with Joe, Doug and Dick Renshaw. They first attempted the West Ridge, the route that we had tried in 1978, but abandoned this a couple of hundred metres higher than our previous high point. Doug Scott returned home but the other three made two very determined assaults on the Abruzzi Spur, getting to within 600 metres of the summit before being avalanched off on their first effort, and beaten by bad weather on a subsequent foray. Two years later Pete and Joe, with Alan Rouse, joined me on Kongur, at the time the third-highest unclimbed peak in the world. It proved a long-drawn-out, exacting expedition.

Joe Tasker was very different to Peter, both in appearance and personality. This perhaps contributed to the strength of their partnership. While Pete appeared to be easy going and relaxed, Joe was very much more intense, even abrasive. He came from a large Roman Catholic family on Teesside and went to a seminary at the age of 13 to train for the priesthood, but at the age of 18 he had begun to have serious doubts about his vocation and went to study sociology at Manchester University. Inevitably, his period at the seminary left its mark. Joe had a built-in reserve that was difficult to penetrate but, at the same time, he had an analytical, questioning mind. He rarely accepted an easy answer and kept going at a point until satisfied that it had been answered in full.

Their climbing relationship had a jokey yet competitive tension in which neither of them wished to be the first to admit weakness or to suggest retreat. It was a trait that not only contributed to their drive but could also cause them to push themselves to the limit.

Joe had served an impressive alpine apprenticeship in the early seventies when, with Dick Renshaw, they worked through some of the hardest climbs in the Alps, both in summer and winter. These included the first British ascent (one of the very few ever ascents) of the formidable and very remote East Face of the Grandes Jorasses. In addition they made the first British winter ascent of the North Wall of the Eiger. With Renshaw he went on to climb, in alpine style, the South Ridge of Dunagiri. It was a bold ascent by any standards, outstandingly so for a first Himalayan expedition. Dick was badly frostbitten and this led to Joe inviting Pete to join him on Changabang the start of their climbing partnership.

On our K2 expedition in 1978, I had barely had the chance to get to know Joe well, but I remember bring exasperated by his constant questioning of decisions, particularly while we were organising the expedition. At the time I felt he was a real barrack-room lawyer but, on reflection, realised that he probably found my approach equally exasperating. We climbed together throughout the 1981 Kongur expedition and I came to know him much better, to find that under that tough outer shell there was a very warm heart. Prior to that, in the winter of 1980–81, he went to Everest with a strong British expedition to attempt the West Ridge. He told the story in his first book, *Everest the Cruel Way*.

Our 1982 expedition to Everest's North East Ridge was a huge challenge but our team was one of the happiest and most closely united of any trip I have been on. There were only six in the party and just four of us, Joe, Pete, Dick Renshaw and I, were planning to tackle the route. Charlie Clarke and Adrian Gordon were there in support going no further than Advance Base. However, there was a sense of shared values, affection and respect, that grew stronger through adversity, as we came to realise just how vast was the undertaking our small team was committed to.

It remained through those harsh anxious days of growing awareness of disaster, after Pete and Joe went out of sight behind the Second Pinnacle, to our final acceptance that there was no longer any hope.

Yet when Pete and Joe set out for that final push on 17 May I had every confidence that they would cross the Pinnacles and reach the upper part of the North Ridge of Everest, even if they were unable to continue to the top. Their deaths, quite apart from the deep feeling of bereavement at the loss of good friends, also give that sense of frustration because they still had so much to offer in their development, both in mountaineering and creative terms.

Chris Bonington
Caldbeck
September 1994

THE MOST-SACRED MOUNTAIN

Space, and the twelve clean winds of heaven
And this sharp exultation, like a cry, after the slow six thousand
      feet of climbing!
This is Tai Shan, the beautiful, the most holy.

Below my feet the foot-hills nestle, brown with flecks of green;
      and lower down the flat brown plain, the floor of earth,
      stretches away to blue infinity.
Beside me in this airy space the temple roofs cut their slow
      curves
      against the sky,
And one black bird circles above the void.

Space, and the twelve clean winds are here;
And with them broods eternity – a swift, white peace, a presence
      manifest.

But I shall go down from this airy space, this swift white peace,
      this stinging exultation;
And time will close about me, and my soul stir to the rhythm
      of the daily round.
Yet, having known, life will not press so close, and always I
      shall feel time ravel thin about me;
For once I stood
In the white windy presence of eternity.

Eunice Tietjens

PART 1

SNOW MOUNTAINS OF NEW GUINEA

1   SACRED SUMMITS

30 November–5 December 1978

It was the last day of November. It was a quiet uncluttered day, and over ten years since I had last stood on this mountain. Then I saw only an exciting, jagged blur of sweeping snow and rock shimmering in summer heat, and dark hazy valleys twisting away below and beyond. Now I saw with different eyes, with a sense of intimacy, almost possession.Each mountain I could see from the Aiguille de Tour held a different adventure shared with a different friend. Memories, trivial and moving, surged inside me. Time had not diminished them. I saw tiny figures of the past picking slowly across the snow and heard their voices. Among those mountains I had found a kingdom that had seemed infinite. Although a newcomer, I had felt apart from the tourists. I was one of the climbers who lived in the woods. First I had climbed urgently, to escape, rather than to search for something that I loved – the absorbed, animal struggle up the crack at the top of the Aiguille de Purtscheller when I was seventeen, the storm on Mont Blanc, when the snow covered our tracks, the lightning shocks on the Gervasutti Pillar, dawn on the Frendo Spur, and the heights of freedom and happiness, emerging into the evening above the precipices of the Dru. And more gentle, recent memories of just a few months before, a walk across the Trient Glacier with my mother and father, and a traverse with Hilary of the Aiguilles d'Orées, the needles of gold.

Different memories of early mad rushes to fill up my postcards home with lists of routes I had climbed, to tick off the hardest routes as if they were a shopping list, and of later calm, when

I discovered the long ridges and filled out the landscape within my mind, seeing these mountains from all sides, in all weathers, and understanding them.

Many people know these mountains – some grow to love them, others try to rape them.

It was cold, and humanity huddled in their oases – dark smudges below the thrusting white snows of winter's defence. The ski season had not yet started and the new, packaged human colonies above the snow line had not yet awakened. Man the exploiter and nature for some moments stood apart.

In the east a distant spire rose from a crown of rock. The Matterhorn. Eight years earlier, and again three months ago, I had stood on its summit. Little more than a century ago, the natives of its surrounding valleys felt an invisible cordon drawn around it. To them the Matterhorn was not only the highest mountain in the Alps, but in the world. They spoke of a ruined city on its summit wherein spirits dwelt; and if you laughed, they gravely shook their heads. To them the mountains were to be feared and suspected as haunts of monsters, wizards and crabbed goblins – and the devil. Something had gone wrong. In earlier times the Matterhorn, the Alps and the trees, rocks and springs of Europe were loved and respected as sacred places. Man had felt his links with them. But then he had broken with this heritage and had buried this delicate magic of life.

I thought of another mountain with a Matterhorn shape, thousands of miles away in the Himalayas. 'Menlungtse, Menlungtse looks like that, I must look at the photographs.' The wind veered beneath the cold dark blue sky and I turned my back. There were the tiny rock spires above Leysin, where I lived. And the sun swung down to the west, picking out the deep line of my tracks etched across the glacier below. Shadows grew on the mountain and a great silence was descending too. I knew the mountain, earth set upon earth, would remain silent, long after I had stopped. For some moments I listened, with a still open soul, until I had to turn from a surging feeling of love, before it overwhelmed me. Dear old planet, stay awhile, wait for me. Now I had to go down also.

Four days later she sat next to me in the car. A quick ready shy smile behind a cupped hand and an uncertain, beautiful voice – and we were going on an adventure together! We wound through the ground-hugging fog of the Jura, the headlights beaming a moving wall of white.

We curled out of the mist, and on to the plains of France. The car winged like a bird through cold night air past snow-covered fields, following the arrow of the autoroute to Paris. Hilary's face was softened by the darkness and she was wrapped in her own silence.

The headlong rush of the car brought plans juggling in my head. Two expeditions to the Himalayas were projected for the coming year. In the spring there would be Kangchenjunga – the arrangements had been made with a casual air in a pub a month before. To attempt this, the third-highest mountain in the world, four of us would leave for Nepal in March. Then, in the autumn, I would return again to the Himalayas to attempt Gauri Sankar, the finest unclimbed mountain in the world. And in between these highlights, I would have to make some money. Peaks in Nepal have to be booked many months before you can approach and attempt them, and my life was booked up in advance. I was on a conveyor belt, carrying me from one booked peak to another. In my mind I tried to stem the rush of these pre-determined commitments and to think clearly, but stopped at the question 'Why on earth should I fling myself into all this? What was the rush?' I could not answer. A tiny, not-yet-drowned part of me stood helplessly as the flotsam crashed past, squeaking, 'I'd rather not,' and 'If you don't mind,' and 'Help!' like Alice wallowing about in the pool of her own tears.

The Snow Mountains of New Guinea, the mountains of the Stone Age, however, could not be booked and that was where Hilary and I were going now. Not only were we uncertain about reaching their summits but also uncertain that we would even reach their feet.

In Paris, our friend Marie, a painter, said: 'Mountain climbing, brutal dangerous mountain climbing, is too extreme for me to express. But exploration I can understand. You go not for the people, not for the mountains, but for them together. Climbers, they are lucky in that they have mountains to justify journeys across continents.'

Projects, hopes and resolutions jostled in my brain, clamouring for attention. I could not wander from day to day. I had to plan. The Victorian explorer Tom Longstaff always warned his protégés: 'Once a man has found the road, he can never keep away for long.' The germ of travel was working inside me like a relapsing fever.

2 TROUBLED PARADISE

6–22 December 1978

'We saw very high mountains white with snow in many places which certainly is strange for mountains so near the equator.' So wrote Jan Carstensz, the Dutch navigator, in 1623 as he sailed on the Arafura Sea, between New Guinea and Australia. Snow mountains in New Guinea? Nobody believed him when he returned to Holland. Centuries later the mysteries of these mountains are still being unravelled. At 16,020 feet (4,883 metres), the highest peak in South East Asia and the highest point in the range has been named after him, the Carstensz Pyramid.

At some time during their careers, all great explorers are monomaniacs – imagination seized, they identify with a mountain, a pole, a blank on the map, then gather will and energy together to fling themselves in effort after effort towards it. The history of exploration is punctuated with the intensity of such relationships: Scott and the South Pole, Mallory and Everest, Shipton and Tilman and Nanda Devi, Bauer and Kangchenjunga, Herzog and Annapurna. The Snow Mountains of New Guinea have obsessed two great explorers – A.F.R. Wollaston, who tried to reach the mountains from the south early this century, and the devoted and energetic New Zealander Philip Temple, who, in 1961, became the first explorer to approach from the north. Both were fascinated by the unique isolation of these mountains.

However, even in the late 1970s, very little was known about the Snow Mountains in the mountaineering world. The allure that had attracted Wollaston and Temple was still there. These mountains were far away from the main mountaineering regions, they were difficult of access, usually covered in cloud, and rose from a strange uninhabited plateau surrounded by jungle, swamp and tribes of primitive peoples still living in the Stone Age. In the autumn of 1976, these isolated mountains had slowly begun to take hold of my imagination.

Whilst Joe Tasker and I were climbing the West Wall of Changabang in the Himalayas that autumn, we often talked, during the forty days of cold struggle it took to climb the mountain, about how it would be so much more pleasant to go to a mountain range in the tropics. We longed for the excitement of travel in an unknown land as a change from the lonely black and white struggle of extreme climbing. But it would have to be the right place, with the right person. Half in fun, we made a pact to find two young ladies and go to New Guinea together.

I was lucky, I found the other half of my expedition very quickly. The first public slide-show I gave about Changabang was at Belper High School. The lecture was organised by Hilary Collins, who ran the school's Outdoor Activities Department. We had met before in 1974, when she attended a course on which I was an instructor at Glenmore Lodge in the Cairngorms. Not long after the lecture we went rock climbing together for the first time, at the Tors in New Mills in Derbyshire. I fell off, clutching a large flake of rock that had come away with my weight. Hilary managed to stop me with the rope after I had fallen thirty feet – a good achievement considering she was only two thirds my weight, and I had nearly hit the ground. It boded well for our relationship. Over the New Year of 1976–77 we went climbing together again in Torridon in North West Scotland. All the girls interested in mountaineering I had met previously seemed either aggressively fanatical, or obscenely healthy, noisy, strong, rosy-cheeked types, inseparable from their anoraks and bobble caps. Hilary was different, and we shared a passion for mountains rather than climbing for competition or health. She had a common-sense, hard working practicality that I lacked. We were compatible. She was talking about going on a trip to the Himalayas when I suggested she came to New

Guinea with me. She agreed. Then she started a new job, teaching geography and biology at a private school in Switzerland.

On 9 January 1977, I began writing a lot of letters – to Papua New Guinea, Australia, Indonesia, Hong Kong, America, West Germany and Holland, with the intention of following up all leads and of piecing together, like a jigsaw, a picture of the Snow Mountains of New Guinea. I devoured all expedition reports and all the books I could find on the area: *Pygmies and Papuans* by A.F.R. Wollaston, *Nawok!* by Philip Temple, *I Come From the Stone Age* by Heinrich Harrer and *Equatorial Glaciers of New Guinea* by Melbourne University. I also read many evangelical books by American Fundamentalist Protestant missionaries, describing their work in the highlands around the mountain. Unfortunately, the most comprehensive books were written in Dutch, including the tantalising *To the Eternal Snow of the Tropical Netherlands* by Dr A.H. Colijn. This book described the 1936 Dutch expedition to the mountains and had very useful aerial photographs. All this research was immensely satisfying. New Guinea was completely outside my previous expedition experience, and every piece of information I gleaned and stored was, for me, a little inroad into a dark unknown.

On 17 January, Dougal Haston, with whom I had climbed on Everest, was killed in an avalanche whilst skiing above the village of Leysin in Switzerland. The mountaineering politics I was involved in at the time, in my work for the British Mountaineering Council, suddenly seemed petty when I heard the news. I went to Dougal's funeral. By coincidence, the school where Hilary was working was in the next valley, and she was able to meet me at the station in Leysin. The service, the coffin, the grave, the blue sky, deep snow and the mountains, and my walk away, hand in hand with Hilary beneath the tall trees, all combined to make one of the saddest, most moving days of my life. I had come as a pilgrim, to reaffirm a faith in extreme mountaineering, but felt only doubt. Many people said that Dougal had been doomed — that he was an Ahab after a White Whale, that his life had a restless, fanatic pace, and that he had been bound, sooner or later, to over-reach himself. To me he had seemed indestructible, and his death was a sudden shock. Nevertheless, our New Guinea plans were a comfort, for they were a step off the conveyor belt of a career of a professional high-altitude mountain gladiator, and a step towards a wider emotional development.

At Easter we met Jack Baines, the leader of RAF Valley Mountain Rescue team in North Wales. Jack had been to the Snow Mountains in 1972. An effusive talker, he was positively garrulous about New Guinea. It had been the greatest experience of his life. He brought seventeen hours of tape recordings and, as he bubbled a commentary, his enthusiasm caught us and we absorbed his every word like blotting paper. Jack kindled in us a fire of enthusiasm for the Snow Mountains that was to burn steadily for the many frustrating months that were to pass before we finally saw them. We planned our departure for July 1977 and, as time passed, our New Guinea file became thicker. The mountains were appearing in my dreams. However, I would never really be able to believe in their existence until I saw them for myself.

New Guinea is divided into two halves – Irian Jaya and Papua New Guinea – by the 141° line of longitude. The highest mountains, and the only mountains with glaciers, lie in the western half, Irian Jaya, which used to be a Dutch colony but is now controlled by Indonesia. The whole of the area is under military control and previous expeditions advised that we would have to keep a very low profile and travel as tourists, rather than as an 'official' mountaineering expedition. I wrote to the British Embassy in Jakarta asking about access to Irian, and within a few days the whole situation was taken out of my hands. One of the staff at the Embassy, coincidentally, was organising an eleven-man joint Indonesian-British expedition to the mountains at the same time, and Hilary and I were embraced into their ranks. The Deputy Chief of the Armed Forces of Indonesia had agreed to be the expedition's patron. Since most of the positions of power in Indonesia are held by army officers, it seemed that all our problems were solved.

On 6 June, however, our expedition was cancelled. Apparently there had been some trouble in Irian Java, and outsiders were not welcome. A proposed visit by the American Ambassador to the copper mine south of the mountains had been cancelled. Most of the missionaries in the interior had been flown out.

Quickly we changed our plans and spent a month climbing in Kenya and Tanzania, reaching the summits of Mount Kenya and Kilimanjaro. This, however, was mere 'tropical training', compared to our determination to go to the Snow Mountains of New Guinea. We planned another attempt to reach the area during Hilary's Christmas holidays in December 1978. There is no settled weather season in Irian, but we hoped that this choice of date would give time for political problems to calm down. For seventeen months we traced and contacted people for first, second and third-hand reports of what was happening in Irian Jaya, and kept our eyes on the papers. Reports were conflicting. While the Indonesian government said its troops in West Irian were merely settling tribal disputes 'over trifling matters like dowries, cattle and women,' the Free Papua Movement was claiming the Indonesian Air Force had napalmed the jungle villages which gave the guerrillas their chief support. It did not help us that the Carstensz Pyramid was so near the Freeport copper mine at Ertsberg, a prime target for guerilla attack. We were told it had had its pipeline blown up in 1977 and a helicopter shot down.

By November 1978, however, the trouble in the Carstensz region was thought to be largely over and we were encouragingly reassured that in Indonesia all things are possible, regardless of what officials say in the first place. So Hilary and I decided to go to Jakarta and try to sort things out from there. But as we arrived, at the first stage of our journey, Charlie and Ruth Clarke's house in Islington (on 6 December), we were no more certain that we would ever reach the Snow Mountains than we had been when the idea first germinated, two years before.

The Clarkes' home has one of those rare generous atmospheres that allow you to walk in, struggle past the dog, cats, toys, children and put the kettle on to make a cup of tea. Ruth's dramatic manner and Charlie's air of detached nonchalance provide hours of entertainment – they could play themselves on television. When

Charlie asked Ruth's father for permission to marry her, he was told: 'Good God, you must need a psychiatrist,' which was fortunate because she is one – and he does.

Their house has become, over the last few years, a climbers' London Base Camp. Climbers' wives, girlfriends and widows find a comforting haven there, professional freelance climbers use it as their London office, and expeditions use it as their springboard – the last night before Heathrow, and on their return for the first bed and bath they've seen in weeks.

Chris Bonington and his road manager were there, in London on a lecture tour. I got out some photographs and unfolded the large Australian 'Operational Navigation Chart 1:1,000,000 1968', on the kitchen table. I described our journey to them all.

'From Jakarta we'll fly to this island here, called Biak, and from there to Nabire on the coast of the mainland. Then, we'll charter a light plane to Ilaga, just five days north of the mountains, and walk in. See these large white spaces, "Relief data incomplete". It's very difficult to map the place from the air, because it's always so cloudy.'

'Blank on the map, eh?'

'Where are these gorillas?'

'Ooh look, they wear those things on their dicks.'

'I'm worried about you two, I hope you'll be all right by yourselves.'

The telephone rang. It was Bernard Domenech from Marseilles. He and another French climber, Jean Fabre, were also going to try to reach the Snow Mountains. We had heard about each other's plans during the summer, and had met in Chamonix. Now we exchanged last-minute details. We had agreed not to travel together, since a group of four would attract more attention and imperil our chances. However, we hoped to see each other in the hills.

'We're leaving next week. See you somewhere perhaps,' he said.

Hilary and I spent our last day hunting through London shops for mosquito nets and silica gel bags to keep our cameras dry. Her hands moved quickly and intelligently as she squeezed vast piles of equipment into our rucksacks, after carefully hiding our ropes and climbing hardware at the bottom – we were to travel as tourists.

'Just think – that biscuit you're eating'll come out in Indonesia,' Ruth said.

'Or over Bangkok,' said Charlie.

On 8 December we left Heathrow for Frankfurt – the first leg of our journey to Jakarta, the capital of Indonesia. Frankfurt was gripped by a fierce winter storm and we were delayed there for six hours whilst ice was cleared from the runway. Free drinks were provided and a boozing team developed, mostly comprising Welsh rugby players who started singing songs. When at last we settled back into the DC10, night had fallen and most of the rugby players fell asleep. Hilary and I sat on the port side. As we took off there was a loud bang and flash from the engine on the wing next to us. A few minutes later we heard the deep growl of the captain's voice:

'Ladies and gentlemen, the port engine has just blown up. We shall go up to 20,000 feet, eject all our fuel and return to Frankfurt.'

The careful delivery in a foreign accent gave the message an extra impact of uncertainty. There were a few nervous titters from the passengers.

'How many more engines are there?' I whispered.

'Two, I think.'

'These things don't glide, do they?'

We saw the fuel being ejected as the wing lights flashed. Then the long descent began. It was difficult to believe that this brightly lit tube containing hundreds of people was not on the ground, but plunging earthwards through the night. I felt my pulse rate. It was soaring. I glanced at a few passengers to see if they were as nervous as I was. Two rugby players were fast asleep. Hilary and I put our boots on and stuffed our pockets with money, cameras and passports.

The plane bumped down, and as we landed fire engines and ambulances raced towards us from all directions and strung out behind in a line of moving, flashing lights.

'He can't just reverse two engines or it'll spin round.'

At last, at the end of the runway, we stopped. Everyone started talking at once. The two rugby players behind us yawned and stretched.

11

'Where are we?' one of them asked.

'Frankfurt.'

As we stepped out of the plane we heard the pilot confess to someone: 'When the engine exploded, I did not know whether to try to stop or to keep on going and try to take off. We just got up.'

So ended the second of the twenty-six take-offs that were to carry us to Irian Jaya and back. It was an unnerving beginning. Two days later the port engine had been replaced and we took off from Frankfurt again, this time without incident.

This was Hilary's first expedition. On the previous two expeditions I had been on, to Changabang and K2 in the Himalayas, my climbing partner had been Joe Tasker. We were of equal abilities, and a poker-faced, competitive edge to our relationship gave impetus to our efforts. I had relied on Joe's organisational drive a lot. Now I was with Hilary, I felt more responsible about the whole thing. I worried about obtaining the Surat Jalan (travel permit) and all the travel ahead of us. It was awesome going into a big Asian city for the first time, knowing no one, with so much to do. Still, one obstacle had to be taken at a time. I opened *Teach Yourself Indonesian*, and tried to learn some words.

Jakarta seemed many cities rolled into one, with tall international skyscrapers pushing into a hot, drizzly sky and contrasting with the tight cluster of small houses – the kampongs – where most of the people lived. Waves of tiredness washed over us in the sultry heat as we tried to find the correct police office initialled M.A.B.A.K. When eventually we arrived it was closed for the day. It was the first encounter of an eleven-day trail through corridors of officialdom. We went to the Garuda Airline office.

'Can we have a flight to Biak, the day after tomorrow?'

'Let's hope so,' smiled the girl behind the desk. At five foot two, Hilary seemed tall beside the tiny Javanese girls.

The next morning we went back to M.A.B.A.K. It was the start of a busy day. Nobody seemed deliberately obstructive, but nobody wanted to take the responsibility of saying yes or no.

'We are tourists and we want a Surat Jalan to visit Irian Jaya. We would like to go to Biak, Nabire and Ilaga, if possible?' I said.

'Ilaga, in the interior? You must apply to the police in Biak for permission to go there, I can give you a Surat Jalan to go to Biak and Jayapura only. Will you come back at 2.00 p.m.?'

At 2.00 p.m. the permits were ready and, elated, we went shopping. Jakarta supermarkets contained all the lightweight foods we needed – at expensive prices. Fortunately, the Indonesian rupiah had been devalued by thirty per cent a few weeks before. Everyone in the shops grinned helpfully.

Early the next morning the domestic airport of Jakarta, Kemajoran, was in apparent turmoil and hundreds of people were waving and thrusting with tickets in their hands. Nobody spoke English. I tried to persuade Hilary to check in: 'They won't push a woman,' I said. We strained to hear the words that would tell us our flight was about to leave.

'Why did Sukarno change all the place names? We didn't learn those in geography at school.'

'Ujung Pandang, Amon, Biak.'

'That must be us!'

At Ujung Pandang, which used to be called Makassar, we changed planes in the shimmering heat and were soon flying through towering clouds above coral islands. When we landed on the island of Biak that afternoon we saw our first Papuans, smiling in yellow uniforms as airport porters. They looked African, with their black skins, woolly hair and broad noses and feet, but apparently they are not closely related. They have no affinity in language, culture or race with the other peoples of the Pacific, the Malayans and Polynesians, and have only tenuous links with the Aborigines of Australia. Although the Papuans were not tall by European standards, they seemed huge to the tiny Indonesians, and Indonesian legends are full of conflicts between the good princes and the 'giants' who inhabited the jungles. The Papuans of Biak speak one of the hundreds of languages of New Guinea – the world's most complex linguistic region.

We found a large, damp hotel near the airport. It used to be popular in Dutch days. Now, many Papuans wandered around it doing little jobs, as the whole mildewed edifice seemed to be crumbling around their ears. These were the lucky ones. There were many others still roaming the town who had also come from the mainland looking for work. We were the only guests in a large dining room. Outside we could see hot steamy coral and the blue sea. Small lizards ran around the walls. In one corner was a bar with no drink behind it, and in another stood a large Christmas tree with cotton wool and flashing lights. A cassette player was blaring out old Beatles' numbers and traditional Western Christmas carols to Indonesian words.

There used to be a Biak legend that vast wealth would one day arrive from the East. After the Second World War, the Japanese departed and generous Americans, rich in material things, arrived. It seemed that the prophecy had been fulfilled. But now they, too, had gone.

In the morning we were interviewed by a policeman. In his immaculate uniform he looked firm and tough. I remembered what a climbing friend, John Barry, had said about Indonesians: 'Bloody good scrappers'. He had fought against them as a Royal Marine in Borneo in 1964.

We presented a list of the villages north of the mountains: Bilorai, Beoga and Ilaga. 'We want to fly to them from Nabire,' we said. 'We want to see the people who live there.'

'I can only give you permission to go to Nabire. You must ask there about places further on.'

Our Surat Jalan was duly stamped, and the immigration office extended our visas.

'Things are going too well,' I said, 'we haven't had to bribe anyone yet.'

At an efficient little travel agency run by a Chinese – always the business men of South East Asia – we booked places on the scheduled flight next morning to Nabire. The travel agent warned us that we would not be able to charter a plane in Nabire because there was a fuel shortage in the whole of Irian Jaya. We decided, nevertheless, to take the chance.

There were only four other passengers in the Twin Otter. We veered around enormous clouds towards the mainland of Irian Jaya.

The tiny outrigger canoes of Biak shrank to specks on the ocean below us. We crossed the island of Yapen in a few minutes. Isolated tall trees reached out of the dense jungle and there were no signs of human habitation. The clouds became thicker. We could see the long fingernails of the pilot's hands on the controls.

'I hope he knows where the coast is,' said Hilary.

Then we saw the long airstrip pointing out to sea, first built by the Japanese during their years of occupation. On the shore a white ship with a rust-stained hull was being unloaded across the surf by tiny figures in little boats. Behind the flat town of tin roofs rose a steaming jungle.

Once we had landed, would-be helpers buzzed around us. A small lively European with a goatee beard stepped through a milling throng, shook our hands and introduced himself as Father Tetteroo, a Franciscan missionary.

'I am saying goodbye to a Sister who is leaving on the plane. Come round to my little house this evening for coffee. It is next to the airstrip. Everyone knows where I live.'

A friendly but insistent policeman perused our Surat Jalan, and this inspection attracted an even larger crowd of onlookers. We were whisked away to the only hotel in the growing town of 15,000 people.

The hotel manager spoke good English – his father was Dutch. He asked if he could help us. I told him we wanted mainly to go to Ilaga.

'Why?' he asked abruptly. His manner was grave and stern.

Momentarily, I dropped my guard, and forgot our strategy, confessing that we wanted to go to the Snow Mountains.

'Impossible. Impossible,' he repeated adamantly.

The whole area was closed. Only two weeks ago a missionary at Ilaga was 'taken'. He did not even think it worth asking the police, but eventually agreed to introduce us to them. As we walked with him, he puffed at a pungent cloves cigarette and remarked that he used to be the Chief of Police. We had lost the chance of secrecy.

At the police post we discovered that the Chief of the Nabire Police was not there – he was in Biak. So we went round to the house of the second in command. I produced my Australian map – it was the best they had seen – and systematically asked about all the other approaches to the mountains. We all sat at a table and chickens scratched around our feet. It was difficult to follow the gist of the conversation, because they were laughing and smiling at the same time as stonewalling our plans. Had I been to the Himalayas? I showed them a little photo of myself on the top of Everest. But why did we want to go to the mountains of Irian? Was there gold there?

Anyway, it was impossible; we could not approach the mountains from the north. However, the southern approach via the Freeport Indonesia copper mine was in another police district – they offered to ask the Jayapura authorities to see if they would allow us to use that way of reaching the mountains.

I knew that even if the Jayapura authorities allowed us to go to the south, the people at the mine had already refused us entry in response to an earlier request. We had heard at Biak that when the guerillas blew up their pipeline, the mine had been put out of action for three months. It seemed most unlikely that tourists would be allowed now.

In the evening we went round to see Father Tetteroo, the man we had met at the airport. He was among the first group of missionaries to come to the interior, in 1937. He knew Colijn and Wissell, who had explored part of the Snow Mountains in 1936. In the early days, he and other priests had crossed the jungles of Irian on foot, often travelling for months at a time with a couple of porters. Very few of the tribes they met had seen Europeans before. He had not heard about Pearl Harbour until a month after the raid had occurred. He had been in a Japanese Prisoner of War camp for three and a half years – a camp which had been bombed mistakenly by the Allies. He delighted and fascinated us with his insights about Irian. His stories were simple, like parables, and directed outwards with a lively sense of fun – and mischief.

Father Tetteroo was sixty-seven years old.

'Why should I go back to Holland, where I shall be retired?

I prefer to stay here and help life wherever I can. I shall stay here until I die.'

He was full of joy, as if he would bounce back no matter how hard life knocked him. He lived simply. When we left him a present of a large bunch of bananas had appeared on the porch. He did not know who had left them there; it could have been anyone in Nabire. We walked back across the airstrip, feeling selfish in our pursuit of the mountains. We could absorb so little, compared with the lifetime experience of a missionary. In the distance, lightning flashed beneath anvil-shaped clouds.

'Ah well, it was worth coming, just to meet him.'

'Perhaps we should make the best of a bad job and try to get to those mountains in Borneo.'

'We could go on a trek somewhere in Irian where there are no problems – then we would at least meet the people.'

But we were sad at heart.

All this way, all this money, to be refused on the doorstep of the fabled mountains. We decide to stay till Monday and give the police another try.

Next morning they seemed to relent. As long as the Jayapura authorities agreed, we could fly to Bilorai and walk out via the mine. No political troubles in the interior were mentioned, but we guessed that the main problems near the mountains were north east of them, in the Ilaga Valley. Bilorai lay to the north west. Obviously, the Indonesians would not want to risk the international outcry if two Europeans were kidnapped as a symbolic protest by guerillas. The police promised to radio to Jayapura immediately.

Caught up in a mood of optimism, we went to see Tom Benoit, a pilot who serviced the Catholic missions in Irian. An American from Minnesota, he lived in Nabire with his wife Mary and two little daughters – with another on the way. He had flown over ten thousand hours in Irian.

Tom was short and stocky, relaxed and practical, and wearing a pair of long garish surfing shorts. 'He likes to help people,' Father Tetteroo had said of him. I asked him if he could squeeze us in on a flight to Bilorai. I was very aware of using people, capitalising on their open goodwill, and I apologised.

'Somebody's got to climb mountains,' said Tom. He could fit us into his schedule on Monday morning. 'I'm rather busy at the moment. One of our pilots – an Indonesian – disappeared a few months ago. He got lost in the clouds and flew into a mountain.'

'We're white parasites waiting for permission for our own ego trip,' Hilary whispered to me after we had left.

Nabire slept during the hottest part of the hot day. When the shops reopened, we went provisioning to the blare of a loudspeaker van bellowing the name of the evening film at the cinema. The shops, mainly owned by Indonesian small traders from all over the archipelago, stocked a wide variety of Western goods, and we bought food for three weeks.

Over the centuries a trickle of Indonesians had settled on Irian's coasts, leaving the interior's forbidding jungles to the strange Papuan tribes they had found there. However, the shopkeepers of Nabire had arrived in the wake of a more recent influx of immigrants, resulting from the Indonesian government's transmigration scheme. This scheme arose initially from President Sukarno's opposition to birth control, and was aimed at relieving the population problems of farming in Java, and also at increasing the strength of Indonesia's ethnic toehold in Irian. The government wished to make the moves as attractive as possible to the Javanese, and offered transportation, land, the corrugated iron for a roof, and sufficient food until the first harvest to those families who agreed to relocate. If the transmigrants become homesick, however, the return ticket is discouragingly expensive.

In the evening Tom showed three home movies he had taken in Irian. They whetted our appetites.

'This is Bilorai a couple of years ago,' he said.

'Sure you don't mean 3,000 years ago?'

'You won't find them much changed now.'

Bad news arrived the following afternoon. The police had received an instruction from Jayapura that we would not be allowed into the interior until we had received authorisation from two organisations, LAKSUSDA in Jayapura and LIPI in Jakarta. To obtain this we would have to fly a circle – a thousand miles to Jakarta and then over a thousand miles back to Jayapura at the other end of Irian Jaya. Hilary and I started miserably snapping at each other. Now we had tasted Indonesian bureaucracy, we knew that, even if we could afford the travel, we could never obtain such documents. Next week the rules would probably be different. Our pile of recently bought food and all our packed equipment in the corner looked pathetic – mute but lucid witnesses to the state of our fortunes. We would return to Biak the next day.

Dawn was the best time in Nabire, and we made the most of our last few hours there. Despite our setbacks, we felt affection towards the Indonesians as we watched the transmigration camp come to life. When the first rays of light sprayed skyward through the tall trees, the jungle chorus started as if at the signal of a baton. The noises faded just as suddenly when the sun appeared. There was a roar of engines as Tom took off on his first flight. We walked along the road to the settlement and were soon walking against the tide of hundreds of people, on scooters and on foot going to school, to work in the shops, government offices and at the airport, and perhaps just going for a walk like us. Everyone greeted each other and us gaily with shining eyes and contagious smiles. 'Salamat pagi!' Our faces became fixed grins. We walked to the Javanese market, past houses on stilts, fields of maize and bananas, a mosque, and a few cows, goats and dogs. Then we returned to the hotel for breakfast.

The manager came up with another straw of hope to clutch at: 'At Biak you must go and see Mr Engels, who owns two hotels and a building company and exports wildlife to European zoos. He is a very powerful and influential man. He will help you to ask the Major General for permission to approach the mountains via the mine.'

At the airport building there was a confusion over the tickets. We pushed our way on to seats in the aeroplane. Our precious dollars were melting into flights and hotels as the days ticked by.

'If we want to move away from problems, I think we'll have to move away from Indonesia,' said Hilary. The flight between Nabire and Biak had lost its excitement now.

At Biak we checked into one of Mr Engels' hotels. It had a vast, extravagant painted Toroja roof, built of thousands of matched pieces of bamboo laid one upon another like tiles, sweeping up in a great curved prow at either end. A legend says that the design of the Toroja roof reflects a folk memory of the ships in which the distant ancestors arrived from China.

Mr Engels had a strong personality. He gave us a rapid résumé of his life history and sent us to the Freeport office with his son, William, but all in vain. Even when I phoned the mine direct, the word was a firm but polite no.

'Come back next year, I shall organise everything for you,' promised Mr Engels.

Eventually we decided to do the one thing nobody had suggested, fly to Jayapura. At least then we would have tried everything.

We pressed our faces against the windows of the aircraft as it followed the coast, gazing longingly at the jungle, which harboured unknown wandering tribes of sago eaters. These people, we had read, hunted and collected food from the sago forests and occasional small-scale shifting cultivation. They had no contact with white people or administration, and spoke their own languages. Sometimes they traded in this jungle, leaving and collecting stone axes, salt and cowrie shells in traditional clearings, without ever seeing the tribesmen with whom they were exchanging goods. Through the jungle wound great meandering rivers which left a trail of oxbow lakes and emptied many channels into the sea.

Jayapura was once called Hollandia by its Dutch administrators – a name flashed around the Western world when General MacArthur spearheaded a battle against the Japanese there in 1944. Even now the rusting hulk of a partly sunken Japanese transport ship projects out of the town's beautiful blue bay. The change of place names reflects the tide of political fortunes. Hollandia has been re-named Kota Baru (new town), Sukanapura and, recently, Jayapura. Meanwhile, West New Guinea has been known as West

Irian and Irian Barat and has only in 1973 become Irian Jaya (literally, Irian Victory).

Before landing, the plane circled over a landscape as gentle as a Chinese watercolour, open pale-green hills, red volcanised soil and large blue lakes whose shores and islands were clustered by houses built over the water on stilts. 'At least it's a change of scenery,' I said. Hilary was busy taking photographs for her geography classes.

Jayapura's airport is twenty-eight miles out of town, so before leaving I decided to investigate the possibility of flights to Bilorai, and left Hilary guarding our equipment. First I went to a large hangar run by a missionary alliance of the twelve different Protestant sects who operate in the highlands. Two tall Americans with crew-cuts ignored me, but eventually I found an office with two Indonesians inside it. The conversation lasted about a minute. There was no possibility of chartering a plane until the second week in January. Christmas was coming and they were too busy to have anything to do with us.

I decided to try the Catholics. A small boy pointed out a house where a Catholic pilot lived, but nobody answered the door. I walked back to Hilary, feeling as helpless as I have ever felt in my life and tiring of the indignity of asking people for favours. We found the large brown police building where our fate would be decided next day, and went away to type a letter to take with us describing what had happened so far. We looked for someone to translate it, and met Father Frans Verheijen, who agreed to come to the police building and help us. There was a pragmatic, straight-talking air about him, of someone used to getting things done – a quality he shared with the other Franciscan missionaries we had met. Next morning we followed him in, past guards and secretaries and along corridors until we were outside the room of the Chief Intelligence Officer of Irian Jaya.

'Wait outside,' said Father Verheijen. We sat down, trying to gauge the mood from the ebb and flow of conversation next door. Hilary had her fingers tightly crossed. Long minutes passed and eventually we were summoned in.

Politely, we were shown our seats. Humbly we looked across at two immaculately uniformed Indonesians sitting beneath a large map of Irian Jaya. One of the men was holding an ominous-looking folder full of papers. Evidently it was the mountaineering file, because he recited the familiar words of the letter, written one and a half years before from Jakarta, cancelling our previous expedition plans. It was the last official – and thus definitive – statement on mountaineering expeditions 'until I have better news from Irian Jaya.' Red rings around many of the districts indicated trouble spots. The village of Bilorai was in an all-clear region, but the area south of the mountains was clearly 'no go'. We were told that an agreement had been reached to allow us to visit Bilorai as tourists, but we were to promise not to go to the mountains. If we went near the mountains, we would be thrown out of Indonesia. The police considered all scientific, surveying and mountaineering expeditions to be forbidden. We were issued with new Surat Jalans, and asked to sign them after these conditions had been typed upon them. We agreed. Everyone smiled and we left.

We blinked in the sunshine outside and thanked Father Verheijen, who rushed off to attend a meeting. He had used all his powers of persuasion and influence, and lain his integrity on the line – and that of the missions he worked for – to help us, two complete strangers.

'We'll see the people at least,' said Hilary, 'and perhaps we'll be able to see the mountains from a distance. But if only they hadn't found out we wanted to go to the mountains!'

'Let's just see what happens,' I said. 'Anyway, the next problem is to try and get a flight organised.'

Back at the airport we found a commercial charter company with one Australian pilot. Although he was away for the day, there seemed a possibility that he could fly us – until we calculated the price. We could not afford 1,000 U.S. dollars. We trailed round to the Catholic pilot's house. His flight schedule was stretching him to the point of tears. He told us that in Irian the Catholics had only two pilots with four planes, but they had enough work to keep six busy. However, he had a suggestion to make. The Seventh

Day Adventists had a grass strip a few miles away, and maybe had more spare time to help. He didn't know much more about them, except that they had split from the main Protestant missionary alliance owing to a disagreement about which day of rest to take at weekends – the Seventh Day Adventists refused to fly on a Saturday but, unlike the other sects in the alliance, they were willing to fly on a Sunday.

Eventually we found the strip, carved out of the jungle. Next to it were two modern houses and a hangar. The property was lavishly modern and well-cared-for – evidence of the support of a wealthy religious commitment. We were nervous.

'Watch out for the death-adders – stay away from the long grass.' The wives of the sect's two pilots were listening to their husbands conversing on the radio. 'They'll be back in a couple of hours,' one said. 'I'm sure they'll try to help you.'

We went for a long walk along a narrow road through the jungle. We joked and flirted, trying to fill in time. Then, within minutes of each other, two tiny, snub-nosed Cessna 185s flew in noisily over the trees, arriving from opposite directions. We walked with slow steps to the hangar, bracing ourselves to bother people again. What would my response be, I thought, if a couple of strangers walked up to me in Leysin after I'd spent a hard day on the hill, and asked me to drive them to Geneva? I need not have worried.

'It sounds like you need a bit of luck,' said Ken.

'I'll fly you in tomorrow morning,' said Leroy. 'Be here at 5.00 a.m. I'm going to Jayapura right now – do you want a lift?' The old American frontier spirit of help and co-operation had not died in the new age of competition. The tide seemed to be turning.

We had left most of our food in Biak – it was costing too much to pay the excess baggage every time we flew. Now we had twenty minutes before the shops closed to buy our rations. We found a large shop with a lot of Australian food displayed, and dashed from shelf to shelf until we had accumulated a large pile on the counter before an amused shop assistant.

'I hope we haven't forgotten anything.'

'Look up Indonesian for "bulk-buy discount", Hilary. You've got the dictionary.'

Leroy had not flown to Bilorai before, and before taking off we listened apprehensively in the half-light of the dawn as he discussed with Ken where it was:

'Turn right at Ilaga ... '

I wondered if climbers discussing a route up a mountain sounded so casual. Then God was addressed very directly, in a strong clear prayer.

We flew along a compass bearing into the interior.

Already, the crisp morning air was being invaded by the first wisps of cloud floating up and starting to gather in bulbous shapes. After crossing some low mountains we approached the vast plateau of the Idenburg River. Below us stretched a dense jungle of sago swamps.

'Where would you land in an emergency?' I asked.

'I'd look for a river,' he said.

'Where are the Snow Mountains?'

'Over there somewhere – I've only seen them twice; usually they're in the cloud. Mind you, I've only been flying in Irian for nine months.'

The river took a hundred detours, but our direction was straight. We surrendered ourselves to our pilot's skill. Clouds picked out ridges in the dark green below. The ground started to move up towards us until we were enclosed in steep-sided valleys, skimming ridges, searching for the needle of an airstrip. After two hours of flying we still had not found the landing ground; we were peering in all directions and we had our maps out. Leroy admired them – they were better than his. I wanted to spend a moment inside his head, so I could find out how worried to become. Then Hilary saw it – a dark brown, unmistakable stretch of level ground above a tin-roofed hut. It was the first sign of habitation we had seen.

We wheeled around and I saw many dark figures race up a track towards the airstrip. As we landed, small grey pigs ran squealing out of our way.

'I'm going to Wamena to pick some people up for Christmas,' said Leroy. 'I'd better go now, before these clouds become any bigger, and the mid-day winds pick up.'

The plane was out of sight within minutes. The Time Machine had dumped us. Hilary and I sat down and waited for the reception committee to arrive.

3 AMAKANE

22–28 December 1978

We were looking at the figures painted on the wall of a cave come to life. Our eyes turned and darted in their sockets like tropical fish. A large crowd swarmed around us. Men of all ages wearing nothing but long yellow penis sheaths were waving bows and arrows. Women in grass skirts peered from behind. All our baggage was picked up and people started carrying it off down the hill. I had not done up my briefcase properly; the contents fell out and I rushed around in a panic picking up the papers.

'Hurry up, let's get after them,' yelled Hilary.

We were half-scared, half-thrilled.

A few hundred yards down the hill the mob stopped and our equipment was put in a pile. We were relieved when a European, in his mid-thirties, appeared and introduced himself as Jan van der Horst.

'Welcome to Bilorai! Excuse me, I have not spoken English for a long time and am a little rusty. I am just here for a few days over Christmas. I work in Enaratoli now but used to live here. Would you like a look around?'

We hesitated, not wanting to leave our equipment unguarded. 'Don't worry,' he said, 'you can trust these people. They will not harm or cheat you.' He plunged off into the undergrowth and we steamed after him. It was the start of a vivid afternoon.

'Walking is hard work in this country. I weighed eighty-four kilos when I first came to Irian – now I weigh fifty-six.'

Eagerly we peppered him with questions – first about himself.

He had studied for seven years at university – maths and chemistry and then philosophy and theology. Working as a priest, he ran a school for children with behaviour problems before coming to Irian when his bishop asked him to. He could speak several languages – Dutch, German, English, Indonesian; and the language of the people of Bilorai, the Monis.

'The Moni language is very difficult – it has twenty-eight tenses. I can use six or seven and they seem to understand what I mean. Before I learnt it, I had to use a small boy, who had been to school and understood my Indonesian, as an interpreter. Sometimes this was embarrassing, particularly when talking to the older people. Now, however, I can ask the questions that I want.'

He was at the moment trying to learn the language of the Ekagis who lived in the west, in the Paniai Region, around the Wissel Lakes.

After a few more questions Jan warmed to describing his work, and the culture he lived in, with the eagerness of an expert lost in his subject. 'When I arrived I did not talk about religion for a long time. I wanted to understand the people without preconceptions, without automatically condemning the beliefs and lifestyle I found. I soon learnt that their social norms and rites have the same right to be respected as our own. I had done courses in agriculture and medicine before I came, so I was able to help. Not long ago infant mortality was seventy per cent. Now it is thirty per cent. But that isn't everything. What I really want to do is to raise their level of consciousness in a Moni way to prepare them for their inevitable future contacts with the outside world. I am trying to help them settle their problems themselves and not trying to see how many people I can baptise in as short a time as possible.'

I did not comment, for I too had much to learn and absorb.

We slid down a muddy track. Little boys were running backwards and forwards around us, like lively dogs out for some exercise. One of them was firing arrows into the trees, for fun. Jan showed us the different arrow heads:

'This one for birds, this one for rats, this one for pigs, and this one for people. They still have not developed flights for them – perhaps so that when they aim at each other they are not too accurate. There is a delicate balance here between chance and competence.'

We arrived at a rectangular wooden hut. Smoke was filtering out of its roof, which was thatched with grass and sedge. 'The smoke keeps the roof tarry and waterproof,' said Jan. 'It rains every afternoon here.' Inside, the floor was raised eighteen inches off the ground and six Monis sat on it. They were eating steamy jungle greens – it looked like spinach.

'*Amakane,*' they all grunted. Then grinned.

'That's a good word to learn,' said Jan. 'It means hello, how do you do, that's good, thank you and goodbye.'

'*Amakane,*' we said.

'They have no cooking utensils,' said Jan, 'and so never have hot drinks. They cook sweet potatoes in the fire and greens in a pit with hot stones – sealed by large leaves like a pressure cooker.'

We passed a longer hut. 'That's where the richest man in the area lives,' said Jan. 'He has six wives, many cowrie shells, and his pigs live inside that enclosure. Each wife has a separate room, and their children sleep with them until adolescence, when the boys move into the father's room. But not many men have enough cowrie shells to have many wives.'

We saw a tightly-woven fence about six feet high. 'Sometimes wild dogs can jump the fences,' said Jan. 'They like to eat pigs.'

The Monis did not have village structures, but since the airstrip was built they had been slowly beginning to settle higher up towards it and the mission and government huts. The valley sloped two and a half thousand feet below the airstrip and Monis who lived lower down tended to class all the Monis, missionaries and Indonesians who lived higher up as 'them up there'. 'Whenever there is a local dispute,' said Jan, 'they think we are automatically on the side of those higher up. When the mission was lower down it was the other way round.'

'How do they know what water is safe to drink?' I asked.

'They know exactly where the good water is,' said Jan. 'You see they are not stupid. They are just as intelligent as anyone else, but they use their intelligence for different things. They know the names of all the pigs around, they can identify and recount the age and history of their cowrie shells, and when there is a local war, they know exactly who is on their side and who is not. They know the names and properties of hundreds and hundreds of plants, and can identify all the seventy species of sweet potato … '

We came to another clearing and saw an old man crouching next to a pig. The pig's eyes were contentedly closed, and the man was affectionately stroking its stomach.

'*Amakane*,' we said.

'He's the oldest man in Bilorai,' said Jan. 'He's about sixty-five years old. Of course no records have been kept until recently, but the average life expectancy of these people is just under forty.' At 6,000 feet, it was too high for the malarial mosquitoes that had plagued us in Nabire. However, civilisation had brought TB to Enaratoli in the west and the Baliem Valley in the east. There had been a lot of goitre problems in the area owing to the lack of iodine but recent injections had cleared this up – with the side-effect of giving the cured a soaring IQ.

'What sort of concept of time have they got?' I asked.

'They remember two or three generations back, although nothing precise, beyond morning, afternoon and evening and two or three moons. Of course, they have no seasons, although they carefully rotate their fields. You see that sharp pointed mountain over there in the east? No one has been there. But they have noticed that for half the year the sun rises on one side of it and for the other half of the year on the other side.'

Another man in the clearing was smoking a cigarette made of locally grown tobacco, rolled in a pandanus leaf. He was smoking it through the side.

'The tobacco was here long before the Europeans came,' said Jan. 'Here, try it.'

I coughed and spluttered with the thick acrid smoke – a great joke. The man showed us a cowrie shell, which he prised out of a tightly woven purse. The shell was filled with beeswax and the man pointed to its teeth, its mouth and gums and its backside. It would have bought a small pig.

A woman nearby had lost the top two joints of three of her fingers. 'They were cut off by her parents when she was a child to express grief when one of the family died,' said Jan. 'It is a sort of adolescent rite. The funny-bone is knocked, as an anaesthetic, before amputation. This tends to be the only time, nowadays, that they use the stone axe.

The same mutilations are depicted on the walls of caves in France. I tried to imagine how a child could submit to such an ordeal – the grim symbolic mood cast by the spell of the ceremony, the suffering of the amputation, and the mixture of pride and relief the child must have felt to come out at the end of it all.

We passed a lot of planks placed carefully against a large tree. 'There is a female symbol behind there,' said Jan, 'and it marks the boundary between those above and those below.' Lower down the hill, away from habitation, was a sacred grove of trees with a broad swathe cleared from jungle around it. 'No one is allowed to enter that,' said Jan, 'spirits and ghosts are supposed to live there. The Monis used to put their dead in tree houses for the birds, but now they bury them, particularly near the missions. They believe that the ghosts of dead people are around all the time helping or playing tricks. Sometimes whole forests are forbidden because they are said to be full of spirits. But also they have a word "Ebu", which means many things – blood, earth, life-energy, Supreme One, nature. If a man steals an axe, then the Ebu knows.'

Did he know what the Seventh Day Adventists believed in?

'The same God as you or I,' he snapped.

I asked for that, I thought, from such an aggressive, committed intellect.

'Many Monis come to church, and sing Moni hymns. You can decide how Christian they are,' he said.

I asked him about the penis sheaths – they were obviously important. What did they wear them for? Was it to affirm their virility, or to protect them from bad spirits?

'They feel naked without them – any other reasons have been

forgotten, and now they wear them for modesty only. They come in all shapes and sizes and usually they have a wardrobe of one or two others. And it's easy for them to change styles – they just go into the jungle and cut a different shaped gourd.'

We started walking back up the hill. Jan studied for four hours every day and we did not want to interrupt his schedule. I asked him when the airstrip was built.

'1967. It took 300 men six years to carve it out of the ridge. These people saw jets a long time before they ever met Europeans – they have some amazing stories about them. The first wheels they saw were on aeroplanes. They accept outside phenomena very quickly – although seeing things, of course, from their own point of view. Nowadays, when an aeroplane goes overhead they hardly look up.'

'Do they use money yet?'

'They have started to do so over the last three or four years. It is very important that they learn about money, otherwise they will be cheated if, in the future, they trade with the coast. Of course there are about 11,000 people in the valley, and a few other places with airstrips like this, and I suppose about a hundred people in Bilorai earn a wage of some sort – doing jobs for the mission and the government, and maintaining the airstrip. The rest of the people work in the gardens, and they are very clever and successful agriculturalists. They are lucky in some ways, too, because they are not troubled by seasons, drought, floods or pests. It is not an easy life but a good one – unhurried but purposeful.'

'We ought to check in at the government post,' I said, 'and tell them we're here.'

'The place is empty, there's no one there,' said Jan. 'You see we had a war here about two weeks ago, and all the Indonesian police and teachers escaped to Enaratoli. They were worried that the emotion of the battle would boil over on to them.'

'Why did the war start?'

'It was between the Monis of Bilorai and those of Titigi – a place about two hours' walk down from here, but further up the valley. It started when a man from Bilorai was drowned in the river near Titigi. The Bilorai Monis thought that a Titigi ghost had pushed him in. You see, if an accident cannot easily be explained by common sense, they accept that a ghost is involved – even if it is something as simple as tripping up. Anyway, casualties have to be even, and a ghost will not rest until he is avenged, so a battle was arranged on a sort of no man's land halfway between the two villages. Of course an inter-clan war is not as serious as one between tribes and, unlike the Danis in the east, the Monis do not damage property or harm women and children; they do not forget themselves and go mad with slaughter. The battle is an elaborate, stylised event, so there are a lot of women and children watching from a safe distance – like a football match. They know the names of the people on the other side, and shout insults and taunt each other. Whereas the Danis use spears, these people only use their inaccurate bows and arrows. They crouch very low when fighting, so that they are not injured in the chest. In this last battle, nobody was killed but about forty were injured – some of them quite badly. Many of them think that the risks involved in fighting the battle are not as bad as if they ignored the unavenged ghost. But they have never harmed me – I once walked through a fight, and they stopped firing when I was in front of them, but started up as soon as I had passed.' Jan explained that he had been trying to call a meeting between the two sides, not to shout at them for their sins, but to encourage them to discuss why they had fought each other. However, those little wars brought so much excitement, it was unlikely that they would stop. I did not ask Jan whether he thought they had a function as population control.

When Jan had gone, Hilary and I discussed what to do. It was a moral dilemma. There were no police around to stop us going to the mountains, so should we take a chance? No one had spoken of guerrilla warfare, and the Monis seemed friendly towards us. But if a police patrol did stop us, and saw the statement on our Surat Jalans, we could be in trouble. The consequences of becoming entangled with a guerrilla unit were unthinkable. To know what is right and not to do it is cowardice. But what was right? Missionaries seemed to be able to wander about without being kidnapped, as did Europeans at the Freeport mine, so why couldn't we? In the

Himalayas one respects a government's ban on climbing mountains in politically sensitive areas because there are so many open areas to choose from. But here, in Indonesia, there was only the one area, and I was sure that the Indonesian authorities did not understand the innocuous nature of mountaineering. We were not journalists out to sensationalise Irian's problems to the outside world, we were not spies or mineral prospectors. We were not going to do anything dramatic, like Mrs Wyn Sargent, the American anthropologist who reached the world's headlines and upset the Indonesians by becoming the fourth wife of a tribal chief in the Baliem Valley. And we were so near the mountains; the idea of repeating the same effort and expenditure in trying to reach them in another attempt in the future was appalling.

I was so determined to climb in these mountains that I would break a promise to do so. We would go.

'We must make sure we don't involve the missions at all, though,' said Hilary. We would be on our own, with our Indonesian dictionary, the knowledge which we had gleaned in our reading before, and what we could try to understand as our adventure unfolded.

No one from Bilorai would come with us as porters to help us carry our equipment to the mountains because everyone wanted to stay for the Christmas celebrations – and also did not want to go through or near the enemy territory of the Titigi Monis. We decided to go down to Titigi and see if we could obtain porters there.

A broad muddy track stretched down to the other settlements. Jan had said it was the best track in the area. The next day we slithered down it, past the huts of the empty government offices and school and away from the cultivated area of Bilorai, through the jungle and out into a broad clearing on the hillside. This was the neutral zone between the two clans, where the prearranged battles were fought. Here we met some Danis, proud warriors with bows and many arrows, pig tusk ornaments and painted foreheads smeared with pig fat and soot. The Danis, fiercest and most ruthless of the Irian tribes, could travel outside their own areas with impunity. Although they had internal feuds of their own, they were not involved in the local war between Bilorai and Titigi and were free to move between the settlements. They appreciated our 'Amakane'.

As we crossed a side stream in the river bottom by a recently built bridge, a group of distant figures by the main river rose, tall and lithe, to follow us. They kept a hundred yards behind us, with the intimidating stealth of a band of Red Indians stalking two white settlers.

'Retreat's cut off,' said Hilary under her breath.

In Titigi a large crowd of men of all ages, from two years upwards, accumulated under a tree to discuss our proposals. The worn ground told us it was an habitual meeting place. The first hopeful sign was four large pits dug in the ground and lined with leaves: the sign that a festive occasion had occurred.

'Hari Natal,' someone said. Some aspects of Christianity were evidently widely spread through the northern highlands, but the religious calendar was flexible. Titigi had already celebrated Christmas two days before, and there would be no problem about obtaining porters. The trip would be an opportunity for the Monis to make some money from us, and to trade with the tribes south of the mountains, and perhaps obtain cast-off loot from the copper mine. They had only one misgiving, and Hilary was upset when they expressed apprehension about accompanying a woman of unknown endurance on such an arduous expedition.

We could not distribute loads heavier than ten kilos for each porter because Monis eat vast quantities of sweet potatoes each day, and they would have to carry sufficient food for the journey. A fee was fixed and we had far too many volunteers – we wanted eight, picked ten and ended up with eleven.

We plodded back up the hill to Bilorai. Hilary quickly packed up our equipment into ten-kilo loads, whilst I sorted out our papers, maps and films. Ten young boys picked up the gear and ran off down the hill, whooping, shouting and barking like excited dogs. Two old ladies carrying large bales of grass up the hill were almost knocked over in the exhilaration of the rush – they were muttering bewilderedly when Hilary and I jogged past. At no man's land we were met by the men from Titigi, and the boys from Bilorai quickly withdrew.

We were confused by the blur of faces. 'I'm sure they aren't the men we took on,' I said.

The eleven men of the grinning armed escort drew their bows like a firing squad. We persuaded them to point their arrows in the air. It was evening by the time we had arrived in Titigi and anxiously checked and reassembled the loads. We gave out mirrors, which caused hoots of merriment. The Monis chanted and sang late into the night, relishing the last hours in their homes before starting on the journey. Because of the loss of altitude, it was much hotter than Bilorai. I was excited and did not sleep well.

'Happy birthday, Hilary.' It was Christmas Eve. Two of our porters were now wearing shorts and vests rather than just penis sheaths – or *kotekas*. They had received the shorts from the Indonesian authorities in 1971 under Operation Koteka – a short-term plan to bring clothes and western culture to the natives within Irian. These muddy torn clothes looked less dignified and less healthy, without the pride of a secure culture. We had some spare rucksacks and the men, never having seen such contraptions before, spent a hilarious time putting them on. They stuck their hands straight up in the air, whilst another jumped up and tried to lasso the upraised arms with the straps. Soon the sacks were coated with greasy soot from their smoke-blackened bodies. The rest of the gear they either put into their string bags, or just carried in their hands. After prolonged goodbyes to their friends and families, the porters eventually set off at a fast pace through the terraced fields.

At the last huts, a husband and wife, busy splitting logs into planks paused to grin at us. Nearby, sweet potatoes grew in gardens of individual mounds, set two feet apart. We stopped by a field of sugar cane and tried to emulate the men as they dextrously stripped the cane with their teeth. They had brought pre-cooked sweet potatoes for trail snacks, and ate different varieties for breakfast, quick nourishment, lunch and dinner.

We tried to follow our direction on the map in *The Equatorial Glaciers of New Guinea*. The information for this had been provided by Bob Mitton, a geologist who had perhaps travelled more of the paths in Irian Jaya than any other foreigner. His fascination with the country had led him to learn Dutch, so that he could read more about it. We calculated from the map that we were following the most direct route to the mountains. On this first day we were following a 'major track' which, according to the map, climbed out of the bed of the Weabu River and then across two steep slopes separated from each other by a swampy plateau, to reach a ridge-side at 9,100 feet. Then it descended to the Kemabu River Valley. This was a horizontal distance of eight miles, and was to take us eleven hours without stopping. The jungle demanded maximum effort for minimum distance. After a few minutes walking we voiced suspicion about what the next day's 'minor track' would be like.

The porters knew the route. They wound their way through the jungle with the nonchalant ease of trained gymnasts. Following them, even though we were only carrying cameras and lightweight anoraks, we felt as if we were trying to break a world speed record on an Outward Bound assault course.

The dark, fetid jungle was a sudden change of atmosphere from the open, garden valley of the Monis. The canopy above us dripped. Mud, roots and vines, dead leaves and trees, fallen and upright, were strangling and struggling with each other. Our footfalls were softened and sucked into the mud, and no birds sang. No doubt we were surrounded by animals, birds, snakes and insects, but our eyes and ears were not attuned to detecting them. We ducked under fallen trees and balanced along sloping greasy logs for fifty feet at a time, nervously glancing at the intangible depths of decay underneath.

'I wish we had crampons on,' said Hilary.

We waded along the beds of streams and wobbled across natural bridges of splintered jigsaws of vegetation. Branches swung at us, thorned vines hooked at us and pulled us back and greasy steps seemed placed with the hidden precision of banana skins in a cartoon prank. The ground was never flat, but was a succession of steep, slithery, vegetable barriers. It was similar to caving, except that the effort was even worse and occasional glimpses of daylight told us that we were still above ground.

Soon we were battered and scratched and tiring with the use of half-forgotten muscles in the constant crouching and bending. The many slips and falls turned our legs to jelly. Hilary, being a foot shorter, seemed to be faring better than I. Most of the porters were even smaller. The path, I decided, was not designed for people six feet high. The Monis ran down logs, gripping effortlessly with their prehensile toes. We blundered along, our eyes glued on the zigzags of the men in front. They, however, were chatting and looking around as if out for an afternoon stroll. We were grateful for the occasional stops, when the men paused to chew potatoes and to fish dry tinder out of a spare *koteka* to light cigarettes. I vowed I would never be impatient with a mountaineering beginner again.

The Monis took us in their care. To us the interminable jungle looked all the same and if we could not see them for a minute we became lost, but if we waited another minute one of them came back to look for us. Whenever I slipped on a log or teetered on a river crossing, a rock-like, steady grip held my arm from behind, although I had heard no one coming after me. One of the older porters, who had a perpetual runny nose (we called him Sniffer) and a short bulky koteka, became particularly concerned for Hilary's welfare, and doggedly hung on her heels. 'You never look after me like that,' she said. Hilary bewildered the porters by constantly changing the combination of jumpers and anorak she was wearing to adjust to the humidity.

The porters liked disposable ornaments and, as the mood took them, they picked up blades of grass and various other small bits of the jungle and put them through the pierced holes in their noses and ears, or made them into armbands. This was a change from the safety-pins and biros the Monis used near the missions in Bilorai.

At two in the afternoon it started to pour with rain, and did not stop for six hours. We put on our cagoules, but were already so wet with mud and perspiration they did not make much difference. The porters unfolded long pandanus-leaf raincoats – a simple long rectangle fastened along two sides, exactly the same as is used by porters in Nepal – and hung them over their heads. Two of them put on our climbing helmets, and became very attached to them. The rain was to start progressively earlier each day for the following eleven days.

I was engrossed in the ground immediately in front of me and suddenly came face to face with a ferocious-looking Dani coming in the other direction. I flinched as he shrieked in astonishment. Then he shouted with delight when he saw Hilary. 'Amakane', we all said. It was the only encounter of the day. Very few Europeans have ever been harmed in Irian, and one of the reasons for this must have been the tradition of fair dealing by the missions. However, at first it was easy to imagine hostility before we recognised their trust.

When we crossed the final ridge at 9,100 feet, the porters started up with high-pitched cries of two or three notes – their own code for sending messages over great distances. Far down in the Kemabu Valley, 1,100 feet below, came answering cries. The porters were calling: 'We're coming from Titigi – light a fire, give us some room, we're coming to stay for the night.'

It took us an hour and a half to descend, and it was dusk when we reached the first habitation. We stopped in a clearing with two circular huts made of upright planks. One of them was full of women, children and pigs. The other one, the 'boarding house', had smoke steaming through its thatched roof but was empty, and the porters dived in. I followed them. A fire was burning in a box full of sand in the middle of the floor. The room was dry and warm, but I could not stay long in the suffocating smoke. No wonder most of the porters had bad coughs! Tents were colder, wetter, but less claustrophobic and more healthy. Despite the rain, a curious crowd of locals peered at us until long after dark.

'You would stare if two Martians camped in your back garden,' I said to Hilary. We felt like zoo exhibits.

Hilary was upset that I had not offered to cook her birthday meal. I argued that I was sorting the films out. Eventually we ate instant spaghetti and a Chinese tin of pork and a Christmas pudding carefully nurtured all the way from England. Whenever we took food out in front of hungry, watching eyes, we felt guilty. For this reason we did not eat during the daytime, in front of the porters. We wanted to give them some, but our precious rations were so stretched that we had not enough for an emergency or to hand out.

The porters seemed to have skins of leather, but they liked having their scratches fussed over by Hilary, who became chief plasterer. They decided she had magical medical powers. Hilary was relaxed company – a lovely change from the usual tough-guy talk with 'the lads' on a Himalayan expedition with a big, serious mountain dominating the horizon all the time. Our mountaineering, I hoped, was going to be relaxing after all the hard work in the jungle.

Below us, the turbulent Kemabu River divided two settlements at the point where we had to cross it. On the far side, to the south, lay Ugimba, a sprawling Moni settlement of predominantly rectangular huts, and on the side where we had arrived was the more cohesive unit of circular Dani huts – Wanibugi. Across the river between the two places was a magnificent rattan suspension bridge built without nails or modern tools. It had to be replaced every few years as it rotted.

On Christmas Day it was my turn to have a birthday. We decided to open all cards in the evening, for we had problems to take our minds off the day's religious and festive significance. Two of the porters were deserting us. One of them, the leader the previous day, had a badly swollen leg. The other was complaining of toothache. We gave the first some antibiotics and the other aspirin and looked around, hoping to recruit local substitutes. Eventually we found two Danis – one tall, with a competitive air and very greasy face, and the other wearing a bizarre collection of loot from the copper mine – old Wellington boots and sunglasses and a yellow waterproof construction worker's jacket. The purpose of some Western goods must fascinate them, for in 1974 Bob Mitton had found in this place a large marquee, erected but unused and weighing fifty-five kilos, which must have been carried for at least three days' walk from the mine.

No sooner had we acquired two new porters than all the others ran off down the hill, leaving us standing in the camp site with all the gear. Suspecting mass desertion we shouted after them, but they kept on going. In despair we gathered all the gear on to our backs and under our arms and followed them. By the time we had staggered and slipped through the mud to the suspension bridge, one of the porters spotted us and came back. I went with him across the river to Ugimba to investigate the cause of their rapid departure. After I had primed myself with a few words of Indonesian, I soon found out. They were simply obtaining sweet potatoes for the rest of the journey and soon returned to pick up our equipment.

Ugimba was high enough for the morning to be cool. We were surrounded by little children, huddling themselves to keep warm. Two women were weaving net from bark, to make carrying bags. They still had enough finger ends to do it; often of necessity it was a man's job. They paused to touch Hilary's long hair – she was probably the first European woman they had seen.

Our eyes, accustomed to scanning the open spaces of mountains and networks of city streets, could barely discern the minor track we were now to follow. If we had been left alone, we would still be there. The porters, however, managed the terrain with the air of detached confidence of a London commuter on his way to work. The tall Dani from Wanibugi seemed eager to demonstrate his local knowledge and jungle mastery to us and the Monis, and he set off at a half run. 'We'll give him a heavy load tomorrow,' said Hilary as it started to rain. We bent double through the undergrowth and waded and crawled through the murky waters of a stream for hundreds of yards.

We were heading into a deep, vegetated box-canyon, with thousand-foot walls. How were we going to reach the plateau from here, we wondered? The Dani sprinter started climbing up a wall of vegetation that made us gasp. When we followed him we found a hidden staircase of holds clipped and scraped out of the network of roots and mud. With the weight of thirteen of us on it, the tree ladder trembled. We forgot the rain and did not notice the leeches between our fingers until we reached the top.

It was like popping over the top of a crag climb in England. We breathed with sudden relief as we reached the horizontal. Our eyes adjusted from the darkness of the forest. The sense of space was exhilarating after the jungle prison. At last we were able to walk a few steps without tripping and slipping. Outcrops of white carboniferous limestone hinted at the mountains far ahead. But we could see little of the future, for the plateau appeared and disappeared in swirling mist. However, the view opened out below, and a general discussion began as to which way we had come, and as to where we had crossed the ridges the day before. The porters had found their way through the jungle without discussion, but the total picture of their route from this airy viewpoint was hotly disputed.

The rain only collected in a few places on the porous plateau, and we worried that the porters would stop far from a water supply that night. Sweet potatoes seemed to provide them with most of their fluid, for they rarely drank, whilst we were always thirsty. However, they found a lean-to shelter not far from a spongy spring. Within minutes they had their bivouac organised, with the roof mended and a fire crackling. The height gain had brought a sharp drop in temperature and some wind. Wrapped in warm woollen clothes, we sat around the porters' fire and opened our damp, smudged cards.

We were ten hours ahead of the festivities at home. Instead of opening Christmas presents, we were protecting our belongings from the rain. Life was a perpetual opening and closing of polythene bags. Outside frogs croaked in unison.

Dawn brought a new world. The sunshine turned the grass to gold and the bushes and cobwebs were fresh with yesterday's rain. We twisted and wriggled through them along the side of a spur until the thin track veered up on to a natural clearing on the crest. From here we could see the line of the scarp cliffs of the Ekabu Plateau, stretching away to the west – its pillars edged sharply in the morning sunlight. I was enthralled by the sight of the high ground. In 1962 Heinrich Harrer exclaimed of the same range, 'Everything an explorer ever dreamed of could be satisfied here.' He had christened the valley next to our route 'Fairy Tale Valley' and called the lakes in it 'Hansel and Gretel'.

We dropped from the spur and wound across two grassy marshes to reach a limestone pavement. 'It's just like the Pennines,' said Hilary, busily photographing the clints and grykes, 'and higher up there's giant groundsel and lobelia like there is on Mount Kenya and Kilimanjaro.' She was noticing more than I was.

My left knee was becoming painful – I had stretched a tendon in its side. Our tennis shoes were being ripped by the limestone. The porters did not notice the razor-sharp edges. Their feet naturally slotted into the best places, as if they had spent a lifetime practising the route in the dark. Hilary, being of similar size, followed one of them and placed her feet identically. I tripped and stumbled behind.

A natural dry rift, punctuated with caves and sinkholes, cut a swathe across the grain of the high plateau and we realised from the map that this would lead us to the Bakopa Pass at 12,000 feet. The valley retained vegetation but the limestone on either side stretched white and bare. The Monis called the plateau 'Tugapa', comparing it with a flat hairless skull. I savoured the rest when the porters stopped to cook some sweet potatoes.

'Which porter's got the bandages, Hilary? You did the packing.' I was not used to things going wrong with myself and was tired and grumpy. I blamed my fatigue on the jungle, and on the two weeks we had spent trailing through Indonesian bureaucracy. Hilary diagnosed my injury as 'just New Guinea knee, a well-known missionary complaint.' The afternoon rain swept in and the valley seemed endless.

After a quick discussion, the porters stopped, although it was still only early afternoon. We had reached the last water, and so we would have to wait until morning before committing ourselves to crossing the Bakopa Pass. They split into three groups and used bracken to light smoky fires under rock overhangs.

Perhaps, like the Australian Aborigines, the Papuans have a very efficient system of heat exchange between the outgoing arterial and incoming venous blood in their arms and legs. But physiological advantages were not enough. The temperature was below freezing.

'*Dingin, tuan,*' said one of them. It was the first complaint of the cold we had heard. We felt guilty in our down sleeping bags. We lent them all our spare clothes and wished we had brought more. Their teeth and the whites of their eyeballs gleamed in the low firelight. They crooned monotonous chants into the night, and started talking long before dawn.

We never identified the Bakopa Pass, because the path undulated across the plateau. The Dani in the yellow raincoat kept on racing away to the next in the procession of cols. He stood there waiting for us, barking with a mixture of fun and impatience, amid a desert of bare rocks. He had taken off his sunglasses in recognition that the weather was bad. Across the plateau we caught our first glimpse of a giant dark fin of rock scattered with fresh snow – the North Face of the Carstensz Pyramid. It was a very long day before we saw it again.

We were losing height, and the plateau was behind us. At the point where the path began to plunge downwards from the pass stood a wooden platform on poles. Inside was a half-decomposed body. I was curious. Air burial was also practised in Tibet, and many American Indian tribes exposed their dead on scaffolds, because Fire and Mother Earth were both sacred and so bodies could neither be burned nor buried. The porters said it was a Dani who had died of cold.

The two sprinting Danis started a race downhill and as we limped after them I became increasingly worried that we were losing too much height. I had anticipated a high-level traverse across to the Meren Valley in the midst of the Snow Mountains, but high cliffs barred our way and forced us ever downwards. When we came out of the mountain cloud and looked at the valley to the south, my heart sank to my muddy feet.

We were seeing the most extreme cultural confrontation in the world. One thousand feet below we saw great white buildings blocking the narrow neck of the valley, beyond the dull green swamp which we knew from our map to be the Carstensz Meadow. We could hear the hum of generators and the sporadic roar of giant earth-moving machines. High floodlights pierced the mist like alien eyes. It was the Freeport copper mine – Ertsberg. We had not realised it was so big and so near the mountains and that our approach would be so close.

Army patrols! Surat Jalans! Detection! Arrest! We stumbled and ran in near panic, trying to stop the porters from being seen. It became apparent that to reach the mountains we would have to pass within 800 yards of the high wire fence that surrounded the mine. I wanted either to rush up into the mountains immediately, or to wait in hiding until nightfall. However, most of the porters were out of sight, unaware of our worries, and the remainder were struggling far behind. We caught up with the front runners at the foot of the hill, at a little bivouac hut improvised out of corrugated-iron salvaged from the mine.

The two porters who wore shorts had produced shirts out of the depths of their string bags, and were dressing. They announced that they and two others were going down in the cable car to Tembagapura, the mining town far below the copper mine, Ertsberg, to obtain some food. Their sweet potatoes were 'habis' – finished. It was beyond their comprehension that we wanted to avoid a visit to Tembagapura, a town full of people of our race and colour. Apprehensively, we watched the four figures cross the two swamps and two rivers to the first outbuildings of the mine. By this time the remaining seven porters had arrived. We told them to stay inside the bivouac hut.

An hour later the two clothed porters returned with instructions from a 'Commandant' that we were to pack up all our things and to come across to the mine immediately. I pretended not to understand the message.

'The other two must be being kept as hostages,' said Hilary. 'If we go over there we'll be arrested and thrown out of Indonesia.' Once again, we told everyone to stay put.

The hide and seek manoeuvring forced a new initiative from the Commandant. Two figures left the mining perimeter and came towards us – soldiers with guns. Hilary and I, as well as the porters, became very agitated.

'You stay here with the gear and the porters. If we all go down there we'll never get back. I'll go across and talk to them,' I said to Hilary.

I met the soldiers when they were a third of their way from the mine. One of them was the Commandant himself. He had dark, curly hair, a moustache and wore a green uniform, and smiled with the panache of a South American bandit. They seemed to be friendly. The Commandant spoke a little English. I told him that we were just walking in the mountains and had no intention of visiting or going near the mine. He asked to see our Surat Jalans and glanced over them. I was calm now, and wondered if he would discover our guilt. I looked at his face for the change in mood when he saw the indicting 'no mountaineering' clause that had been written in by the security authorities in Jayapura. Either he did not see it, or he misunderstood, for he said nothing about it. But I could not be sure. He offered lodgings inside one of his guard huts. Politely, but insistently, I declined. He insisted that the porters spend the night there and ordered the sergeant to accompany me back to the camp-site and to wait there until 6.00 p.m., when it grew dark. I returned to Hilary under armed escort. She thought we were being arrested and I thought we might be. The sergeant dispatched all the porters across to the mine, firing his rifle wildly into the air as if trying to provoke them to stampede.

Hilary and I entertained the sergeant until dusk, plying him with cups of tea. We were uneasy about him and did not trust the casual way with which he fingered his rifle. We told him that we wanted the porters back early in the morning, and would he make sure they were released? At 6.00 p.m. we heard a rifle shot from the mine and, turning to go, the sergeant fired some answering bullets towards the mountains. 'My Commandant is very stupid,' he said, and he winked.

'What a cowboy,' muttered Hilary after he had gone.

I woke at two in the morning, thinking it was dawn. It was not the sun, but the floodlights of the mine, casting a yellow light across the valley and turning night into day. Instead of the chatter of the Monis, I could hear the throb of motors.

Hilary and I were packed and ready to move by 6.15 a.m. We had no idea how long the walk up the Meren Valley into the mountains would take – our sense of scale was deceived by the cloud and by the size the mountains had assumed in our longing imaginations. At 7.30 a.m. there was still no sign of the porters.

'What if the police have taken them all down to Tembagapura?' said Hilary. 'We may never see them again!'

I went across to the mine to investigate. Two hundred yards away, behind a wire fence thirty feet high, white men sat astride great caterpillar-tracked, ground-eating machines. But before I could make contact with them, I was greeted by the Commandant from the door of the hut. The interior walls were covered with graffiti and pictures of Javanese beauties. Four booted soldiers sprawled across bunk beds and an electric fire glowed in one corner. In the other, huddled together, were our porters; they had crushed themselves into a tiny space and were a sea of worried upturned faces. They were silent and their eyes were startled and constantly moving, as if they had been cornered in a manhunt. I tried to encourage them with a smile, but they did not even flicker with recognition. They were thousands of years away from the carefree laughing, hooting and barking of the previous days.

'Have the Monis eaten anything?' I asked.

'Who? Oh – these people?' Yes, they had.

I counted the heads. Ten. Where was the eleventh? He had gone down to Tembagapura with the sergeant and would be back about 10.00 a.m. Then the Commandant ordered all the porters out of the hut, and they stood outside in a group, shivering from the sudden change in temperature. He offered me apples, cake and tea, but I was anxious to return to Hilary and tell her of the latest developments. He insisted that he came with me, put on a dark beret, immaculate white gloves and his pistol belt, and appointed two of the porters to accompany us.

The Commandant was very unfit and complained constantly of the cold; he stopped every twenty paces and rubbed his hands together. 'It ees warm at my home in the Moluccas,' he explained. The morning sun was moving on to us but failed to warm him. He contrasted strangely with the two naked porters, but was too pre-occupied to notice it himself. Four hundred yards away from his hut, he admitted that he had never been this far from the mine before. The walk took a long time, and Hilary came to meet us, unable to stand the strain of waiting.

'I think it's O.K.,' I whispered. I gave her a green apple – her favourite fruit.

The Commandant was amazed to see the shelter, and warmed himself by the fire. Then he started writing an official document.

'What's he writing?' whispered Hilary. 'A parking ticket?'

'Zees my address – now you take photos of me and send in letter.' He put his arm around Hilary. 'You don't mind?' he asked, flashing a smile. I took a photo. Then he put his arm around me and Hilary took a photo. We all wore fixed grins.

At 9.30 a.m. all eleven of the porters came over from the mine. They had obtained some cooked rice from Tembagapura and were carrying it, wrapped into tin-foil packages. The sergeant with his rifle trailed far behind them. Thirty minutes of baffling uncertainty ensued. The porters refused to go any further. Hilary had grown to trust and respect them deeply, and their sudden reversal in behaviour shocked her. She lost her temper. She pulled all the loads out of the shelter and shouted at them to go away – she and I would carry the gear into the mountains ourselves. I asked her to calm down, telling her that porters always go on strike from time to time – it was traditional. The Commandant, impressed by Hilary's anger, decided to take over on our side. 'Excuse me, speak little English, I speak Indonesian with zeeze men. I tell them Christus says they must help you.'

After five minutes we learnt that it was all a misunderstanding. The porters were demanding 10,000 rupiahs for food. Such was our communications problem. I had told them days before that they would receive 2,000 each when we reached Base Camp.

All seemed settled, and Hilary stormed off across the marsh of the Carstensz Meadow whilst I agitatedly dispatched porters off after her. I thanked the Commandant for his help but it was a relief to move away from his jurisdiction and out of sight of the mine.

We climbed up into the hanging valley of the Meren, beneath steep limestone walls 2,000 feet high. These slopes had been climbed in 1936, by the Dutch explorers Colijn and Dozy, after they had penetrated the southern jungle from the coast. The two men had found untracked, virgin ground. Forty-two years later we were following a muddy path flanked by boulders on which had been sprayed Indonesian graffiti. Rounding a corner, we came face to face with a human skull perched on top of a pole – a forceful reminder that we were in New Guinea.

'They must come up here from the mine for Sunday afternoon picnics,' said Hilary. 'I can see a glacier.'

In the distance, part of the snow cap swept gently down into the Meren Valley, along the backs of the steep north walls of the range. It was a desolate place. We walked along fresh moraines. There was no vegetation. We passed two of the three lakes which gave the valley its Dutch name. Beside the third lake we found four big oil drums, left by the Melbourne University scientific expeditions of December and January 1971–72 and December – February 1972–73. The porters stopped. A brisk wind blew across the camp-site and it started to hail.

We had decided to keep two of the Monis, Fones and Ans, with us. Since the Base Camp was on a trading route from the north over the only gap in the ice cap – the New Zealand Pass – we did not want to risk leaving our equipment unguarded whilst we went climbing. We also hoped that keeping two would ensure that their friends returned to carry our equipment back to Bilorai. We wanted the rest of the porters to wait for us south of the mountains for seven days before rejoining us. Communicating the plan was a difficult task. I counted by sticking my fingers up, whilst the Monis brought their fingers down across their palms. Eventually I tied seven knots in a string and told them to untie one as soon as they woke each morning. Now Hilary and I took a turn to feel hungry. We watched them eat their packed lunches, fingering the rice out of the foil and sheltering from the hail behind their pandanus-leaf coats.

Before leaving, two of the Monis picked old tins from the ground and rushed up to the glacier with our ice axes, returning with the tins full of large lumps of ice. Then they all hurried back down the valley, leaving the four of us to settle into our Base Camp. Fones and Ans were to make daily ritual of this ice-collecting, continually replenishing the stock whilst we were in the mountains. Some Irian tribes call ice 'white arrow', because of its sharpness, whilst perhaps the Monis associated the white ice with the white fat of their pigs, or with salt, but for whatever reason it held an enduring fascination until it melted.

To us, the Snow Mountains of New Guinea were the most inaccessible mountains in the world – and yet our first impression on arriving in their midst was that they also had the most rubbish. For fifty feet in all directions were strewn mounds of tins, broken glass and old pieces of green canvas. It was like an industrial waste dumping ground. Owing to their scientific character, the Melbourne University expeditions had won the co-operation of the mining authorities, and their camp had been serviced by air-drops and helicopters from Tembagapura. However, the helicopters had not made the last trip to take the expeditions' debris away. The contrast between such carelessness and the scientific discipline of their book, which displayed an intense ecological concern for the area, was bewildering. I spent two hours clearing up the mess and putting it into the oil drums. The drums were full of rain water and melted snow, and when I emptied one of them a large drowned rat fell out.

'There are supposed to be marsupial cats and rats the size of sheep around here,' said Hilary. 'This rat must be a young one.'

Fones and Ans were soon settled in, wrapped in many layers of clothing and cocooned in bivouac bags. Hilary and I went on an orientation walk on to the ridge between the Meren Valley and its parallel depression, the Yellow Valley. To the north the snow fields were wreathed in mist and we guessed where they crested before the plunge of the north walls on the other side. We estimated where the New Zealand Pass was, but then its narrow rocky defile appeared to prove us wrong. It was a deep dark slice out of the iced cake of the glaciers.

To the south, pillars of mist filed down the Yellow Valley. Segments of a mountain slid in and out of view. Soon we had pieced together its picture. The Carstensz Pyramid was before us and nothing else mattered.

4   CARSTENSZ

28–29 December 1978

In London in March 1920, a paper entitled 'The Opening of New Territories in Papua' was read before the Royal Geographical Society. As the speaker, E.W. Pearson-Chinnery, droned on, one member of the audience, a Mr. A.F.R. Wollaston, became increasingly agitated. Wollaston knew as much about the interior of New Guinea as any other European at that time, and he did not agree with Pearson-Chinnery's opinions. Wollaston was one of the last of the great explorers of the Victorian Empire tradition – a scientist, a diarist and a leader, who recorded all the minute details his boundless curiosity and powers of observation could discern. Yet Wollaston was also a prophet and an idealist, with the rare gift of being able to sense the future consequences of exploration, and the damage and the exploitation that would follow. When Pearson-Chinnery finished speaking, Wollaston could contain himself no longer. He stood up and protested, making what was to be his final statement about New Guinea:

> 'Mr Chinnery objects to inter-tribal warfare. Well, we have spent many years in killing each other, at great expense, to make the world free for democracy … he says we must alter – modify – their traditions (institutions, I think is the word) so that they may 'fall into line with the needs of progress'. I hope this modifying of institutions will be very slow. You have in New Guinea the last people who have not yet

been contaminated by association with the white
races. They have an extraordinarily interesting culture of which we know very little, and we have much
to learn from them ... I believe that the whole of the
interior of New Guinea should be kept as a vast eth-
nological museum, a native reserve where these
people can live their own life, and work out their
own destiny, whatever it may be. Into that country
no traders, no missionaries, no exploiters, not even
Government Police themselves should be allowed
to go ... Perhaps it is an impossible dream, but I am
looking ahead through two or three more centuries,
and the example of the fate of the Tasmanians and
the present condition of the aboriginal Australian
native ought to be a sufficient warning.'

Wollaston had pioneered a way from the Arafura Sea to the South
Face of the Carstensz Pyramid in 1913. Ironically his reports were
the basis of exploration which eventually culminated in the 1970s
in the largest economic undertaking in Irian Jaya – the exploitation of the Ertsberg mine, and the growth of Temagapura – 'copper town' – just to the south, where 2,000 people now live. It had
taken Wollaston ninety-two days to cover the last thirty-one miles
to the mountain. Now, a few miles to the west of Wollaston's route,
a road runs from the coast to service town and mine. This road is
the longest in Irian Jaya. It took three years for it to be bridged and
tunnelled through the jungle to the mountains, using massive
earth-moving equipment, trucks, large helicopters and huge
amounts of explosives. The Free Papua Movement and economic
demand permitting, the Freeport Mining Scheme will continue
for another thirty years, until the ore is exhausted – dramatic proof
that Wollaston's dream was, indeed, impossible.

After Wollaston, the interior of Irian defended itself from the
outside world until the 1930s when pilots in small amphibious aircraft began to explore and map the main valleys. When Hilary and
I were planning our route on the South Face of Carstensz we

consulted the first photographs of the area taken by the Dutch Lieutenant J.F. Wissel, while making reconnaissance flights in an S-38 for Colijn's 1936 expedition. The Dutch failed to climb the Carstensz Pyramid, but did discover the unique copper node at Ertsberg, the largest above-ground outcrop of base metal ore in the world.

On his various reconnaissance flights Wissel reported the presence of a large native population and the people called his plane 'the roaring prow'. No Western explorer has ever discovered a substantial area of habitable land that is not already inhabited.

In the wake of the flyers came the missionaries, setting up a network of missions to the north of the Snow Mountains in the 1950s, and after the missionaries came the mountaineers.

The Carstensz Pyramid had a Gothic splendour. Mist, rain and hail increased its remoteness and inhospitality – and accentuated its size. Hilary and I were never to see it subdued beneath a strong sun and lost beneath the expanse of an open blue sky. Its North Face comprised large, monolithic blue-grey slabs of steeply tilted limestone bedding. We identified the easiest line up the wall, where Philip Temple and the Austrian mountaineer, Heinrich Harrer, had led their team when they made the first ascent of the mountain in 1962. They had followed a ramp that stretched up to the West Ridge, and then made a lengthy traverse along the ridge to the summit.

Between 1971 and 1974 the Carstensz Pyramid was visited by five different expeditions, most of them approaching the mountains from the north west along the path found by Temple from Ilaga. The original route up the mountain was straightened out with an approach to the West Ridge nearer to the summit. This route was repeated three times, the East Ridge was climbed and the North Face was criss-crossed with four new routes. This face obviously offered some superb climbing, but Hilary and I wanted to tread on new ground.

It had been a copy of a letter from Bruce Carson, to Hermann Huber of a 1974 Munich expedition, that had first drawn our attention to the South Face. Carson, a brilliant young American rock climber, had climbed the Pyramid three times in 1973, but had been killed in the Himalayas in 1975. He had written:

> The best climb yet to be done is the South Face. It would be a major undertaking, however. If you were going to try it, it would be good to climb the easiest northern route first, to have the descent memorised, and to get a look at the hanging glacier and 'schrunds near the top to the climb. Also, I'm not sure how one can get down to the base of the face. It might be possible to cross the ridge at the notch between the Pyramid and Wollaston Peak and then descend to the foot of the face. We didn't get to that notch, so I'm not sure if it would work. If it doesn't work, then it's a very long way around either side – several days. The South Face is definitely a challenging objective.

As Hilary and I looked across the tail of the Carstensz Glacier, we could see the notch which Carson had referred to. We tried to memorise the route to it across scree and glacier, so that we could start our approach to the route in the dark.

Back at Base Camp we scanned the two aerial photographs we had of the face – Wissel's of 1936 and one taken by Richard Muggleton as part of the Melbourne University project. The 'eternal snow' of the 1936 Dutch book title had shrunk. It was like looking at two different mountains. In 1936 the whole face had been plastered by a huge, hanging glacier, but in 1972 the glacier had receded, buttresses projected from it and its icefalls looked more complex. It was now seven years since the last photograph had been taken, and we had seen no clues as to the state of the southern side in our view from the north. It was like discussing the dark side of the moon from a couple of satellite photographs.

Since we would only have a week among the mountains we allowed ourselves just that first afternoon's walk to orientate ourselves. There was no time to climb the easiest route up the Pyramid first so as to become familiar with the descent as Carson had suggested, or to do a training climb to acquire a feel for the area. We decided to start early the next day for the South Face. Overawed by the aloofness of the mountain and by the seriousness implicit in Carson's letter, we selected our equipment carefully.

Fones and Ans looked puzzled as we sorted out our bivouac equipment and the hardware of crampons, ice hammers, screws, nuts, pegs and karabiners. They coughed a lot during the night, their noise combining with the sniffing of a marauding rat to keep me awake.

At 5.30 a.m. we set out into the mist and darkness. Shapes and distances were confusing and our sketch maps were only a rough guide because since they had been drawn the glaciers had obviously melted. I took out my compass and we stumbled towards an occasional glimpse of whiteness in the night, which we knew to be the Carstensz Glacier.

The toe of the glacier was an ice slope, which tilted back at sixty degrees for 300 feet. We put on the rope and ice gear. It seemed as if our feet had been cloyed in mud for days. Despite the heavy rucksacks we were carrying, we revelled in the clean, balancing movements of front pointing on crampons. As we climbed into the dawn the soft, silted colours of the Yellow Valley beneath the North Face of Carstensz opened out below us; we could see the freshly ground browns, yellows and reds left by the retreating glacier. It took us half an hour to cross the notch between Wollaston Peak and the East Ridge of Carstensz, and we hoped that the patches of blue that illuminated our walk heralded a clear morning. But all views have to be snatched in Irian, and cloud was rushing in again as we reached the notch. The Pyramid's East Ridge swept up on our right side. It was easy angled at first, but soon disappeared into a tangle of cloud-swept towers. Looking to the south we saw a hundred feet of scree vanishing into a cauldron of mist. We took long strides downwards, peering apprehensively for hidden cliffs and thrilled with the prospect of untrodden ground. It was a hundred years since exploratory climbs of this type were done in the Western Alps.

We had chanced upon a cliff-free descent, and lost height rapidly. The mist was so thick that the sudden clearings gave the fleeting insights of an erratic lighthouse – we picked out a prominent boulder, memorised the ground between, and as the mist closed in again, we followed the memory until it faded.

We squinted around, looking for the South Face glacier. According to the most recent photographs, we should have been standing on it. We crossed two great ridges that stuck out of the mountainside like the ribs of a skeleton, following a horizontal break in the strata that cut across them. I glanced over my shoulder and saw, for thirty seconds, the Arafura Sea seventy miles away appear in a cloud window. It glimmered beyond the coast and then the hole closed up.

'Hard luck, Hilary, you've just missed it.'

But where was the glacier? I reached the second ridge a few feet ahead of Hilary and for a minute I sucked in the only view of the South Face I was to see all day. It looked blank and forbidding, like an alpine north face in the grip of a summer storm. I tried to describe it to Hilary when she arrived: 'There's an enormous amphitheatre of sort of tiered shelves and the glacier's really high up, split into two. At least it doesn't look as if we'll be pegging over soggy ice walls. I couldn't see the top, though. We'll just have to guess where the middle is and wander up. It looks really loose.'

We zigzagged backwards and forwards, climbing over bulges in between the sloping shelves. Small stones were falling constantly around us from out of the mist, and we put our helmets on. We did not dare tie a rope between us, for fear that it would snag around the large poised rocks and disturb them on top of us. Although we were placing our hands and feet carefully, we occasionally nudged large rocks which bounced and thundered into the abyss below.

'Do you think you can manage that bit, Hilary? I'll climb next to you. Just say if you get gripped or need any help.'

'Course I don't.'

I wondered what would I say to her Mum and Dad if she slipped? If it were Tasker I'd just let him get on with it and think of myself. What a place to bring her for her Christmas holidays. Why were we climbing this tottering heap instead of those clean, solid slabs of the North Face?

The sky was baptising us in the masochistic Irianese art of climbing in the rain – water was pouring down, loosing more and more stones on to us. After two hours of steady climbing we reached the two ice slopes. We followed the thin ribbon of rock between them until it petered out. We put on our crampons and I set off soloing. It was steep, hard, water ice, and sixty feet up I remembered Hilary.

'Hang on and I'll drop a rope.'

After another 150 feet of steep ice we flopped into the shelter of the bergschrund where the ice terminated beneath a ring of rock overhangs. The rain had turned to sleet and we could hear the wind blow from the north across the ridge a few hundred feet above our heads. We were in the Stalls, and wanted to reach the Circle.

It was like climbing in a recently blasted quarry. An unstable pillar of rock dropped down towards us from the lip of the overhang, like an unwrapped packet of yellow biscuits twenty feet high. Flakes of rock broke off beneath my hands and feet, as I edged gingerly up trying to put my feet on the most stable holds. I breathed carefully, concentrating so as to avoid any sudden movement that could endanger my precarious balance. Moving over the top of the overhang was the crux. Instead of a ledge to heave on to, there was a steep slope of half-frozen sand. I hacked into it with my ice hammer and short ice axe and clawed around the lip, stepping high with my feet. The sand moved as I eased my weight on to my boots and kicked furiously up the slope above for fifty feet, as if I were rushing up a down-moving escalator, my blood warming to the excitement of the action. The debris I dislodged cascaded over the overhang above Hilary and blocked the sky from her like a curtain.

If that had been the Circle, now I was in the Gods. When she arrived, Hilary admired the two-foot-wide ledge I was standing on. It ran continuously across the wall, like a pathway carved out of a limestone cave, so that it could be opened to the general public.

'Oh, what a lovely ledge, a good place for a bivouac,' she said.

'We might need one, I can't get past this overhang,' I muttered. Although it was only mid-day, we had arrived at an impasse that blocked all hope of continuing directly to the ridge. Ten feet above our heads a smooth, ten-foot-wide overhang stretched into the mist in both directions.

We had nearly reached 16,000 feet, and were tiring in the thinning air. Our heavy rucksacks had become unwelcome partners inhibiting our movements. I left mine with Hilary, sitting on the ledge, and sidestepped like a crab, into the murk, to make a solitary reconnaissance. The shelf petered out into a shattered rib of rock. I stepped round this into a wide chimney that split the obstacle of the overhang. I wriggled up the chimney until I could see the ridge, shouting: 'We're there. We're there!' I returned to Hilary, picked up my sack and we climbed up the chimney together.

The wind across the ridge quickly pierced through our sodden clothes. We lay down and peered cautiously over the edge of the north side. Flurries of hail and sleet blew into our eyes and made us duck. The world beneath was divided from us by hours of mountain. Through scudding cloud we could glimpse patches of the Yellow Valley, 2,000 feet below. I felt giddy at seeing the drop, for the thicker mist of the south side had cushioned our previous downwards view.

'Are we on the top, then?' asked Hilary.

'I don't know, I think so,' I replied. But we were not. Higher towers of rock taunted us on our left, in the west. We peered for a long time along the ridge to the right, trying to extract rock images from the moving cloud, until we were sure there was no point higher than us in that direction. We turned left.

The ridge was as razor sharp as the rock itself, but at least it was stable. Soon the ends of our gloves were torn away. At one awkward step Hilary caught her anorak sleeve and it ripped apart. She cursed the sleeve and rock as if they had plotted the tear, and then cursed the rucksack for pulling her backwards and making her clumsy. She often gave life to inanimate objects, and I told her so.

'Well, I prefer talking to plants, but I can't do that up here,' she said, and then confronted me for giving her such a heavy sack to carry.

Our progress along the ridge was halted by a deep gap. I failed to climb down and across it. We had to retrace our steps back along the ridge and down the chimney into the comparative shelter of the South Face. At two o'clock that afternoon we were back on the shelf of the Gods at exactly the same place we had been two hours before. The good progress of the morning had been lost.

The remaining hours of daylight began to tick away in my head like a metronome. This time we traversed left, westward along the shelf. I yelled at Hilary for not trying to climb more quickly, left her again and soloed off on another reconnaissance. I was becoming angry with Hilary, the mountain, the rain and wind and myself. I tried to rationalise and to channel my frustration into energy. I moved faster and faster, alone in a private world of mist and rock. 'Why does she always seem to move so slowly when the going gets rough? Why do I shout at her and long for an equal? I'd never do that to any other climbing partner – it's unfair, it's not that serious a situation. But I don't want to spend a night out in this and we must get a move on. What if the summit really was to the east? What if we're going the wrong way up?'

I followed the shelf beneath the gap that had turned us back on the ridge's crest. The ground began to open out and I spotted a line of ramps and gullies leading out of the South Face and on to the ridge. I returned and collected Hilary and my rucksack. We dumped our expensive ice screws in a symbolic attempt to shed some of our loads and set off again.

We regained the ridge beyond the obstacles of major gaps and towers. The rising crest indicated that we were climbing in the right direction. I raced out ropelength after ropelength, towing Hilary behind. Every time she stopped I took a photograph of her, which infuriated her. If she could spare a hand she put it on her hip and shouted into the sleet: 'Don't take photographs of me looking like this, my face is all puffy with the altitude,' and 'Stop bullying me and treating me like a sack of coal – let me climb it properly.' She could not hear my replies because her anorak hood was drawn tight against the wind.

A wooden pole lying on the ridge was the first evidence of the summit. We soon found other relics. We opened two rain-drenched tins and found soggy notes from the 1974 Munich climbers and Carson's party the year before. There were little flags of New Zealand and Indonesia in a polythene bag, and inside a plastic film container were locks of hair. In the mist these were the only signs that we sat on the summit. 'Just think, you're the only bird that's been up here, and there's no one higher than us from the Andes to the Himalayas.'

'Except in planes,' she said. They were brief moments of relaxation. It was 3.00 p.m. and in two and a half hours it would be dark.

I tried to goad her into hurrying. 'Come on, Hilary, pull yourself together, an hour's effort will make the difference between a night out up here or not. You don't want to sit up here for twelve hours in the wind and rain, do you?' My tone was deliberately unpleasant.

Our descent of the West Ridge was checked by a forty-foot-deep cleft. It was too steep to climb down on our side. Then Hilary noticed an aluminium nut and nylon sling in a crack – it was a reassuring signpost that we were coming down the normal route up the mountain. We doubled the rope, passed it through the sling and abseiled into the bottom of the cleft.

'I'll go down a bit further and have a look,' I said. I threw the rope down again and slid a hundred feet down the wall of the North Face. I stopped and became a gently swaying pendulum, surrounded by moving mist. Screwing up my eyes, I looked into the gloom beneath my feet. Four hundred feet below I saw the reddish blur of a sandy ramp, cutting diagonally downwards across the Face. It was our descent route, but this was not the way to reach it. I hauled my way back up the ropes and rejoined Hilary. We climbed out on to the lower lip of the cleft, and continued down the crest, soon arriving at the point where the top of the ramp met the West Ridge.

The ramp was filled with fine scree. Hilary suddenly started moving more quickly. Eager to lose height, we half ran down, digging our heels in. Within twenty minutes we had dropped nearly a thousand feet. Then the ramp stopped and the rock slabs of the North Face curved away convexly, concealing from us a view of the valley floor. The slabs were scored by shallow channels and water was sheeting down them, turning them into a steep weir.

'Come on, let's go straight down,' said Hilary. 'It can't be far.' Facing inwards, she started soloing down one of the water runnels.

Worried, I clambered after her, thinking that she was becoming over-confident and accident prone. Water was pouring down our sleeves. I feared the rock would be slippery, but it remained rough and clean despite the deluge.

'Let's stop and abseil,' I said. 'It'll be safer.'

Three times we slid down 150-foot ropelengths until our feet touched gentle ground. We were safe. We would not have to bivouac.

'I never realised you could get so angry,' said Hilary.

Within minutes it became totally dark. We realised how wet we were. My head torch failed to work and the darkness was so dense that Hilary's torch was not strong enough to light the way across the boulders for both of us at the same time. I took it, walked twenty feet and shone the light back for Hilary. Stop. Go. Stop. Go. The rain pelted across the beam of the light and the distance to Base Camp stretched beyond our imagination.

'*Tuan!*' Fones and Ans sounded happy to hear the clinking of our hardware as we walked into the camp. That night even the rat did not wake me up.

5 DUGUNDUGU

30 December 1978–1 January 1979

We spread out our equipment with ceremony. It was a great event. We had climbed the Carstensz Pyramid, the sun was shining and we hoped that our equipment and clothes would be dry, for the first time since we had entered the interior of Irian Jaya. It was our first rest day since the tide in our fortunes turned in Jayapura ten days before. We discussed the weather – it seemed to be getting better, and perhaps we might now have alternate good days. However, we spoke too soon, for the sunshine was a brief respite. The early morning wind picked up cloud and rain, and we scuttled about packing everything away again. The gear was still damp for our next adventure.

A wild dog came up the Meren Valley to investigate our arrival, and howled at us. The retreating glaciers of the Snow Mountains had left our camp surrounded by bleak, recently exposed screes and gaunt moraines. It was an inhospitable place, and we wanted to move on.

On New Year's Eve we set out to explore the northern side of the mountains, where the highest cliffs of the range rise out of the tussocky grass of the Kemabu Plateau. Fones and Ans did not want to go with us and preferred to stay at Base Camp. Hilary and I left on our own, carrying enough food for two and a half days, and all our climbing equipment.

To reach the path up to New Zealand Pass, it was necessary to re-trace a few hundred yards of our approach route. We walked around a corner and suddenly came face to face with five Indonesians, dressed in yellow industrial jackets and Wellington boots. My first reaction was that they were an army patrol sent to arrest us. Our paranoia at encountering officialdom at the mine had not worn off. It was too late to avoid them, so we smiled as if to imply the normality of our being there. They were startled but friendly, and said they were going for a New Year's Eve picnic.

In Wissel's aerial photographs in 1936, New Zealand Pass did not exist, for it was still choked with ice, and the snow cap of the mountains stretched around in an unbroken horseshoe to the Carstensz Pyramid. When Temple found the pass in 1961, however, it had probably been ice-free for about ten years, and was already used by the natives from the north and south on hunting and trading trips. At 14,764 feet (4,500 metres), it is the highest pass in New Guinea.

It was an impressive canyon, and the prospect of new country lightened our steps as we crossed it. Now without our Moni guides, we could explore the land ourselves. We felt privileged to be there.

At the highest point of the pass, on the path in front of us, was a ring of nine small stones, carefully arranged inside another large ring about two feet in diameter, of eighteen stones. We looked around and saw a human skull on a rock, peering hollowly at us. We had heard that in 1976 twenty-three natives had frozen to death in a storm whilst crossing the pass – perhaps this ritual arrangement was a symbolic remnant or plea for the benevolence of their ghosts.

The wealth and curiosity value of the mine had certainly increased the amount of travel over the mountains during the 1970s. As we descended the northern side of the pass we met three tiny men and two boys, wearing only kotekas and carrying bows and arrows. They were coming up to the pass, having travelled from Beoga, a settlement to the north of the mountains. They greeted us by pulling our fingers, and hastily produced a typed Surat Jalan, which we guessed had been prepared by a missionary. We looked at it, although we could not understand it. We gave them a sweet each and watched, worried for them, as they threaded up into the cold mists that were now building up on the mountains.

There was something lemming-like about this vulnerability to the allure of Western curiosities, that caused people to walk into such a dangerous place, naked and unprepared. It seemed an attraction they could never be inoculated against. When Wollaston was approaching the mountains from the south coast in 1913, he had received daily visits from hill people, come to investigate the strange sights they had heard about. As he neared the mountains, he found many dead huddles of them – forty in total – who had run out of food on the return journey or succumbed to the cold. He was puzzled, because they did not appear emaciated, and concluded that they must have just given up and died.

Below us we could see Lake Larson, named after the American missionary at Ilaga who had been met by the expeditions of the early 1970s when they approached the mountains from the airstrip there. Our first priority was to find a boulder to bivouac under, for we had left the tents at Base Camp. We knew that near the lake there was a huge erratic block – the Mapala Boulder – which many expeditions from Ilaga had used as a Base. This was a traditional bivouac, for Melbourne University had found evidence in the remnants of cowrie shells, fire and bones there that suggested man has traded and hunted wallaby and echidna on the plateau for between three and five thousand years, and eaten and slept under the shelter of the boulder. However, it was at too low an altitude for our purposes, and we contoured eastwards under the vast 3,000-foot north walls of the three summits of Ngga Pulu. The walls were a dramatic contrast to the rolling snows of their other side, and rose out of the gently undulating Kemabu Plateau with the ninety-degree abruptness of sea cliffs. My eyes were increasingly drawn to the crags, searching for possible lines of climbable weakness, and neglecting the discipline of the boulder search.

Hilary found a boulder before I found a possible route. It was an ideal bivouac with a jutting roof that would provide enough shelter to keep the rain out, and a little spring running out from underneath it. There were the tracks of wild dogs nearby, so we placed our food and equipment under heavy stones before going on a reconnaissance.

As we were about to leave, we heard the metallic soaring clatter of a helicopter overhead. Instinctively, we dived back under the rock, ducking like Vietcong evading an airborne gunship. We soon realised how unlikely it was that we were being pursued – the helicopter was probably surveying for the mine, or taking Freeport executives on a New Year's Eve sightseeing trip. Nevertheless, it seemed best to stay out of sight. Twice the helicopter swept backwards and forwards, along the base of the cliffs, then disappeared over New Zealand Pass as suddenly as it had arrived. Its whirring engines echoed for a few moments, and then the sound died away.

Owing to the constantly shifting patchwork of mist, it had taken us until now to become familiar with the topography of the mountains. They were laid out like a rectangle with an open end in the west – the Meren Valley, up which we had come initially with the porters. Base Camp was in the middle. The bottom south line with the Carstensz Pryamid and the north line was interrupted by New Zealand Pass. Glaciers sloped down towards Base Camp from north and east lines, and six miles of vertical cliffs plunged down on their other sides – under which we now stood. The highest of the three summits of Ngga Pulu, Sunday Peak, was on the top corner, where the north and east lines met. It was the North Wall of this that we wanted to climb.

Reinhold Messner compared these North Walls to the Civetta, and they looked as awe-inspiring as any Dolomite cliff. They were broken into several complex towers by steep gullies down which ice from the snow cap occasionally fell. The walls had been climbed previously in only three places, and there were countless other tempting possibilities. But we never saw the complete face in the mist and teeming rain. We sat under our boulder and watched lightning flash down a valley to the east, brewing a huge storm that moved towards and over us. It was like being in the Ark.

'Happy New Year.' My attitude clarified, and at ten minutes past midnight I said: 'I think this weather's trying to tell us something.'

Immediately, Hilary advocated strongly that, instead of the Sunday Peak wall, we should attempt one of the two pillars on the

North Face of Dugundugu – the mountain immediately west of New Zealand Pass. 'At least we might get up it,' she said.

Towards morning the rain slackened and shafts of sombre light broke through the leaden clouds and chased them away towards the west. We left in the half-light, and by the time the sun lit up the backcloth of mountains I had seen enough of Sunday Peak to confirm the decision against an attempt. Dugundugu looked much more tempting. After picking up the cache, we once more sorted out the gear, sifting a different selection for the new objective. This time we did not take bivouac equipment, thus committing ourselves to having to climb the mountain or retreat before nightfall. It was a serious step, and Hilary re-plaited her pigtails in preparation for a hard day.

We gained as much height as possible on the path up to New Zealand Pass, and then traversed across. The North Face of Dugundugu was divided by a great chasm into two pillars, 1,600 feet high. At the base of this chasm we could see the blue gleam of the ice cap on the other side of the mountain. Dugundugu was the Danis' word for snow mountain – but it was the glacier on the other side of the mountain that gave it the name. The North Face was all rock. The right-hand pillar seemed the more feasible climbing proposition. Its bands of overhangs were split by a long crack which, in the morning sunshine, appeared to be a fabulous line – a clear solution to an improbable buttress. The first 200 feet looked the most difficult.

We crossed the bed of the chasm and gained a hundred feet of height by unroped scrambling. Hilary anchored herself to a large flake of rock on the edge of the pillar and admired the view. Loops of rope swung down into the abyss. I started climbing, breathing deeply. I had bought some new boots for the expedition, and this was the first steep rock climbing I had done with them. I tested them, balancing on little toeholds. The rock felt familiar. It was, I told myself, just another limestone rock pitch, like carboniferous limestone anywhere – steep, loose, with unexpected pockets and too many holds to choose from, but none of them big enough. I focused all my attention on it, trying to forget that I was in New Guinea and that Hilary was holding the rope. She was soon out of sight.

I launched myself up the rock, swinging out on to the central edge of the pillar. The rock was cut away below me and there was a drop of a thousand feet beneath my boots. Now, with my nose pressed against the rock, the route was not as obvious as it had seemed from below. The crack did not emerge from the gentle overhanging sweep of rock beside me until it broke through a four-foot-wide horizontal roof, thirty feet above my head. I decided to follow a rib of rock to the roof and hand-traversed right to the crack. I tapped in a piton at eye level, clipped the rope in and balanced up.

For fifteen feet, holds curled under the tips of my fingers. Then the rib became smooth. I hung out from one hand and slipped a tiny wire nut into a thin crack, clipped the rope in and started lay-backing, feet and hands pushing and pulling, braced against the rib, drawing nearer and nearer to the roof. I knew it was essential to remain calm and to keep on going. All that existed was myself and a few feet of rock.

My arms were tiring and my fingers were beginning to open out. With one hand I quickly hammered a piton in, hoping to grab it before my strength drained completely. But before I could clip into it I started to sway off backwards, in slow motion. I had levered off the top ten feet of the rock rib and was keeling over with it! I screamed as I fell, pushing myself away from the blocks of rock that were falling with me. Rock blurred past, until I swooped on to the end of rope and the downwards plunge stopped. I was hanging clear, slowly yo-yoing up and down on the stretch of the nylon, and spinning at the same time.

'Are you all right?' shouted Hilary.

Although I was now back on the same level, we could not see each other because of the curve of the pillar. 'I don't know, I think so. Must have gone about twenty feet. I'll try and swing back in.' I grabbed a projecting spike to stop myself spinning, and pulled myself towards it. 'Take the rope in, Hilary, I'm just transferring my weight back on to the rock.'

As I did so, the two enormous blocks I had stepped on, and the spike I was holding on to, all detached from the mountain and disappeared below me in a thunderous roar. I slipped again, shrieking with surprise. When my weight hit the rope the strain was too much for the nut runner, which snapped out. I fell another twenty feet, jerking Hilary so hard she let the rope slide another ten feet. A few small rocks fell past me, and then there was silence. I was scratched and bruised and my clothes were torn. It was a long climb back up.

I clipped in the rope to the piton of my previous high point and stood up in a sling. It was better to go straight back up on to the climb than to return to Hilary, lick my wounds, rest and risk second thoughts. I traversed on my hands under the roof and pulled myself over it, bracing palms and elbows across the crack. It was 'off-width' – too wide to handjam, too narrow to wriggle inside, easy to get stuck in, and difficult to move up in – and was caked in mud.

'It's like Right Eliminate at Curbar,' I yelled, 'bloody desperate and no protection.' I panted and heaved, wriggled and pulled, inching slowly upwards. After fifteen feet it became wider, and I scraped some finger holds out of the mud, wrenched myself upwards and sprawled on to a ledge, gasping like a landed fish.

Hilary did not waste time and energy by climbing after me. She just fastened on her jumar clamps and came up on the rope, swinging off on the traversing parts and bouncing up and down like a demented puppet. 'I hope that was the hardest bit,' she said.

'Well, at least we've got going.'

Retreat, we decided, would now be difficult, and the roof and overhanging rocks below us gave an extra incentive to struggle on upwards. We had been so absorbed in our acrobatics that we had not noticed it had begun to drizzle. We donned waterproofs.

Above us the main crack opened up into an overhanging chimney, but by traversing a ledge rightwards I found some easier cracks. I swarmed up them, infused with a sense of abandon after the hard climbing below.

'It's about grade four,' I yelled. 'You'll love it.'

She did. 'I enjoy that sort of climbing,' she said when she reached me.

The climb was starting to flow. The route-finding was deliciously intricate. Overhangs and bulges barred our way but always there was a way to thread around them. The wall leant back in a shallow corner 200 feet high, like a half-open book on a great tilted lectern. We pranced up it, savouring the freedom of balancing on tiny, solid incut holds. We were feeling in tune with the rock. Clouds slid beneath our feet, opening windows on the valley floor.

The pillar reared up again and narrowed, squeezing us back into the line of the chimney crack. With one boot on either side of the chimney, we bridged up it. Suddenly, the clouds opened. When the deluge began we were trapped in the largest natural water course of the entire pillar. I dodged under an overhang and tied myself to the rock, taking the rope in as Hilary climbed up towards me. This shelter gave me confidence. I was warming to the excitement of the fight.

'Come on, Hilary – with your Geordie mining blood, you should be enjoying this. We've got enough time! We're going to do it!'

She was hit by a shock-wave of water that almost knocked her off the rock, pouring all over her. She blamed me, tossing her sodden, tangled pigtails out of her eyes as she shouted: 'Don't take pictures of me. I hate you.'

When she started shivering, I felt guilty that I was drier. We continued up the waterfall, and escaped from the chimney as soon as the pillar allowed. In the alternating cycles of rain, sleet and snow, I soon became as drenched as Hilary.

Like most mountain tops of the world, the summit of Dugundugu was elusive. Every time we stopped on a ledge we ensured it was under an overhang out of the rain, and said 'The next pitch must get us there. It'll give in soon.' But more of the mountain rose up in front of us.

Faced with a smooth slab, fifteen feet high, covered in water, I balanced five rocks on top of each other and teetered on top of them to reach a hold at full stretch. Such tactics would be seen as cheating on British rock, but I was too wet for ethics. I tiptoed up a blank, leaning corner. The climbing was airy and exhilarating and I was lost in it when the air around me lightened, and then blew across my face. My boots crackled on the fractured limestone of the summit. Ten feet away sloped the glacier of the other side of the mountain. Twenty feet away, sky and snow blended together in whiteness.

The wind bit deep into my elation. Hilary seemed an age arriving and I started a shouting match again, which dissolved when her head popped up over the ridge.

'Sorry I yelled, but it did seem to work,' I said.

'Which way now? Left?'

'I suppose so.'

'I think Dugundugu means slush mountain.'

We sank up to our knees as we wallowed down through the snow and haze until we found New Zealand Pass. We dumped our ropes and hardware to pick up the next day and stumbled down for an hour in the relentless rain, hurrying to find the boulder before darkness fell. On the plateau we tripped over tussocks and splashed across small, shallow lakes that in the morning had been doughy, silted flats. The ground dimmed and we stumbled; in the dusk and cloud, all the boulders looked the same. Hilary found it but it was the last thing she did that day.

'You'll have to cook the tea for once,' she said.

It had been a savage New Year's Day.

6 AN IMPOSSIBLE DREAM

2–18 January 1979

When we saw our Base Camp below in the Meren Valley, we halted in alarm.

'Hey, there's a big white thing next to our tents.'

Something or someone had arrived at our Base Camp and I felt a sudden wave of resentment. But the new arrivals were not a threat. They were the Frenchmen, Jean Fabre and Bernard Domenech, with whom we'd been in touch back in Europe. Now we compared notes happily on what Bernard described as the administrative steeplechase of Indonesian bureaucracy. Fones and Ans looked on, playing their bamboo mouth harps. All day it rained and rained.

One day remained before the seven knots in the string Hilary and I had given to our porters would all be undone, and they would soon return to collect us. So we invited Jean and Bernard to join us in a relaxed high-altitude wander along the summits of Ngga Pulu.

But next morning, Jean decided to go down to the mine to plead for medical aid. He was complaining of a terrible pain in his shoulder and suspected the wet weather was the cause.

'In the South of France,' he said, 'the cliffs are warm with sun. I am not used to all this water.'

Bernard, however, was still enthusiastic to come with us on the snow traverse. We told Fones and Ans that we would be back in five hours and walked towards the toe of the Meren Glacier. The dawn sun soon became watery behind the mist and sleet. We passed occasional cairns that described the dying glacier's one-mile retreat over the previous forty years. Without winters to recoup its strength, it was a mystery how the glacier survived at all.

Pitted across the lower slopes of the glacier were many ponds ten feet in diameter of black, sun-absorbing, ice-eating cryoalgae. Scientists have not decided how these growths of specialised bacteria originated. Perhaps they were brought by birds from the nearest ice areas, thousands of miles away. But it is certain they combine with the climate to melt away the tiny remnants of the great ice sheet that once spilled over the Kemabu Plateau from the mountains. We rose into perpetual cloud, ploughed through the slushy snow, and became more lost than a couple of professional guides should admit to, and took in all three summits of Ngga Pulu – including the highest, Sunday Peak – almost by accident. At the third summit we found a short note from the Munich men who'd been there in 1974 and a visiting card in a tin tube – 'Alpine International, Reinhold Messner.' After a long descending traverse we emerged into drizzle below the white blanket of cloud. Having gone into the cloud at one side of the range, we had come out of it at the other.

Next morning our porters bounded up towards us like long-lost friends. Everyone except the two Danis from Wanibugi had returned. Our loads were quickly taken off us and distributed.

Suddenly, two of them sprang off into the mists towards the glacier, in the opposite direction to the homeward journey.

'What on earth are they doing now?'

'It'll be raining soon.'

'Not more complications!'

Twenty minutes later the two Monis returned, grinning, and carrying under their arms large chunks of ice.

We met Jean Fabre coming up the path. He had avoided any contact with the police at the mine, and instead had approached some sturdy Australians driving bulldozers, who had stared at him, gaping with disbelief as if he had come from the moon. They quickly ushered him through the Ertsberg mine site and down the cable line to Tembagapura, where an American doctor gave him an analgesic and a luxurious bedroom suite for the night. Although he had been kept hidden, Jean had seen much. He was brimming with stories about the town – its 2,000 people, cinema, super-market, cold beers, showers, tennis courts, restaurants, and a loud-speaker playing Tom Jones singing 'The Green Green Grass of Home'. The people below thought him strange to have come to the mountains and had treated him suspiciously, as if he were slightly mad.

After descending to the Carstensz Meadow, we hurried under torrential rain to the makeshift shelter we had used on the way up. The Monis soon lit a fire and showed us some of their loot from the mine and from the journey they had made whilst we were in the mountains – mainly tin cans and boxes. Inside their string bags were precious smaller objects, wrapped with leaves into bundles. They had brought some food for us too – six big tins of fish, some rice and two packets of biscuits. We seized them greedily, for our food supplies were nearly exhausted, and we were perpetually hungry. Now was not the time to indulge in idealistic objections to the existence of the mine. Because it was there we took advantage of it, just as Jean had done in hurrying down to seek medical help.

There were bursts of laughter from the Monis as they gathered around the fire. I longed to understand what stories Fones and Ans were telling the others about the strange antics of the *tuans* among the Snow Mountains above. The mine must have seemed even more mysterious to them. What did they conclude from the appearance of apparently inexhaustible supplies of metal, cloth and food? For in this slice of the West amid the wilderness, it made better economic sense to replace rather than repair most equipment. As a result, vast quantities of refuse and unwanted materials were simply moved out of the way and abandoned.

Deprived of explanation, the Papuans tended to see only the most superficial aspects of Western techno-culture, and tried to imitate them. We had read of a number of cargo cults that stemmed from the arrival of the copper mine. There was the man who claimed to be a Messiah and convinced a village group to stop the cultivation of crops in the expectation that unceasing riches would be provided if a key could be found to unlock a stone on the mountain. In 1971, helicopter pilots had reported that villages south of the mountains had built large copies of helicopter pads, presumably so as to attract the flying machines to land and lay wealth like golden eggs.

Looking at the Monis around the fire, we felt very protective towards them and apprehensive about their future.

In that long, first day's walk, we covered ground that had taken two days to cross during our approach to the mountains. The rain stayed away until 4.00 p.m. As we traversed the Kemabu Plateau the wedge-shaped tower of the Dugundugu and the dark mass of the Carstensz Pyramid receded behind us, looking like great heads, their dark North Faces shadowed by the sunlight. All their details of chimney, wall and traverse where we had stretched our ropes and our limbs were hidden from us in their distant bulk.

A snow quail whirred away from amongst us and the Monis seized bows and arrows and split up quickly into different directions like a well-deployed rugby team, trying to fend it off and catch it. They ran, crouching, hundreds of yards over the tussocky grass and limestone pavement as the bird flew unconsciously about, apparently unaware that it was being chased. Its every move caused its pursuers vast expenditures of energy. It stopped on a large bush but flew again as Fones raised his bow, and the arrow skittered across the empty branch. Eventually the snow quail cackled away towards inaccessible crags, and the Monis returned to their loads, laughing with the fun of the chase.

Next day we reached Ugimba – civilisation at last. The sweet potato terraces, huts, smiling children and women in a gentle sunlit breeze were ordered and sane after the ferocity of the jungle. I lay down with my head on my rucksack on a deliciously wide stretch of grass and looked with affection at the leisurely pace of old men, toddling babies and rooting pigs. The brand-new rattan bridge was golden in the afternoon sun and the previously muddy waters of the Kemabu River were blue and smooth.

From our map we recognised the track branching off towards Bilorai. I was keen to follow it, so as to avoid losing height. But the porters refused to go into enemy territory, and insisted that we descend towards their village of Titigi, four hours away.

'Damn their stupid war,' I said. 'I'm shattered. Now we'll never get to Bilorai today.'

As the day wore on the shouting and hooting of the Monis died down as they also became tired. However, we knew that we were nearing their home, because their mirrors emerged from their string bags and they put fresh green grass through their noses. One of them even washed his legs.

The outskirts of habitation brought social demands which slowed our pace down further. Every hundred yards there were neighbours to greet and adventures to relate after over two weeks away from home. The tastes of a freshly-picked lime and a constant supply of sugar cane revived our thoughts of different foods. As we waited for the porters to finish their successive visits to different huts, I lay down with my hat over my face, looking at the fine tracery of twigs and leaves through perspiration eyelets.

We were now in mission-land, and different seeds grew from the earth.

'*Titigi,*' announced Fones.

I asked to buy food and, after we had paid two people, word spread that we were hungry. Soon a pile of jungle greens, bananas, sweet-corn, cabbage, onions and beans appeared. Ans cuddled his little boy and his father appeared – an elderly, straight-backed grandfather with a lovely bright smile. The grandfather started to shell beans for us, and soon five other Monis were helping him.

'They're no different from us, are they?' said Hilary.

Without discussion she did the cooking, whilst I sorted out the clothing and equipment we would give away.

'I think we're just a quiet pair, aren't we?' she said.

'Be careful, released prisoners-of-war have died from over-eating.' We stuffed ourselves with food.

The next morning we gave each Moni a little pile of gear: shedding the excess baggage reduced our responsibilities and was a gesture of gratitude to our team. Nothing entrusted to their care had been lost. A large, excitable crowd accompanied us up the hill. The lads were whooping with high spirits, singing, shouting and hooting with laughter. We stopped on the edge of no man's land and paid them their well-earned cash. Although we had given them much more than the negotiated fee, they seemed quiet and disappointed and their lack of enthusiasm upset and puzzled us.

'A few notes must be an anti-climax after all that time. If only we'd got a lot of smaller notes,' I said, 'they just don't seem to understand money. Perhaps we should have given them more – oh, I don't know – I mean, in the Himalayas you don't spoil porters, you have a responsibility to travellers who come later; it's not fair to cause inflation and encourage them always to expect more every year. I just don't know whether I can apply the lessons I've learned in the Himalayas here; I mean the Monis are so different, perhaps we ought to encourage them to change as much as possible, or they'll be cheated some day.' It was a sad note to our goodbye.

We engaged a group of women and children to help us carry our few belongings to Bilorai. They seemed to revel in their impunity as they crossed the frontier, and declined our offers of gifts for their help. One woman carried our purple rucksack on her head, whilst on her back, in a string bag, she carried her baby wrapped inside a bark cradle. The wizened grandmother carried a green polythene bag full of climbing hardware in one hand, swinging it slightly to the rhythm of her gait. Feeling pink, overclothed and overfed, we followed them up the hill beneath the hot sun. We walked past a group of men working on a hut. One of them sang a lead and all the others answered in chorus. It was a song to greet a return.

The change of diet had been too much for Hilary's stomach. She spent a weepy, wobbly day being sick, listening enviously to me bluffing and bartering with the Monis for string bags, stone axes and cutting tools and a penis sheath. I ran a hilarious instructional seminar on how to put a complicated lightweight tent up, with velcro attachments and tension lines. In return they tried to teach me to light a fire by twirling sticks. I enjoyed my last day with the Monis.

On 10 January, Pilot Tom flew in out of a showery sky. The little plane tossed about as the jungle spread beneath us. Immediately Bilorai receded into the dimension of a vivid dream, I would never return to the Monis and their mountains. Too many forces seemed poised to change and exploit them. It had taken thousands of years for the Moni society to develop in a stable but precarious balance, but it would take only a few years for it to alter totally. The Himalayas will always call me, but these people, this place, seemed too fragile. This would soon be a land of lost content. A solitary, pure-white bird winged from a tall tree, mimicking our flight. We left it behind.

Forever in my memory would be a bird flying.

At Nabire the circle of our Irian Jaya travels was complete. After the garden serenity of Titigi and Bilorai, Nabire was a bustling colonial boom town. We sat on the beach in the long afternoon sunshine, watching boats unloading a ship. Driftwood, whitened by the sun, and sand-scoured by the wind, lay scattered around us. Little grey crabs scurried like shadows on the sand. We heard the distant babble of young voices, like those of children in a far-off school playground. I realised I had never heard a child cry in the highland villages.

'The Papuans don't seem as dignified with clothes on,' said Hilary.

'When in Rome … ' I said. 'I suppose they have to learn to wear them when they deal with the outside world.'

'Anyway, I hope they always put their kotekas on when they go home – they must be more healthy to wear in the jungle than dirty clothes.'

'Well, you don't look as if you've stepped out of the pages of *Vogue*.' Our clothes were torn and stained by the jungle. To me she looked like a princess in disguise. Our eyes met.

A thought had crept up on us, unannounced until now. So happy was the reciprocity between us that we had reached a level of understanding that was no ordinary friendship or sympathy. We came out of the highlands on an upper floor, sharing an eternal secret.

Father Tetteroo seemed to know why I had come to see him. Our conversation was broken, as he nipped away every few minutes to check a loaf he was baking in his oven.

'No,' he said immediately. 'I cannot marry you. It might lead to many complications with the authorities if I were to marry strangers passing through the town, and marriage requires much preparation. You are not Catholics, are you?'

'Well, I just thought I would ask,' I said.

Whilst trying to recover from the effort of having asked the question, I changed the subject to the Papuans. I had heard of missionaries attempting to eradicate the old beliefs and superstitions by encouraging the natives to make huge bonfires of charms and fetishes. Did this still happen? Father Tetteroo told me a long story.

'I was living in a village and the people, the men, came to me and said "Father, we are tiring of all our taboo objects, we want to put them in the past. But we have this churn and nobody dares open it. It has never been opened, and nobody knows what is inside it – perhaps it is a crocodile's testicle. We want you to help us and for you to open the churn for us." So I said: "Who do you think I am? I am an ordinary man – you are just as capable of opening it as I am."

'"But if we open it," they said "many calamities will come to us, the rivers will rise and we shall all be sick. Evil spirits will become angry and destroy us."

'Of course I still refused to have anything to do with it. Eventually a few of them got together and opened it. And what do you think was inside? Crocodile testicles? No, of course not, I will tell you what was there. It was a beautiful, truly beautiful stone axe. And then the people waited and waited – they were very frightened – but the rivers did not rise. And they asked me "What shall we do with this axe?"

'And I said "Well, it is a very beautiful thing, you must put it in the church!" And there it stayed until it disappeared when the Japanese came.'

In Biak I went to the telephone exchange. The call bounced off the satellite to my parents' home, thousands of miles away, wavering and fading and becoming strong again.

'Hello Dad, sorry to wake you up … in Biak … it's an island off the coast of New Guinea … Sorry, but it was impossible to send any letters from the interior. We had a great time … We're on the way home now – just going to spend a few days in Bali and we're flying from Jakarta on Friday.'

Centuries of civilisation have not helped the Balinese become robust enough to survive a few years of tourism. Tour operators harangued our every move and treated us like dollar-distributing idiots, we were pestered by Balinese who performed unnecessary services for us and then asked for payment and, when I photographed a field, ten people of all ages asked me for money. It reminded me sadly of how we had been told that even in New Guinea, Papuan natives in their tribal regalia were now demanding a dollar for a photograph. This was yet to reach west to Irian Jaya.

Passengers queued through the security check of Bali's international airport, struggling with bags full of paintings, carvings and batiks and other souvenirs. The girl on duty found the *koteka* I had bargained for in the hills of Irian Jaya.

'I know where you've been,' she smiled.

For a moment I felt proud.

7 BACK FROM THE STONE AGE

19 January–13 March 1979

On my return, for a while I responded to things spontaneously without defensive or self-conscious screens. Back with the tap water, television and telephones, I could assess the life around me from new contrasts. I was seeing human beings as one of earth's species for the first time.

Hilary flew straight back to her teaching job in Switzerland, and I spent a few days at my house in New Mills in Derbyshire before driving back to Leysin.

In Paris I stayed with friends, Vincent and Marie Renard, who live near the Eiffel Tower. When I walked into the flat, I was surprised to meet Jean Fabre and Bernard Domenech, who had arrived a few hours before from Jakarta. The world seemed small. After Hilary and I had left the mountains they had enjoyed perfect weather and climbed the North Face of the Carstensz Pyramid, and a rock tower near Base Camp. Their porters had not come back to help them move out of the mountains, so they had had no choice but to leave via the copper mine. In such a situation the Freeport authorities could not refuse them entry, but Jean and Bernard were disappointed to have missed their return journey through the highlands.

Back in Leysin it was the ski season. The winter was deliciously cold, clear and sharp. Unlike the soggy sleet and slush of New Guinea, the snow crunched underfoot. In a few weeks' time I would be going to Kangchenjunga, and I went cross-country skiing in training for the mountain. I breathed deeply on the frozen air, and savoured its crackle in my nostrils.

Leysin nowadays exists mainly because of tourism, which supports over eighty per cent of its economy. However, the village's cosmopolitan, tolerant atmosphere was born early this century, when the world's rich sufferers came there to breathe the alpine air and either die or recover in its many TB sanatoria. When TB became curable, following the introduction of streptomycin in 1950, the economy had to change, and now the many sanatoria with their old lifts, and their wide bed-sized balconies, house hotels, Club Méditerrannée, colleges, schools, clinics and transcendental meditation centres. These old buildings contrast with the new concrete ski hotels and téléphérique buildings that stick out of the ground like artificial teeth. During the winter the village swells with tourists giving the place the self-indulgent air of constant carnival. Nobody seems to wear or use second-hand gear, and everything's brand new.

The departure date for Kangchenjunga was approaching and I had some items of equipment to organise. I went over to Chamonix to arrange boots for the expedition. No trip to Chamonix is complete for a British climber without a visit to the Bar Nationale. Hilary and I walked in late one night, after a moonlit drive between white snow-ploughed walls over the Col de la Forclaz and the Col de Montets. The glass doors of the Bar were steamed with condensation. It was like walking into a pub in North Wales on a Saturday night, just before closing time. There were about thirty British climbers there that I knew, all reeling and drunk. Multiple rounds were being ordered and intermittently glasses crashed to the slippery floor. A snuff-snorting competition was taking place in one corner, and in another some girls were arguing loudly. Behind the bar Maurice served calmly and detachedly. His style had not changed since I had first seen him, some eleven years before. The noise was deafening. I reeled back from the culture shock, took a deep breath – and joined in.

It was a busy weekend in Chamonix, in the middle of the French holidays. Hilary and I went skiing from the Grands Montets, a téléphérique station high on a flank of the Aiguille Verte, 9,000 feet above the Chamonix Valley. The queue was long for the top station, and we waited for an hour in long queues hemmed between railings, like cattle at a market. Whenever a cable car took a load up we all shuffled forward with skis and sticks pointing in the air, with the intensity of a host of Danis holding spears in a ritual dance, preparing for battle.

Joe Tasker was co-ordinating the equipment organisation for Kangchenjunga. Fortunately, when under pressure, he had an ability to focus hard on a job to be done and to seal himself off from all distractions. Having been away from England for so long, I had missed most of the preparations. I returned on 5 March, and rushed around picking up socks and jackets and breeches, whilst Joe co-ordinated by telephone from his shop in Castleton. Meanwhile, I lectured for six evenings in succession, trying to make some money. We were paying for Kangchenjunga almost entirely out of our own pockets, and it was costing us about £1,750 each.

A week before departure it looked as if we still had a full month of work to do. The day before departure I went to a meeting organised by Dennis Gray, the leader of the Gauri Sankar expedition planned for the following autumn, and it seemed that more was already arranged for Gauri Sankar in six months' time than had been organised for Kangchenjunga in a few hours' time. However, Joe and Doug Scott (who was organising the food) were past masters at last-minute organisation, and Georges Bettembourg, the fourth member, arrived from the States to provide deadline impetus. Eventually, after packing all night, everyone piled into a transit and drove to London Heathrow.

I stayed in London for two days after the others had gone, to collect and shop for equipment that had been forgotten or had not arrived in the rush, and to give a lecture to the Alpine Club.

I had decided not to give any big public lectures about New Guinea – it was easier and more palatable to relate dramatics about desperate climbs in the Himalayas. What would the hardcore climbers say about New Guinea? 'Pete's snaps of his holiday jaunt with his bird'? 'The Noble Savage Show'? 'Comparative Religion in South East Asia'? However, I did show the slides to the Alpine Club, the evening before I flew to Nepal. I felt almost schizoid, talking about a past expedition whilst all my thoughts were focusing on the future.

In the front row at the lecture sat an elderly couple, heroes of an earlier mountaineering generation – Professor I.A. Richards and his wife Dorothy Pilley-Richards. Most awesome of his achievements for me, however, was I.A. Richards' critical breakthrough – *The Principles of Literary Criticism*, written in 1924, which I had spent two weeks trying to understand during an Easter vacation whilst I was at university. As I was showing the slides, I could see the white-haired father of modern criticism nodding and then bouncing back, alert, as his wife nudged him vigorously with her elbow. At the end of the lecture, I.A. Richards stood up and spoke with a vitality that denied his eighty-six years:

> I remember a story about New Guinea told to me by Winthrop Young which, in turn, had been told to him by Wollaston. When Wollaston was returning from the Snow Mountains, he became parted in the jungle from his companions and his native guides. He soon became completely lost, for not only was the jungle very thick but there was also a dense mist and the ground was steep and muddy. For a long time he fought through the undergrowth, completely disorientated. Then, to his grateful surprise, he saw the back of a figure through the mist. This back was moving quickly, so he hurried after it assuming that he had caught up with one of the porters. And sure enough, after negotiating many slippery obstacles, he eventually found himself among the main group. He turned to thank his guide, but could not identify him.
>
> Months later, after many other adventures, and the long voyage back home, Wollaston returned thankfully to London. To celebrate his arrival, he decided to buy himself a new suit and he went to the

tailors. When the suit was ready, he turned around in front of a mirror to admire it. To his surprise, he recognised that the back he had followed in New Guinea was his own.

PART 2

KANGCHENJUNGA

8   SPRING

14 March–4 April 1979

The great white peaks filed past – Dhaulagiri, Annapurna, Himal-chuli; symbolical names that spoke to the soul rather than referred, as in some countries, to historical events or the memories of famous men. Dhaulagiri means 'Mountain of Storms' and Anna-purna, 'Giver of Life'. Waters from these high mountains permitted and nourished life. During the long dry season the waters in the lowlands and the foothills dried up, but the great rivers from the snow mountains never ceased to provide the water necessary for irrigation. As well as storing water, the high glaciers carried down finely ground rock to the meltwater streams, and this reached the lowlands as silt and soil. The mountains gave shelter – but also they attracted the winds, clouds and storms that often caused death and devastation. To the people north and south of the Himalayas, the mountains lit up white in the morning, when the lowlands were still in darkness, and in the evenings they turned rose red and were last to part with the sunset. They towered above all other things. Nobody owned them – they belonged to all! Over thousands of years they had been accessible to people of all races and creeds – through prayer. All Indian and Tibetan mythology praised these vast mountains as the home of the greatest gods.

My expedition to the Himalayas the previous year had been to K2, the second-highest mountain in the world, in the Karakoram range of Pakistan. Our eight-man team had abandoned the attempt early, after the death of Nick Estcourt in an avalanche. In our retreat we left behind thousands of pounds' worth of equipment, and the expedition left a feeling of futile waste – we had not had the satisfaction of having pushed ourselves fully, only having tasted the route's technical problems, and we had lost a cherished friend. For me the experiences on K2 were a spectre I tried to forget, but which often reared up – and which I hoped Kangchenjunga would purge.

Our present enterprise seemed much more controllable. Nevertheless, I worried about developing some weakness. Using oxygen on Everest hadn't told me if my lungs were big enough for Kangchenjunga without it. For many days before departure I had been absorbing the little subtleties of life, laughing and joking with people, trying, I suppose, to leave them sweet in their attitude towards me. I thought morbid but realistic thoughts – could this be the last time I should ever speak to them? I tidied my affairs, signed my will, arranged my insurance. I went to see my two little nieces, one tired and irritable with chicken pox, the other just recovering and bouncy. I hoped and believed the iron was still there inside me to help when the going got rough. But it hadn't been called on for a long time. I was recognising again the half-dread, half-thrill of the prospect of Himalayan climbing.

In Kathmandu the expedition organisation had a studied nonchalance. We hired our sirdar, cook and cook boy; equipment and food were bought, assembled and packed. There was the familiar nasal whine of a Hindi song on a transistor. All seemed normal and smooth running. After the uncertainties of Indonesia, the procedures were relaxed and certain.

Doug Scott and I had been trying to gain permission to climb Kangchenjunga since early in 1977. At that time neither Nepal nor India were allowing foreign expeditions to attempt the main summit. My letters to India had received negative replies. Nepal was more ready to open up the peak, though, and Doug's probings there were successful. We gained the first permission to attempt Kangchenjunga from the north west to be granted for nearly fifty years.

Next we had had to find two more team members, and quickly decided on Joe Tasker and Tut Braithwaite. So we had the expedition notepaper printed first and sent them word on it that they had been co-opted – which proved fine as far as Joe was concerned, but unfortunately Tut had to drop out with lung trouble, which rather upset the names on our letter heading. In his place we then invited Georges Bettembourg. Between us, we had been on twenty Himalayan expeditions and I myself had been on two with Doug and two with Joe.

We soon appointed Georges as our physiological trainer. We had met him in the Karakoram in 1978. He and Yannick Seigneur had steamed past our K2 expedition during the walk-in, and had climbed the 26,400-foot Broad Peak in a round trip of five days. The two of them were back in Islamabad when we had scarcely got a grip on the lower slopes of our mountain. Obviously, the three 'Anglais' had much to learn from Georges. He had us running round the palace walls every morning. It did not seem to matter that none of us had been on an expedition with him before – it helped, for it gave a competitive edge which nudged us into extra effort. He knew what was entailed in climbing big mountains, and seemed bright-eyed, eager, full of energy and bounce, like Tigger in the Winnie the Pooh stories.

We were hoping to make the first ascent of Kangchenjunga by its North Ridge. All the previous expeditions having had any success on the mountain were very large and used traditional siege tactics. Our lightweight, four-man team was only a small hammer to crack a very large nut.

At 28,208 feet (8,597 metres) Kangchenjunga is the third-highest mountain in the world, being approximately eight hundred feet lower than Everest, and forty-five feet lower than K2. Both these two higher mountains had been climbed during recent years without the use of oxygen equipment. On both occasions, however, the successful climbers had been accompanied by large-scale expeditions which had placed stocks of oxygen at the highest camps. We were going to attempt Kangchenjunga without such support, with only two Sherpas to help us carry our equipment between the lower camps.

Ours was a serious enterprise, but it was rarely solemn. We teased each other with quotes from books written by the modern heroes whose achievements we were hoping to emulate:

> In the morning I have a cold shower, run up 1,000 metres on my toes within thirty minutes, and then chew garlic to dilate my vascular walls.
>
> Every Friday I eat and drink nothing, to train my liver and kidneys to withstand deprivation.
>
> Every afternoon I ski cross-country for four hours, at altitudes above 3,000 metres.
>
> My body hardens until I am in total control of it.
>
> My personal physician advises me on everything I eat, everything I do. He tells me I am a superman.

These quoting sessions with which we taunted each other would then gain pace until the superstar gasped up to the 'death zone' summit amid a blur of nitrogen. We would meekly shrug our shoulders and say 'Well, we can only give it a try.'

It was always difficult to dissect truth and useful information from the writing of mountaineers for, naturally enough, an author nurtures his own self-image. We counted up how many climbers had been to 28,000 feet without using oxygen equipment. Many of them were members of the pre-war Everest expeditions who, encouragingly, had all been different ages, shapes and sizes. However, their achievements had occurred a long time ago and it was difficult to relate ourselves to them. Attitudes had changed since those early high-altitude climbers made their masterly understatements. It seemed current practice to inflate achievement. The American jogging craze and the Russian temples of health were both symptomatic of a modern worship of the body, and the public's gullibility to media and advertising pressures continually expounding a belief in 'supermen'. All this was anathema to Joe Tasker's obsessive iconoclastic nature. He did not bow to ego-myths, publicity machines and the human need for heroes, and instinctively he distrusted all dogma about training programmes. Yet during the early days of the walk-in,

I was so impressed with Georges and had read so much about training that I could not dismiss it as lightly.

'But I am worried that there is no doctor among you,' said Lieutenant Mohan Thapa. He had been assigned to our expedition as liaison officer, to make sure we did not stray out of bounds.

'Don't worry,' said Doug, 'we'll be taking an oxygen cylinder with us for medical purposes.'

However, there was a problem in finding an oxygen cylinder with the right sort of fitting for the mask we had brought with us. Eventually, we met Pertemba, the Sherpa with whom I had reached the summit of Everest in 1975. Pertemba, who was soon to leave Kathmandu with the American–Nepali expedition to Gauri Sankar, offered to help. '1,500 rupees,' he said.

'1,000.'

'1,500 – it's a good price.'

'If we bring it back unused can we have the money back?'

'1,500 is what I paid for it. Either you want it or not.'

He knew that we did, and having travelled widely over the world, Pertemba knew what Westerners could afford, even when they pleaded poverty.

Kangchenjunga lies in one of the most remote corners of the Himalayas, astride the north east corner of Nepal and the western frontier of Sikkim – a country that has recently been annexed by India. We had to travel east and start the eighteen-day approach walk to the mountains right from their foot – the hot malarial plains of the Terai. This strip of level alluvial terrain, only 600 feet above sea level, situated between the Indian frontier and the foot-hills, is Nepal's modest share of the Ganges Plain. Our Sherpas took the gear overland in a truck for fifteen hours along the Russian-built west-to-east highway to the largest town of the Terai – Dharan. A day later we flew out via Biratnagar to join them.

At Dharan the British army kindly allowed us to stay in their Gurkha soldiers' recruiting camp. Here I sat down to bring the expedition accounts up to date. The heat was sultry, and a large fan gave little relief. I recognised a familiar face, the narrow eyes and slightly lopsided mouth – our sirdar for the expedition, Ang

Phurba. It was three and a half years since I had seen him on Everest and he looked much older – so, probably, did I. He seemed pleased to see me, although he rarely showed emotion, being one of the most inscrutable of that inscrutable race, the Sherpas. These constantly travelling and trading people are used to renewing acquaintances after long intervening years, and to picking up where they left off. I was looking forward to being with them and to sharing jokes with them again. I hoped that our small expedition would bring us closer to the Sherpas than had been possible on the big Everest trip. In 1975 I had come away with respect for their inner peace and happiness, convinced that they had more to teach the West than we had to teach them. Now I, also, would pick up where I had left off.

'Just leave it to Ang Phurba, he knows what he's doing, he's many steps ahead of us in dealing with the porters.' Ang Phurba had been sirdar to Doug and Joe's expedition to Nuptse in the autumn, and now they were happy to delegate all responsibility to his laconic, self-confident style of organisation. 'All sorts of things go on that we don't know about. If he has to hire a few more porters than are necessary, just to keep them all quiet, then let him, it makes life easier.'

It was 18 March. We set off up the four-hour climb to the Dhara Pass, a saddle providing a crossing place in the Siwaliks, the first foothills rising from the Indian plains. This almost unbroken 5,000-foot range stretches parallel to the Himalayas from the Bramaputra to the Indus. The ancient Aryans called it 'the edge of the roof of Shiva's Himalayan Abode'. The Dhara Pass was the gateway to Eastern Nepal; for more than 120 miles it was the only practicable pass by which people of the interior could communicate with the modern outside world. Commercial movements affecting a population of about two million crossed this pass, and the traffic in both directions was dense. Frequently, we had to queue behind lines of porters. Each wore a curved dagger around his waist like a codpiece, and prominent tortoise-like neck sinews strained upwards to support the tumpline or headband of a load. The greatest traffic jams were caused by porters carrying large sheets of wood and corrugated iron, which blocked the two-way traffic at the narrow places.

Winding in a loop across the ridge nearby, a road was being constructed – a British aid project to link Dharan in the Terai with Dhankuta. This project was a small percentage of the aid which poured into Nepal from all over the world, accounting for half the nation's income.

The steep walk was hard work. 'What are we doing this for again?' I asked Joe.

'I'm thinking the same thing,' he said, and we laughed – the question melted away through the day.

The only previous time I had walked to a mountain in Nepal had been to Everest during the monsoon. In contrast, the Siwaliks were dry and hot, and so was I.

Georges was holding a ski stick in either hand. 'They're really good,' he said, 'they loosen up your upper body, exercise your arms and take the jolts and strains from your knees. Yannick and I used them all the time last year. You should try them.' Joe and I soon copied the technique.

From the Dhara Pass, we could see across a transverse valley the defensive wall of the Mahabharat Lekh. This natural barrier had protected the Nepali mountain people from the wars and conflicts of the Indian plain. I groaned inwardly to see the climb up to Dhankuta, which was to be our next stop, an important trading place perched high on the ridge.

The route up on to the foothills was punctuated with wayside cafes – small, dingy smoke-stained benches where we sat, sipped sweet milky tea and ate biscuits and fresh oranges. Yellow dogs snapped listlessly, and mangy chickens pecked at spit. Flies like particles of dust danced up and down the sunshafts. The way was dusty and weary, but at least we were climbing out of the heat.

Georges did not hesitate from talking about anything, and tackled topics head on. We discussed the mountains, morality, values, religion, everything. Although he always talked quickly and emphatically, he was not completely at ease speaking English, and his opinions came out abruptly, free of nuance.

'I see God everywhere I look,' he said.

Joe quoted Camus mischievously back at him: 'If there is a god, then I don't need him.'

Joe and I did not give in lightly to Georges' direct honesty. However, I was feeling more gregarious than I had been on previous expeditions, more willing to say what I thought and to exchange opinions. Georges was blunt yet impressionable, and he generated an easy atmosphere. He even managed to break down Joe's defences and squeeze some comments out of his habitual opacity. We were testing each other out in conversation, trying to find common ground and understand and trust each other. Women were the usual early theme – a tenuous mental link to the world we were leaving behind.

In contrast to the huts along the trail, Dhankuta was a spotlessly clean town, with a wide stone-flagged street flanked by whitewashed houses with black-tiled roofs and balconies with window boxes full of flowers. On a rocky promontory above the town stood a giant pipal tree. These trees are sacred to both Hindu and Buddhist, and are usually sited at convenient rest stops. Beneath this one was a *chautara*, a stone bench on which porters could lean their loads. The tree's spreading boughs offered reassuring strong shade in a breeze that blew refreshingly across the ridge. The tree glittered, each leaf shaking separately, in a million different rhythms. The ascent on to the foothills was over, and we fell asleep waiting for the porters.

We gained the ridge we were to follow for the next four days and moods changed. The dry winter was over but the grass was still pale and bleached like straw. It was the most beautiful approach walk I had ever made in the Himalayas, along an open ridge, around shoulders, through rhododendrons full of the promise of the bloom before the monsoon – unlike the ups and downs of the way in to Everest. All along the trail there were hamlets and people. But the terraced fields were dry and dusty, with little agricultural work going on. Four great eagles circled around us – above and below. Spring here is a time when the monsoon is awaited; it's not the same as the complete renewal of nature in Europe. The seasons were confusing me. After a mid-winter south of the equator, the dream-like powder blue, the crisp coldness of Switzerland in February, and the rain of northern England, there was a freshness and strength in this special hilltop season which gave hope and delight.

We discussed the rights and wrongs of having ladies along during the walk in to a mountain. The porter stages were short, the days were leisurely and I thought that the walking was so gentle and pleasurable that female company would not hinder us. I was going to send carbon copies of my diary to Hilary, Doug was copying his to his wife, Jan.

'How can you be completely honest in a diary which you know someone else is going to read?' taunted Joe.

'I'm not honest,' I said. 'I lie and show off. Anyway, what's wrong with sharing thoughts?'

'If you were the last person in the world would you write a diary?' asked Doug. 'And if we were the last people in the world, would we still go to climb Kangchenjunga?'

When anything of interest happened within or around me I made a mental note to tell Hilary about it. This habit of thinking of things in connection with her enhanced their meaning, and memories jostled with the thought that at those same instants in time she lived, breathed and thought. However, despite the bond of understanding we had found together in New Guinea, I still could not feel I was talking to her; I wrote into the space between. I used my writing as a means of coming to terms with the fact that, though I could not blindly forget, I had to leave much of my past behind.

We walked along the stone flags of the village of Hille, where we met a British agricultural adviser and a German water supply expert, both involved in aid projects. They told us Hille was a prosperous settlement of Bhoti, Tibetan-speakers from Walongchung, which used to be one of the main Nepali towns controlling trade to and from Tibet, along the Arun Valley before the border closed.

Georges bought a Montreux Jazz Festival tee-shirt.

We walked past comfortable houses. Western music was playing

'Seasons in the Sun' ... 'Goodbye my friends, it's hard to die ... '

Georges' head spun round. 'Hey, did you catch the words of that song?'

A few minutes later, high above children playing rolypoly on the grass where a graceful cowherdess with gold in her ears sat knitting, we saw mountains. Far to the north, hanging with their outlines faintly revealed like ethereal white clouds above the dark valley haze, much higher in the sky than we had expected, we saw the giants of Makalu and Chamlang and the massive bulk of Kangchenjunga, a complete range in itself: multiple-summited from Jannu to Kabru.

Of the world's first half-dozen peaks, Kangchenjunga is the best displayed. Fifty miles to the east from where we were, the mountain is fully visible from the busy crowded Indian hill town of Darjeeling. Meet anyone who has visited Darjeeling, and his eyes will moisten as he tells you of the sight of Kangchenjunga at dawn – it must be one of the most described and photographed views in the world. But unlike a view of the European Alps, Kangchenjunga from a distance is of a scale that cannot be grasped.

It has been worshipped as a guardian spirit since ancient animistic times by Tibetans and the Lepchas of Sikkim. The Tibetans gave the mountain its name, which is physically descriptive of its five peaks and literally means 'the five repositories or ledges of the great snows'. However, when the great lama Lha-Tsan Ch'enbo introduced Buddhism into Sikkim, he told the people that the mountain was the home of a god of that name, a god who was a defender of Lamaism. Lha-Tsan Ch'enbo gave the name a mythological meaning, and the five repositories became real storehouses of the god's treasures. The peak which was most conspicuously gilded by the rising sun became the treasury of gold, the peak which remained in cold grey shade, the silver treasury; and the other peaks were the stores of gems and grains and holy books. When the disciples of Lha-Tsan Ch'enbo came to depict Kangchenjunga in paintings and statues, the idea of treasure led them to represent the god in the style of the god of wealth – red in colour, clad in armour, carrying a banner of victory, and mounted on a white lion.

Kangchenjunga is still regarded as a sacred mountain, and the Maharajahs of Sikkim have always either refused permission or asked for special behaviour whenever European climbers and explorers applied to venture near it. Out of respect for the mountain's sanctity, and upon the request of the Maharajah, the two successful ascents in 1955 and 1977 left the final few feet of summit snow untrodden.

Was the god simply a benign giver of life, a god of wealth, as the name implied? During the 1930 expedition to Kangchenjunga, Frank Smythe detected more than thanksgiving in the attitude of the people towards the mountain. Their main Kangchenjunga dances were held before the harvest, to placate the god, rather than in gratitude afterwards.

> Their prosperity, and even their lives, depend on the good humour of this god, for he is able to blast their crops with his storms, or destroy their villages with his floods and avalanches. There are even dark tales of human sacrifices to this powerful deity, handed down from the remote past.

When Smythe was shown a statue of the god, it had a cruel countenance and sardonic grin. After an avalanche killed one of them, and nearly destroyed them all, he wrote: 'Kangchenjunga is something more than unfriendly, it is imbued with a blind unreasoning hatred towards the mountaineer.'

As recently as 1977 the lamas of Sikkim accused a large Indian expedition of disturbing the god. A loud explosion was heard from the mountain, followed by heavy landslides and avalanches. It was said that thousands of dead fish were being swept down rivers that sprang from the glacier affected by the explosion and that scores of road construction workers nearby had suddenly fallen sick. Not long after, one of the Indian climbers was killed in a fall during an early stage of the expedition.

I had always thought that a mountain was magnificently indifferent; I had regarded local beliefs as superstitions to be tolerated, and always tried to avoid the temptation of attaching human attributes to a mountain. But this year I began to discover how much your physical experience of a mountain depends on your mental attitude. At times Kangchenjunga seemed to have a mind. If you did not match up, you were quickly rejected. But if you approached with a mixture of confidence, respect and caution, it was usually just possible to come through the worst, and discover a special reward.

From over seventy-five miles away, Kangchenjunga dominated the ridge we were following and gave a new sense of purpose to the walk. A chill sharpness at sunset reminded us of the cold hill that awaited us and before we returned to our tents we quoted to each other suitable passages about the mountain, giggling nervously. I found some awesome thoughts in Jack Tucker's book, *Kangchenjunga*:

> ... Kangchenjunga is a mountain which does not respond to normal mountaineering techniques. The psychological effects of the ever-present danger from the terrible avalanches which pour down day and night from the mountain, the extreme difficulty and the awful weather, coupled with the very short period when it is possible to climb on Kangchenjunga, make this peak just that much more dangerous and inaccessible. Any expedition which hopes to reach the summit must approach the mountain with something of the philosophy of a fanatic. Every nerve and every fibre must be devoted to one cause – the attainment of the summit ...

Joe chimed in with the daunting prophecy of Erwin Schneider, an Austrian climber on G.O. Dyhrenfurth's 1930 expedition. 'Attempts on this mountain by small parties are doomed to failure from their inception.'

'I hope we can do this route fast – perhaps after we've made a reconnaissance,' I said.

'We'll just have to try the big breath theory.'

'What's that, Doug?'

'Take a big breath of air at the North Col and go for it.'

Once inside the tent I sealed out a group of whispering children, the bats, insects and mountain fears of Nepal with a pull of the door's zip. Usually we camped apart – it was important to cherish some privacy, for we would be together for long enough on the mountain. Now I was cushioned from our surroundings, and the dominating mountain ahead. I listened to some music on the cassette player, and lost myself in a book by candlelight, relaxing in an imported, sealed bubble of Western reality. Absorbing books telescoped time. Joe and I tended to read the same books after each other, so that we could discuss them, whilst Georges could never manage more than the first few pages of anything, and Doug had a special collection of books and cassettes that helped his own incessant quest for prophets.

At 6.30 a.m. little Nima, the kitchen boy, brought a cup of tea – a soothing way of bringing in the morning. It was the start of another perfect day on the ridge.

'Do you like our music?' I asked Mohan, our liaison officer.

His English vocabulary was vast, but his pronunciation was barely understandable: 'In sweet music is such art, killing care and grief of heart.'

'Where's that from, Mohan?'

'Shakespeare, *Henry VIII*, Orpheus' song.'

'We haven't got a cassette of that.'

After we had wound down from the hectic days that had preceded our departure, we began to wind up for the mountain ahead. Fatigue and stiffness left us and we soon began to feel fit and gloriously alive, happy to know we would be taxed utterly on the climb ahead. The trail seemed like a motorway compared to the paths I had tangled with in New Guinea. Although it was not as crowded as it had been before Hille, a trickle of traders and travellers continued to move steadily by. We walked in the morning and reached the day's camp-site by early afternoon, to laze for a while. Then we played around climbing on boulders – forgotten muscles quickened, and we enjoyed the light-hearted competition. The pace of the expedition was asserting itself.

We camped in a little glade: forty-eight porters, sirdar Ang Phurba, assistant sirdar Nima Tenzing, Kami the cook, Nima Tamang the kitchen boy, Mohan the liaison officer, the four of us. We were glad we did not have a single main sponsor for our expedition, so that our commitment was purely to ourselves and the route.

Four was a good number because there was room for gossip and manoeuvring within the microcosm, but nothing could become too serious because we knew we would soon have to be totally interdependent once on the mountain.

Eighty per cent of our conversation was spent mocking and deflating each other. Joe was best at this, never at a loss for an answer, quick to unmask pretence, a tough teaser, making tight-lipped remarks like gunshots. Sometimes he was a bit too near the mark – he made me wince a few times. We'd been through a lot together, and out of many past altercations a lot of mutual respect and trust seemed to have grown. The comments between us now were just as barbed but neither suspected malice any more. Georges missed many of the jokes, partly because his English wasn't up to it (Doug's Nottingham accent didn't help), but also because I don't think the French – or the Americans for that matter – talk each other down all the time, as a matter of course. We spent a long time one day trying to explain to him what 'taking the piss' means. We trod a fine line in our humour, and it was important for everyone to be tuned in and find the same things funny. Doug sometimes could, sometimes couldn't, or missed a joke on himself, particularly about the 'ego' business and why we were there. He didn't stick with the three of us, but walked alone in a happy haze, scribbling notes in his diary. We all kept diaries:

> Today we sped past him and he said 'Remember
> the tortoise and the hare,' and I replied that the
> hare had more time at the end to dream. But now

I'm not so sure who is the hare and who is the tortoise! I just can't make out Doug's home-baked psychological musings – or gauge his capacity to move within himself. He's either undergoing a second adolescence or he's in touch with something beyond the range of all the rest of us here. He has a clever knack of self-parody and a ready laugh that makes it difficult to sense his level of seriousness when he drops his heavy lines into a conversation like today's: 'with only three trillion heartbeats each at our disposal, we have to focus our energies carefully, on to something worthwhile.' And 'We're all mobile plants – imagine us turned inside out – we are what we eat.' And 'The subconscious is very strong on this trip.' He loves to float off with words, playing and pondering with them. I'm more inhibited than he is – I think it would be a sort of tense anarchy if all of us allowed our feelings to dominate what we say.

The days on the ridge came to an end and we descended six and a half thousand feet to the Tamur Valley. We could see its blue waters far below, glimmering over boulder and pebbles. On the way down into the heat we stopped for a cup of tea, savouring the breeze that sang through the great trees around us. An ex-Gurkha soldier chatted to us in English, with fond reminiscences of his fifteen years abroad with the British army. His pension was five times as large as the income of a peasant and when he had been on active service the ratio had been twenty-five times larger. Yet his experiences and his money seemed to have had little effect on his present life.

At Dobhan, to celebrate our arrival at a lower and more balmy altitude, we swam in a side river which poured into the Tamur. The broad cheekboned, Chinese-looking Limbus have settled in the Tamur Valley. We walked past their three-storeyed, balconied houses, marvelling at one of the highest standards of living in Nepal. The high precipitation – both during the summer monsoon and the winter – accounted for this prosperity, enabling the Limbus to grow not only much rice but also winter crops.

Although Europeans did not pass this way very often, our caravan did not raise an upward glance from them. The Western roadshow had not the same curiosity value or attraction here that it had in New Guinea. Ang Phurba warned us not to stop at one particularly surly hamlet – it was, he reported, a haunt of robbers with sharp knives, and Limbus are famous for their knife-fighting prowess.

We decided that the Limbus were pyromaniacs. Day and night, great fires swept through trees and shrubbery around their settlements, clearing a way for the fresh green shoots of spring. The destruction was painful to watch. On the east side of the Tamur, acres of forest had been gutted, but the Sherpas said that this was not spring-cleaning by the Limbus. Out of mischief, the porters of an expedition to Jannu a few years previously had started a fire that had raged until the monsoon put it out. The government had had to pay compensation.

We had been walking for eight days from Dharan when we arrived on the afternoon of 26 March at Chirawa – a lovely clearing scattered with the blackened stones of old camp fires amid an amphitheatre of great rock boulders fifty feet high. Joe settled down wisely to read *The Seven Pillars of Wisdom*, and we could not entice him on to the boulders by the Tamur River. The bouldering was fun until we arrived at a rock slab fifteen feet high. Georges bounded up this and I struggled up after him. Doug had some difficulty because his ankles, full of metal from his accident whilst descending the Ogre in Pakistan in 1977, wouldn't bend enough. Georges, soon bored, decided to play 'I'm the king of the castle' and gave me a boisterous push off the top of the boulder. I spun round, grabbed for his feet, but he shook me free. I slid down the slab, fingers scratching the rock, and landed awkwardly with my left foot on a tuft of grass. There was a sharp noise like a snapping twig from my ankle.

'Oh no!' shouted Doug and rushed over.

I could not walk any more.

I crawled back up to the clearing and Joe looked up from his book and uttered a few words of sympathy. Mohan's face lost its habitual grin, and the Sherpas shook their heads and tut-tutted. With the strong confidence of a faith-healer, Doug held my swollen foot firmly between his great hands, but I hoped in vain for a miracle cure. It was first-aid by committee, and everyone suggested a different treatment. 'Put it in cold water.' 'Hold it up in the air.' 'Bathe it in warm salty water.'

I tried everything. Georges dashed around performing unnecessary tasks for me, agonising with a guilt that we did not help by our deep amateur probes into his subconscious: 'Why did you really do it, Georges?'

I lay down in total despair, imagining the noisy insects of the jungle screaming into my ears were trying to eat me up. With my eyes closed, I felt I was just a large, throbbing, decaying foot.

'It sometimes does you good to reach the heights and depths, youth,' said Doug.

My grandmother had always said 'Horseplay ends in tears!'

For four days three tiny Limbu men took it in turns to carry me towards Ghunsa – the last permanent village on the walk-in. Perched in a conical wicker basket, I felt like an aged and crippled pilgrim being carried towards holy water.

'Well, at least you're being carried up to the mountain, and not down and away from it,' said Joe.

It took me two days to summon the courage to face my self-pity and write it down. I could not bear forward-looking thoughts, I only wanted to rest, sleep, forget:

> What can I see before me? What can I say? I just can't believe it. It's all so utterly stupid I feel angry. I need these big climbs – I plan my life around them and look what happens! The summit of Kangch seems far away, and I have morbid fears about my Alpine guiding this summer – what if my foot sets itself wrongly? I never realised how much I wanted to

climb Kangchenjunga until this injury cast a black shadow of doubt.

We were paying the three shift-working porters who were carrying me a total of 200 rupees – about £8 – a day. They were earning every note – one slip beneath my twelve and a half stone pre-expedition weight and they could have ruined a knee, ankle or back. A slip could have ruined me too, since at times we were traversing steep slopes many hundreds of feet above the river. I kept rigid, immovable, as they insisted, not wanting to upset the balance, strapped in, with my foot tucked under and fastened with a belt.

The long-distance carry was lonely. I missed the lively chatter and repartee of before the accident, and longed for the tea stops when I would catch the others up for a short time. My head became disassociated from the effort of the bodies that carried me, and as we followed the switchbacks of the path I stared stiffly at the disappearing foliage, the river and cliffs.

Nima Tenzing, our assistant sirdar, had appointed himself as my safety-net and moving stirrup. At fifty years old, Nima was a veteran of eighteen expeditions, including seven to Everest, where he had made carries to the highest camp three times and to the South Col six times. He was like the adventure-book Sherpa of the pre-war Everest expeditions, illiterate, unsophisticated, reliable, loyal, with a ready smile and with a constant, almost servile willingness to help and to seek out any job that needed doing. He ambled constantly behind me, safeguarding my tilting over perilous places, his wrinkled brown face grinning encouragement. Nima's everyday work and his religion seemed to blend without distinction between the two. Most of the time he was sunk into a habitual deep prayer that to him was as natural as breathing air.

For me, there was one distraction. We were joined on the trail by a family of Bhoti, who were travelling to their home in Ghunsa – a mother, two small children and a teenage daughter. The mother had a fresh complexion and a kind but mischievous smile. She had, she said, seven other children, and this daughter was soon to be married to a Ghunsa man.

'She'll tell you anything,' said Ang Phurba, laughing.

She had realised who was distracting us. Her daughter, Dawa, wore an emerald green coat and had a smile like a sunrise. Dawa enchanted us all.

After three days of being carried, I was beginning to feel less sorry for myself:

> One can adjust to anything if one has to. I suppose bad things usually come to an end. I've actually managed to walk a little today, so am feeling a bit more cheerful. Being with Nima is good for me – I'm reluctant to show any signs of suffering in front of the Sherpas. I have to be really careful and am painfully slow, but perhaps there's hope. If will to heal works, then I shall soon be better. I'm focusing all my energies in THE FOOT, massaging, warming, flexing, thinking.

In Nepal, an altimeter can tell you what race of people you are likely to meet. An hour of path separated language, economy, religion and culture. We had crossed the ethnic frontier – the 10,000-foot contour between south and north; we had left the strict caste and conformity of the Hindu Limbus and entered a zone of hospitality. At the village of Pele I found the others eating boiled eggs, surrounded by a group of giggling women and children. Their rosy cheeks and robust appearance, their black, sack-like 'chuba' dresses held in place by striped aprons, their chunky Tibetan silver ornaments and necklaces of amber and turquoise beads all woke me from the rocking stupor of my basket-ridden journey. Here, in contrast to the children in Limbu land, the youngsters were laughing, curious, and vivacious. I felt I was looking at one of those old photographs of medieval Tibet taken forty years before by Heinrich Harrer and described in *Seven Years in Tibet*. Pele, the Sherpas told us, was another settlement of Tibetan refugees who had accumulated there over the previous twenty years since the Chinese invasion. There were Nepali government plans to move them into the foothills, but at the moment they practise transhumance with yaks and grow potatoes, in the same style as the Bhoti, who live mainly in Ghunsa, a few miles higher up the valley.

Nima was now among familiar religious symbols. Carefully, he guided my little party to the left side of stone Mani walls and *chortens*.

'We go round like a watch,' he said. It was an old tradition, to walk clockwise, in the same direction as the earth and universe revolves – a tradition which also survives in the Scottish Highlands, in the passing of a decanter, cattle treading out corn and walking around someone to wish them well.

Ghunsa had the air of an outpost suddenly abandoned before the advance of an enemy. Lines of prayer flags flew like tattered, war-torn banners, flapping spiritual longings into the winds – at first sight these flags were all that distinguished the place from a lonely hamlet high up in the Lötschental of Switzerland. The stone-walled houses were roofed with planks weighed down by big rocks. The village stood on meadows which were once the alluvial bottom of a lake, and on either side steep valley sides blocked out the sun.

According to legend, Lha-Tsan Ch'enbo stopped here on his way into Sikkim, and founded a Buddhist monastery. After leaving the village, he had become lost and sheltered in a cave. There, the god of Kangchenjunga visited him in the form of a wild goose and inspired him to fulfil an ancient prophecy by composing a sacred text to guide the worship of the mountain.

When the first European, Sir Joseph Hooker, visited Ghunsa in 1850 it was a prosperous trading community. Further exploration of the district was taken up by the famous 'pundits' – Bengalis, trained by the Survey of India, who collected data from which the earliest maps of the district were compiled. In 1879, Chandra Das, a pundit and headmaster of a Darjeeling school, visited the monastery and reported it as being one of the finest and richest in Sikkim and Eastern Nepal, containing eighty lamas and a dozen nuns. In 1884, another pundit, Rinzing, noted 150 well-to-do houses. As traders, used to adapting to different cultures, the inhabitants showed no surprise when William Douglas Freshfield passed through the village on his celebrated circuit of Kangchenjunga in 1899 – and readily accepted his Indian currency. By the time the next Europeans passed through – the 1930 International Expedition to Kangchenjunga – much of the trade had declined. Frank Smythe's rather patronising description of the childlike superstitions of the lamas and their open-mouthed reactions to his gramophone, implied a religious decline also.

Few lamas appeared as we passed the *kani*, and the gilded spire of the *gompa* and some of the monuments were in a state of disrepair. Nima said, 'The people here, they give what they can to the monastery, but not so many here now as before.'

We stopped at Ghunsa, in order to pay off the porters who had carried our equipment from Dharan and to hire forty locals for the last stage of the walk-in. When the lowland porters had gone, the four of us sat around the fire, sipping a drink of warm, fermenting millet – *tumba* – from wooden jars. We ate our first and last meal of a three-month-old piece of yak – the Sherpas seemed to relish its high smell and strange taste. Slowly, unhurriedly, some of the 300 inhabitants came to look at us. Ang Phurba was already asking round for porters to carry our gear up to Base Camp. The Bhoti could understand his Sherpa dialect. Both languages are rooted in Tibetan, but have developed as separate dialects because of the lack of east-west contact between the deep valleys of Northern Nepal. I was happy that we were a small expedition – a large one might have uprooted the whole village from their fields. Instead, we were a lucky five-day cash crop bonus – or, more appropriately, a curious flock who paid to be herded up the valley.

The locals were emerging into the spring after a long, biting winter.

Many had bad coughs, ear-aches and smoke-reddened eyes. Doug opened up his clinic at 5.00 p.m. He spoke gently through his long hair and wire-framed spectacles, administering to each sufferer after they had explained to him their problems. In the mountaineering world, Doug's toughness, strength and endurance were legendary, and he also had a reputation for volcanic unpredictability and scarcely controlled violence – yet here he had the tenderness of a saint. A crowd of small children stood watching, quiet and subdued, with shy eyes. One, about four, uncomplainingly carried a baby on her back. Meanwhile, I was looking in wonder at countless pairs of healthy feet – everywhere I looked I saw feet jumping, running, twisting, bending, mocking.

'It's a miracle that so many people function so normally,' I said. 'No,' said Doug, 'the miracle is that we ever stop or fall, we're so well-programmed.'

During the night it snowed, and in the morning the high mountains slowed down the sun's descent to us. As the sun arrived the day gave way at first to winds, and then to clouds and some rain. We decided to stay for two days, to give my ankle a chance to rest and to acclimatise to our present altitude of 12,000 feet.

In a traditional porter behaviour-pattern, the locals started exaggerating the dangers and difficulties between Ghunsa and our proposed Base Camp at Pangpema, so that they could claim more pay. An exorbitant price was demanded for the hire of a yak to carry me, so I set off on 2 April, two hours ahead of the main party, determined to hobble the rest of the journey without help.

Within the space of two weeks we had passed through almost all the climatic zones of the earth; from the sub-tropical jungle of the Terai to the mountain wastes we were now entering.

The last inhabited settlement, recently occupied for the spring, was Kangbachen – a hamlet of ten houses. The children were wild and grimy and had running noses, but they were well wrapped against the cold and completely unafraid of strangers. It was here that in 1879 the pundit Chandra Das, on his way from Ghunsa to the Chabok La and Tibet, had witnessed a grand offering to Kangchenjunga.

> The firing of guns, athletic feats and exercises with
> the bow and arrow form the principal parts of the
> ceremony which is believed to be highly acceptable
> to the mountain deity. The youth of Gyansar vied
> with each other in athletic exercise, the favourite

amusements of their elders being quoits, back-kicking and the shooting of arrows. I also contributed my share to their religious observances. The scene reminded one of the Olympic Games, and like good Buddhists, I too paid my obeisance to Kangchan, the Buddhist's Olympus.

Chandra Das' colourful account of his journey is permeated with legends about the valley along which we were now walking – the holy waterfall where the eight Indian saints had bathed, the cavern where the key of heaven was concealed, the sacred hot mineral spring and the hollow in the slope consecrated to a mountain nymph.

From Kangbachen we could see the vast glittering flutings of the North Wall of Jannu, and beyond that several magnificent unclimbed twenty to 20,000- to 22,000-foot mountains ('nameless Weiss-horns', as Freshfield called them), flanked our route. I limped along the grass-covered moraine beside the Kangchenjunga Glacier. There was still over twelve miles to go – the glacier owed its length to the heavy precipitation in Eastern Nepal. I was relieved when the porters, spinning the day out, stopped to make a cup of tea at Rhantang. There, the vast panorama of white peaks confirmed why the yak herds regarded it as the special haunt of the spirits of the mountains, a place where 'gods and saints dwell in great numbers'.

We arrived at the next pasture beside the moraine, Lhonak, in the early afternoon. It was exciting to see all the mountains that had hitherto only existed for me in books, to be able to look at Schneider's map and think 'Yes, we're really at this point.' We could see Wedge Peak, Nepal Peak, Kangbachen and Kangchenjunga itself. To the north were passes and peaks, dry and Tibetan. I wrote:

> The beauty around us has taken me out of myself, and I know it is right for me to be here. After a starry night with a crescent moon, there's a frosty stillness

until the morning wind starts blowing uphill. Doug and Georges, in particular, are talking about how happy they are and feel. Today I relaxed into a long discussion about commercialism and personality exploitation in mountaineering. Doug's still upset about the publication of that full page mugshot of him wearing fibre pile gear, which Joe took. How can what he says have any impact if he's used a lot in adverts? How can he say anything political about climbing if he appears to have exploited the sport? It's a problem that certainly worries him.

There weren't many boulders on the ground – mostly we walked across great yellow grass meadows, and my foot managed O.K. Last night Georges and Joe both dreamed that I got to the top, so their psyches must think I'm going to get better. Yet I wish I could see my own role in the climb ahead – am I summit-bound, miracle mending, or just a doomed hobbler and lifelong cripple?

The short day had not tired the girls among the porters at all. Throughout the afternoon they danced and sang in circles – at first high on a rocky eminence beneath fluttering prayer flags – and then down on the meadow. Georges bounced around, doing cartwheels and walked on his knees whilst in a lotus position, much to the hoots and delight of the girls, who played rough and pushed him over. His love of nonsense endeared him to them all. It made my ankle twinge to watch!

In the evening the porters split into two generation groups. For the young it was a social adventure. Their journey was a break from their work in the fields, an excuse to talk and intermingle away from the village. While the young giggled and shouted, the old chatted around their fire, nodding with wisdom and sleep. The Sherpas moved easily between us and the two groups. We were the excuse for the journey, but we were irrelevant.

On the morning of 4 April the porters stopped.

'Porters, they say this is Pangpema Base Camp,' said Ang Phurba.

Once again we fished out Frank Smythe's book *Kangchenjunga Adventure*. We checked the alignment of cliff, glacier and moraine against a picture in the book. Yes, we weren't being dumped short, we were at the 1930 Base Camp. I looked up at the mountain.

'See what I've found,' said Doug. 'A 1930 tent peg.'

9   SÉRACS

4–14 April 1979

> Dear Mr Boardman,
> I am sending you two photographs of the wall west of the North Ridge of Kangchenjunga. I have taken them during a flight in 1975. The wall is very steep ice and rock, but no danger of avalanches. Nearly 1,000-metre high. Be careful with ice avalanches from the N.W. Wall! Pangpema is a very nice place for Base Camp. With my best wishes,
> Yours sincerely,
> Erwin Schneider

We re-read letters, and thumbed again through photographs. The information in them took on new meaning, with the subject matter in front of us – the North West Face of Kangchenjunga.

Pangpema was indeed 'a very nice place'. It became our last link with the outside world, a halfway house of warmth, comfort and safety, of grass, flowers and running water, to which we could return and recover after adventures in the upper world of ice and glacier. The kitchen fire at Pangpema became the pillar of our wandering. Here, Mohan the liaison officer, Kami the cook and Nima Tamang the kitchen boy stayed, in touch with the world down in the valley haze.

The relief that we felt when we arrived at Pangpema, and which we were to feel many times on returning there from the mountain over the following weeks, was mirrored in a description by the first European to go there, William Douglas Freshfield. In 1899, Freshfield had approached Pangpema from Sikkim, by crossing the 20,156-feet Jongsong La – the pass of hidden treasures. The Kangchenjunga group lies south of the main Himalayan watershed, pointing a northerly ridge towards it. This ridge separates Sikkim and Nepal, and the Jongsong Pass cuts across it. Freshfield was accompanied by the pundit Rinzing, who had been there fifteen years before, crossing the pass from our present position at Pangpema, into Sikkim, and suffering an epic descent on the other side – two of his porters had died from the cold, and he had run out of provisions.

This tragedy clouded Rinzing's memory as he guided Freshfield down from the pass and he declared the party 'lost'. Freshfield was shaken by Rinzing's uncertainty, but persevered, determined to fill in the missing link, the broad blank on the map between known travellers' routes to the north west and north east sides of Kangchenjunga. It seemed that they were descending into a blind valley blocked by cliffs, until a drifting cloud revealed a hidden turn:

> I was suddenly aware of a winged messenger from the outer world coming towards us. A tiny wisp of white vapour floated into sight quite low down between two apparently connected cliffs. We no longer needed to walk by faith.

It had been five days since they had touched vegetation, or walked on horizontal ground, clear of boulders and ice. The descent, happily, shook Rinzing's memory clear. He led the expedition to Pangpema:

> We had returned to a habitable and living world. A sudden cheerfulness seized us ... A sense of escape, of having come out of their peril, spread itself visibly among the coolies. Their faces brightened, they became more talkative. Our feet no longer

>   hampered by the soft substance of clinging snow,
>   we all stepped out, full of hope.

Eighty years later, Doug, Joe, Georges and I sat on the secure turf of Pangpema, looking up at Kangchenjunga, making occasional detached comments about possibilities and dangers. We were like generals out of gunshot range on a well-protected hilltop, surveying the enemy's positions and discussing the deployment of troops. We discussed some guerrilla tactics, as Georges' binoculars passed between us. We knew not to judge on first impressions and tried to break down the enormity of the mountain into logical, climbable stages. There was an air of unreality, it being understood but not spoken, that if we were the generals we were also the troops. But today, at least, we were safe.

The North West Face of Kangchenjunga might have been designed specifically to repel mountaineers. It is structured in a horseshoe of three tiers of gigantic shelves, separated by cliffs of ice which are the mountain's defences, poised to thunder across any lines of weakness that an eye of faith could imagine. Our eyes wandered up the face, following possibilities, only to be brought to a brutal stop every time by the threat of hanging glaciers. Only the North Ridge looked free from such objective dangers. But how could we reach it without playing Russian roulette with ice cliffs? R.L. Irving and other Alpine Club members had accused Professor G.O. Dyhrenfurth, the leader of the 1930 expedition, of 'having led his men into a death trap'. Yet their expedition was the only practical experience of this side of the mountain that we could learn from.

Freshfield was the first of a succession of mountaineers to recognise that the strategic key to climbing the North Ridge of Kangchenjunga was reaching the 23,000-foot North Col, which is hidden from Pangpema by the double-summited Twins Peak. The first panoramic photographs of this side of Kangchenjunga, taken by the famous Italian mountain photographer accompanying Freshfield, Vittorio Sella, did not show what lay around the corner in the upper Kangchenjunga Glacier, behind the Twins. This 'dead ground' was the missing link which we wished to explore. I had written to Erwin Schneider, one of the few members of the 1930 expedition still living, and Doug had contacted G.O. Dyhrenfurth's son, Norman. As a result, we had a dossier of photographs which showed that we would have to run the gauntlet underneath the hanging glaciers and séracs of Kangchenjunga and Twins Peak before starting to climb a 3,000-foot wall up to the North Col.

'Perhaps we ought to climb Twins Peak first, and approach it from there.'

'We'd be knackered before we started on Kangch if we did.' 'Anyway, we haven't got permission for it.'

'Perhaps we ought to cross the Jongsong La and climb it from Sikkim.'

'And cause an international scandal by getting arrested for spying!'

'It looks a long way to the top from here.'

'Eleven-thousand-foot vertical difference, youth – only the same as the top of Mont Blanc from Chamonix.'

Pangpema was at an altitude of nearly 17,000 feet, and we would have preferred a day of rest and acclimatisation. However, we had decided to keep six of our Ghunsa porters employed for an extra day, to help us to carry enough equipment to establish a first camp beneath Twins Peak and the icefall that linked the upper and lower Kangchenjunga Glaciers. On the afternoon of our arrival at Pangpema, Georges and Doug sorted through equipment and food for the big carry the next day. Nima Tenzing put tents up and Ang Phurba paid off the remaining porters. Kami and Nima Tamang started building a kitchen shelter by slinging a tarpaulin across some rough stone walls left by the 1930 expedition. Meanwhile, I was arguing with a tall, sharp-faced Tibetan who had brought several yak-loads of wood up for us to Base Camp. He had sub-contracted some of the work to two others, and a hundred kilos more than we had asked for had arrived. Also, he had put the price up from the rate we had agreed in Ghunsa. Ang Phurba was avoiding involvement in the argument, but was enjoying translating for both sides. I needed more support.

'Hey, Joe, you're the hard man with the porters, can you come and help me hassle with this bloke? He needs to be stonewalled. He keeps coming up with a hard-luck story about how ten years ago he was a wealthy man in Tibet, until the Chinese came and took his yaks.'

'He looks well-off to me – oh, I know him, he's a real shark. He tried to sell me genuine Dalai Lama hats and boots in Ghunsa.'

'Well, we're in the strong position; since he's brought it all here, he's not going to take it back down again, is he?'

'The Sherpas say they can use it all anyway.'

'I'd be daft to pay that price, he's just on the make. There'll be inflation here like in the Karakoram if we pay them the first price they ask.'

'Just pay him what we arranged in Ghunsa now, let him stew over the problem tonight and open up negotiations in the morning.'

In the morning I offered him half price for the surplus and he agreed immediately. The Sherpas and the six porters who had stayed on thought the whole negotiations were hilarious and I laughed with them, half suspecting that the joke was on me.

We licked envelopes hurriedly, stuffed our letters in a polythene bag and wished our mail runner, Nima Wangdi, a speedy journey. Then we set off towards the mountain. To reach the Kangchenjunga Glacier from Pangpema we had to descend 500 feet of scree and boulders, then for an hour cross a chaos of unstable moraine before our feet touched the ice of the glacier. The wind brought snow, and soon I was slipping and tripping at the back of the group. Realising that my foot was not ready for big-boulder-hopping, and not wanting to put my recovery back or hold the others up, I returned to Pangpema and went into the kitchen shelter. Its tarpaulin roof was cracking like a pneumatic drill, so I retreated to the sleeping bag inside my tent. I could not relax, and decided in the afternoon to go for a walk and face the bad weather, rather than cower inside from it.

Three and a half hours later I was back, having walked through the blizzard for about 1,500 feet up the hillside above the camp, and seen nothing except cloud and scree. Weather like that is never as bad when you go for a walk in it; wind and snow are best confronted. Nevertheless it was so cold it would take us a few days to acclimatise to the change in temperature. The others reached a curve in the glacier which they thought was roughly in a good position for Camp 1, but they were not certain because the visibility was so bad. They had done a phenomenal carry and on their return were consoling about my foot.

'I'm sure it'll be better soon,' said Georges.

'These things usually happen for the best,' said Joe.

'It was meant to be so we could all wait for you and have to acclimatise,' said Doug. The six porters were drinking rakshi. 'Stone Cold Sober Again', sang Rod Stewart on the cassette and I lay in my sleeping bag, writing the daily state of mind and foot bulletin:

> I am eaten up at the moment with a restlessness. I have to do something. I can't bring myself to read serious books. It's easier to face one's soul when it's enclosed by a healthy body. I feel terrible thoughts about Georges when I try to walk, and keep asking myself if there was a subconscious, competitive reason why he pushed me. If he has a third party insurance, I could sue him for all the money I'll lose if I can't work properly this summer! I could scream with frustration and anger sometimes, particularly coming down scree slopes, slopes that normally I could slide and leap down. Yet I must reach the top of this mountain.

The storm grew during the evening. I had never known such winds at this altitude in the Himalayas before, they came in terrible gusts. At 4.30 a.m. the wind abated and by dawn the snow cocks in the meadow were chuckling to each other in a temperature of minus eighteen degrees Celsius. We lay in our separate tents spread over the field, talking across to each other, relishing the peace and calm, waiting for the sun to move down to us. It was a rest day, and passed uncluttered until the evening. But I was still in a self-pity-ing and uncharitable mood:

> 6.00 p.m. The day is dying and Kangchenjunga has appeared red in sunlight, looking high and vast through a hole in the clouds. I managed a crap today without having to stick one foot out like a Cossack dancer – such is progress. An enormous brown Himalayan griffon vulture flew past this afternoon, mobbed by crows. It was only a few feet away and turned its head to stare at us. It looked unbelievably big, and the fast-swooping crows that were pester-ing it made it look stiff and ungainly. Perhaps it was intrigued by our rubbish – the Sherpas refuse to burn any of it, since the kitchen fire is of special sig-nificance to them and also the folks from Ghunsa said that burning smells cause bad weather. The two Nimas have been down to Lhonak to collect some juniper to burn at their daily altar. I'm all for attract-ing as much help as they can summon – a large ava-lanche came off the Twins this afternoon and fell towards the place where the lads think they left the gear yesterday. Why do I respect the Sherpas' be-liefs, yet find Doug's musings too superstitious and emotive and react against them? Perhaps I'm just suspicious of mixing cultures too much. I agree with what he says, but his introspection is enough for all of us to take without my joining in.
>
> Georges and Doug have just returned from an ex-cursion to chase after and try to photograph some Himalayan blue sheep. They've also been boulder-ing this afternoon. Georges is always either hyper-active or sleeping and hypochrondriacal, never in between. He's been bouncing around the Sherpas, discussing with them what makes their wives sing – cooking? washing? chang? Meanwhile, Joe,

naturally so lazy when there's nothing really important to do, has had little Nima rushing backwards and forwards, carrying things to him in his tent. 'That's what we pay them for,' he says, 'it's important to conserve your energy.'

I'm sitting in the entrance of my tent playing music, using the last of the daylight to write by. Dusk has cleared the afternoon's clouds, and a growing moon has appeared above our heads. Doug quotes his Chinese Yellow Emperor's Medicine Book as saying that new moons bring strength. He's full of spiritual and nutritional solutions to the climb. He's recently been converted to vegetarianism so, since he organised the food, we have a lot of different varieties of beans. He's directing cooking operations from his little brown bean book. Tonight it's black-eyed bean stew.

The next day Georges had diarrhoea, and stayed at Base Camp whilst I went up the glacier with Doug and Joe. Walking unladen, I managed to keep up with them – impressed at the distance of the carry they had done two days previously. From the site of the equipment cache we estimated the risks from the encircling séracs. The large avalanche of the day before, from some séracs on Twins Peak, had not reached the equipment, although the run-out slope of fresh debris was only fifty yards away. The only dangers would be from the blasts from avalanches – vacuums and the accelerating air that are generated by a large fall. It was not far-fetched to imagine that everywhere on this north west side of Kangchenjunga was threatened by such blasts. We decided to stay where we were, and put the tents up. Camp 1 was established.

Joe and I had just finished reading *Goodbye to All That*, Robert Graves' autobiography about life in the trenches during the First World War. During all the time we were on the Kangchenjunga Glacier, we were accompanied by the almost constant booming of collapsing séracs, and this book gave us a whole new terminology to play with. 'Cushies' were minor injuries that enabled you to move back from the almost inevitable fatality of the front line. 'Sniper fire' was occasional stonefall. Now, at Camp 1, we tried to distinguish between the splitting and cracking of the glacier beneath us and the different sounds of sérac fire coming from the North Face of Kangchenjunga – the sounds that mattered, that you woke up and tried to run away from, and the sounds that you allowed yourself to sleep through. About every half hour, a sérac fell. It was a fitful night.

'At least when you charge, you're doing something about it, rather than lying here waiting for it to happen,' said Joe.

We stayed until the sun lit up our tents. At 9.00 a.m. we walked out into the middle of the glacier to look up at the icefall that guarded the upper Kangchenjunga Glacier, and to estimate the danger of three collections of séracs poised above it.

'All our Derbyshire experience on the East Face of Mam Tor has brought us to expect this,' said Joe.

Doug repeatedly encouraged me. 'Just come along with us and see how far you can get. It doesn't matter if you decide to turn back.'

We wandered through the ice cliffs and crevasses of the lower icefall, building cairns out of the rocks that lay on the surface. Then we reached a bowl of snow, swept into a smooth slope by avalanches from above. It was not a place to linger, and we steadily moved forwards, probing the snow in front of us for crevasses and discovering many. The 1930 expedition had nearly lost one of their porters in such a concealed trap. Although I had needed a pull on the rope to help me over a couple of steps in the icefall, I now broke trail in the snow for an hour, happy to be involved in the action.

Above the slope the glacier surface was slashed by huge crevasses. Joe, then Doug took over and led us through the area, finding a switchback route in the upper curve of the Kangchenjunga Glacier. We had no alternative but to walk along the bottom of one enormous crevasse with high, leaning walls, and we christened it Death Valley. We wanted to find a site for our second camp and also gain enough height to have a clear view of the west wall of the North Col. Our trail behind us looked like that of a drunken man.

'The 1930 camp was further in the middle, wasn't it?'

'The avalanche nearly hit it, Smythe had set off running when he saw it coming down.'

'We'd better keep the camp over here, those slopes on the Twins above us look too steep and icy to allow much of a build-up.'

We discussed the problem until we all agreed about the siting of the camp. Although we had strong mutual respect for each other's mountaineering judgment and skills, it was important that all of us constantly questioned each other's decisions. We knew that the collective strength and tension of this questioning increased our chances of staying alive. I was overawed by the gloomy history that had haunted the cwm during the forty-nine years since the death of Sherpa Chettan. We were the first people to enter the cwm since then, and the accident weighed freshly on our minds, as if we were ourselves survivors of it.

We had all read various descriptions of the avalanche that nearly wiped out most of the members of the 1930 expedition. They had been trying to reach the North Ridge by climbing the narrowest point of the ice cliff below the first terrace of the North West Face, when a huge portion of the cliff collapsed. Frank Smythe saw it happen from the camp: 'Great masses of ice, as large as cathedrals, were toppling to destruction.'

Dyhrenfurth was in the thick of it:

> A high cracking sound was the first thing I heard. Then I saw that at the very top of the cliff – somewhat to my right – an ice wall perhaps a thousand feet wide began slowly to topple forward. It seemed minutes, though I am sure it only lasted a matter of seconds, before the huge face broke and came crashing down in a gigantic avalanche of ice. The impact of the fragments whirled up a curtain of snow and ice particles which broadened with incredible velocity into a solid, perpendicular wall. I ran towards

the left – if running is the right word for moving
quickly in deep powder snow at 20,000 feet, with little hope of escaping. It was a horrible feeling when
the blast knocked me over, but as I fell I instinctively
shielded my face with my arm. The uproar all around
me was frightening. I lay in the snow and awaited
death.

Smythe estimated that the debris was several feet thick, covered a
square mile of snowfield and weighed one million tons.
Miraculously, only one person, Sherpa Chettan, had been killed.
The sérac had actually toppled over Erwin Schneider, leaving him
unharmed.

During the next few weeks, as we walked below this wall to the
face of the North Col, it was to be our constant fear that a similar
avalanche might occur and we could not rely on the same accompanying luck if it did.

Doug and I left our loads on the rock around which we had chosen to establish Camp 2. Short gusts of wind scurried across the
cwm and we turned to descend. Far across on the other side of the
horseshoe of the North West Face rose the aggressive, challenging
summit of the 22,140-foot (6,749-metre) Wedge Peak. It would
not be long, I hoped, before we were looking down on it from the
North Ridge of Kangchenjunga.

I was glad to have contributed to the forward momentum of the
expedition for the first time. My injury no longer isolated me.

Through the expedition we seemed to pass between us a debilitating baton of sickness and set-backs. Joe and Georges had already suffered from colds and diarrhoea. Now it was my turn. For
three days I was ill. I managed to scribble occasional notes in my
diary:

I can't remember having felt so sick … Joe is rushing
around, fixing his overboots, his activity mocking
my prone inertness. At dinner I tell the others
I won't be able to go back up yet. They're all for

sticking together, and not splitting up the team. They'll wait until I'm better ... The first time I go to the loo in the night is appalling. I can hardly get warm again, and am aching all over with cold. My foot and hands are numb, and I start worrying if I'll pass out from hypothermia. Outside, it snows heavily, and then the moon appears – it's surreal to feel ill in this place. Woke with a splitting head that seems to stretch right round to my back ... I have a lot of hot water to sip and have now started reading *Sense and Sensibility*; a lovely, civilised change and a contrast to here and now. I still go to the cook tent at meal times, not to eat, but to keep in with all the decisions ... I at last fit a pair of crampons to my boots – there now, that was a positive step ... I'm just going to have a go tomorrow. I haven't eaten much for three days, and dread fainting or weakly collapsing on the walk up to Camp 1 – but the foot and body should be well rested. We're all going up to work for a few days till we've stocked Camp 2, and fixed the route up to the North Col. Ang Phurba and Nima Tenzing are going to come and carry loads in support. Then we'll make a quick reconnaissance up the ridge and come back here for a rest and THE MAIL RUNNER. Then we'll climb back up for the summit push. That's the Sports Plan.

The foot was beginning to feel weak rather than broken, and for the first time I carried a load. Crossing the boulder field, I only twinged it once, and Georges and Joe waited for me to chat for a while. The mist swirled in, and we walked past fins and sails of ice to Camp 1.

We were professional old hands, and most of the time assumed that each of us would look after himself. Outward Bound, and other outdoor-education philosophies, would have one believe that mountain climbing develops character, courage, resourcefulness and team work. That may be so, but it is also true that mountaineering expeditions can develop selfishness, fanaticism, glory-seeking and cunning. At Camp 1 we played the opening rounds of a half-serious game that was to develop through the expedition – 'High-Altitude Manoeuvring'. The main aims of this game are personal survival, self-image survival, personal success and personal comfort. The first rule is not to be seen playing by the others. If anyone plays too overtly, or extremely, the game – and the expedition – collapse.

The game requires the participation of all the members, and has been played to a greater or lesser extent since expeditioning began. As time distances one from the events the manoeuvring seems less serious and more funny, and one's own involvement seems self-righteous. I filled my diaries with observations of the others' manoeuvring, but few confessions of my own:

> Next door Georges and Doug are sharing a tent. Georges hasn't brought any books and can't sit still. Bob Dylan howls out for hour after hour from the cassette player. It's like camping next to a pack of wolves. Doug seems to have got us to cook for the Sherpas. He won't let them cook because they're staying in his tunnel tent, and he's afraid they'll burn it down. So now they're in here, gassing us with a primus stove that refuses to light. Sherpas are always useless with primus stoves. Joe has decided that I'm to cook every evening meal, and he'll do the breakfasts. Now I find I have to cook the Sherpas' tea also … Doug seems to have to prove he's strong (we all know he is) by exaggerating the weight he's carrying, and putting the weight the others are carrying down in his estimation. I tried to borrow the cassette deck off him, but he resents Joe's light load and thinks we don't deserve it. But then he apologises. You can't have a maxim 'if I carried it up, only I can use it' … I wonder what the Sherpas think of us.

We decided to carry loads up to Camp 2 for two days, and then to climb on above, leaving Ang Phurba and Nima Tenzing to shuttle more equipment up directly from Base Camp. The first day Georges was nudged up to the front, since he had missed the earlier foray on to the Upper Kangchenjunga Glacier. Wind and snow had erased our earlier tracks. He prodded the surface in front of him vigorously with a long bamboo cane, searching for concealed crevasses. It sank in deeply everywhere.

'Good job you're not that thin,' said Joe.

As we climbed we improved and marked the route for future ferrying – leaving more cairns and canes, cutting steps in the ice and chopping away the lips of the crevasses we had to cross. Reassuringly, the site of Camp 2 had not been disturbed by avalanches since we were last there.

Back at Camp 1 in the evening Joe and I were lying, wide awake and twitching, listening to avalanches.

'You know on Everest, Camp 2 was hit by the blast of an avalanche which threw a tent in the air with five people in it on top of another one,' I said.

'Once hit, twice shy.'

'We're right at the end of the run-out for those séracs on Twins Peak. They would pick up a hell of a speed falling 2,000 feet.'

'Well, there's nothing we can do about it. Anyway, we can identify the shell noises.'

I started up at the first thumping of blocks.

'A trial run,' said Joe. 'It takes two aims for them to line up the target, and then … '

'Who's the spotter, then? God?'

There was an ominous note in the roar of the second avalanche. I unzipped the tent door, stuck my head out and swore. The sky was filled with falling ice and snow, thundering down towards us with a noise like a jet plane hurtling to destruction.

'Grab the tent and poles, Joe!'

For a few seconds the ice beneath us shuddered and the tent heaved and flapped as we hung on to it. Then the blast faded. I stuck my head out again and saw Georges doing the same. No block had hit us, we had just suffered a dusting and shaking. From the tunnel tent I heard Nima muttering insistent prayers. I wished I could propitiate who or whatever had a finger on the sérac button. The third strike was not as powerful.

'They put too much effort into that second one,' said Joe.

"I think we should shift this camp,' I said.

Next door, Georges was saying the same. The moon rose and I looked at my watch, 10.00 p.m., Friday 13th.

'We should be O.K. in a couple of hours.' We never stayed at Camp 1 again.

The next day we moved up to Camp 2. Nima Tenzing had with him a polythene bag full of holy rice which, whilst chanting prayers, he scattered over potentially dangerous-looking crevasses, slopes and séracs.

'I hope he sticks all that snow together,' said Joe.

'I bet there's a Yeti down that crevasse, eating it all up,' I said.

When Nima arrived at Camp 2, he took one look at the tier upon tier of séracs and threw the remainder of the rice in a sweeping gesture at the entire North West Face of Kangchenjunga.

10 THE WALL

15–30 April 1979

We grew self-conscious and fell quiet, afraid to flaunt our smallness beneath the stupendous walls of ice, each of us locked in as much thought as the altitude would allow.

> Are the others as worried as I am? Aren't we being presumptuous? How many times will we have to walk this gauntlet gasping, our legs weaving urgently through the danger-zones? The plod of the light brigade, that's what this is. Once we reach there, we'll be out of danger from the Twins. Once we reach the next point further on, we'll be out of danger from Kangchenjunga. At least the wall to the North Col looks too steep to collect loose snow and ice. It looks steep enough to be safe.

If we could reach the North Col by climbing its West Wall, then we would escape from the sérac-threatened cwm, and above that the North Ridge that curved up from the col to the summit appeared free of objective dangers. We selected a direct route up the wall to the col, tracing a line through its corduroy of rock ribs and snow gullies.

The eyes of 1930 had dismissed the wall as a 'sheer ice-armoured precipice,' concluding there was no possible way to the North Ridge except over the ice wall and lower terrace they had attempted. But in 1930, mountaineers did not have our jumars, curved axes and hammers, twelve-point crampons, low stretch nylon ropes and sophisticated rock and ice pitons. Now we looked at the 3,000-foot wall, knowing that although it was dangerous going to and from its foot, and it would be time-absorbing to climb, at least we had got up similar obstacles in the Alps before. Although obviously very difficult, the wall would be safe and secure, and we would be acclimatising during the effort.

Doug broke the trail into the upper cwm, and we marked our route with canes. It took us two hours to reach a snow bridge across the bergschrund at the foot of the wall, at a point 3,000 feet directly below the lowest point of the North Col. There was no logistical framework behind our approach to the mountain, as there had been on the large, systematic South West Face of the Everest expedition in 1975. This time we had just stuffed ropes and hardware into our sacks and set off to have a look. Our expedition had no official leader – which made us an expedition of four leaders. However, decisions had to be made. Despite his insistence on democracy, it was often Doug who, by strength of personality, made the most forceful suggestions during our continual discussions. Joe probably had the hardest time accepting them, but rather than he and Doug butting against each other like two billy-goats, he often kept quiet when the issue was not important enough to risk a confrontation. One has to swallow a lot of feeling, including pride, to unite to climb a mountain. The best way to communicate an idea was to feed it to Georges and persuade him to take it up. Everyone trusted him as being completely open; he could bluntly say what he thought, without inhibitions, and no one was offended. The three 'Anglais' knew each other's weaknesses too well. However, we accepted Georges without suspicion.

Someone had to make a suggestion. Nobody wanted to be seen to be pairing off with someone else. Our climbing partners would have to be interchangeable, otherwise competition rather than unity would result.

'How about Joe and Georges climbing together and you come with me?' said Doug.

I was flattered that he had chosen the cripple, for this meant that he would be under the pressure of doing all the leading.

'Tak, tak, tak,' exclaimed Georges. It was his favourite French ice-climbing noise, which he followed with his favourite Franco-Americanism 'Let's go for eet.' He tied on to two of the ropes, pulled his way across the snow bridge and bounded up the slope above.

The bergschrund was at an altitude of 20,000 feet. We looked along our tracks which shied across the cwm, skirting imagined danger zones, to the dark smudge of Camp 2, on the edge of the smooth white world of the upper cwm, above the confusion of the icefall. The lines of séracs stretched across the North West Face of Kangchenjunga with the poised menace of serried ranks of nuclear warheads. Seventy miles away in the west rose Everest and Makalu.

'We may as well go back to the camp,' said Doug. 'No point in hanging around here with cold toes.'

'Yes, let them get on with it.'

Forty-five minutes later we were watching Georges' and Joe's progress through binoculars, with the stove beside us melting snow for a brew of tea; then cloud filled the cwm and it began to snow lightly.

When Georges and Joe returned we eagerly absorbed and discussed the details of their day.

'It's a good hard ice after the first couple of pitches. The rock's very compact – it doesn't like pegs.'

'It's an Alpine T.D., like the North Spur of Les Droites.'

'It's a long way — I hope we don't run out of rope before we reach the col.'

'Who led?'

'Georges. I was load-carrying today. What's for dinner anyway?'

'Bean stew.'

'You can't cook beans at this height.'

'You can with a pressure cooker.'

'I'm losing weight.'

'We'll be farting so much we'll be able to climb the mountain by jet propulsion.'

'They'll just be taking the Easter Sunday roast out of the oven at home now.'

The next day the weather was too bad to move, and we read and talked. The snow, however, did not deter Ang Phurba and Nima Tenzing, who arrived with a load. Nima told us that according to his Tibetan calendar the weather would be bad for three days.

'Look at those crows, they've followed us up.'

'Scavengers – they always seem to turn up on every expedition.'

'You sure they're not choughs?'

'Probably. Some sort of Corvidae anyway.'

On 17 April Georges kicked his way through the freshly fallen snow and we filed behind him. Snow slides had buried the equipment left at the foot of the wall, and we burrowed head first for it, our feet kicking in the air. All four of us carried loads up the five ropes that Joe and Georges had fixed and then Doug and I were left to carry on with the climb.

Between 11.00 a.m. and 5.00 p.m., Doug led steadily up steep ice and rock. I climbed up the ropes he fixed, carrying a thousand feet of rope in my sack, my injured foot firmly strapped and braced sideways across the ice, my lungs gasping and my thoughts blurred and wandering with the altitude. The last pitch of the day was a difficult diagonal traverse, halfway up the trail through a rock barrier, and after fighting his way above it Doug was exhausted with the effort and dehydration. He slid down the ropes, and after dumping the load at the high point I followed him.

On the glacier, Doug doubled up with stomach cramps, vomiting from the effort and heat of a day without fluid. We had forgotten to bring water bottles. Beyond him the sun set behind Everest and Makalu. Camp 2 brought refreshment and company. It was becoming our haven, retreat, rest house, our cosy three-tent hamlet. I was encouraged by my foot – it seemed stronger. I was looking forward to a night's sleep, to a rest day whilst Joe and Georges took their turn at the front and to the action the day after that.

The rest day was gloriously hot. Doug stripped to his underpants. We sat in the scorching sunshine, which reflected intensely around the white cwm, turning it into a great oven of ice. The heat made us dozy with glacier lassitude – 'glassy lassy', we called it. Idly, we fiddled with cameras, crampons and head torches, and looked at the two tiny dots of Joe and Georges, working their way up the shining ice of the wall. We felt comfortably detached in our security and inaction.

There was a load roar and our eyes jerked around till we saw the cause. An avalanche was plunging from some séracs on Twins Peak with the energy of a sudden dam-burst. The spearhead was imbued with a monstrous life, and, on hitting the cwm floor between our camp and the wall, it exploded forwards to cross the glacier in leaps and bounds and then climbed hundreds of feet up the North West Face of Kangchenjunga, having swept the entire breadth of the glacier. We were finely dusted, as the fall-out of snow finally settled.

From their eyrie on the wall, Joe and Georges had a bird's-eye view of the whole incident. Later in the day, when they returned across the lumpy debris of the avalanche, they estimated that it had covered their morning tracks for half a mile, to a depth of ten feet.

It was unnerving to walk back over the debris the next day, despite my rationalisations: 'It's taken me about twenty minutes to cross the danger zone. The whole avalanche only lasted about three minutes, which is a tiny, tiny fraction of the time we've been here. And that was probably the most dangerous part of the sérac that fell down, and it'll be safe now.'

Doug went first up the fixed ropes, and when he reached a convenient tiny ledge above his rockband, he lit a stove and prepared some orange juice whilst he waited for me. 'Here you are, youth, have a sip of this. What do you think of whilst you're jumaring?' 'Oh, I don't know; nothing much really. My thoughts just circle around all sorts of things, it's like dreaming, I can't control them, it's as if they're sorting themselves out.'

'Gurdjief would call that sort of thinking a waste of energy – not having direction. Here, will you carry my camera and take some shots of me leading this? I'm going to aim for the end of that ramp. The lads did some steep pitches yesterday.'

'The ice looks brittle and Georges said that roof was hard.'

'At least we're gaining height; we must be about 22,000-feet. Kangbachen's slowly coming down to our size.'

Doug clawed his way on to the smooth ice of the ramp, through the falling snow of the afternoon. A ropelength above his head another rock barrier jutted out. From our binocular studies, we knew it guarded the final slope to the North Col. I was frustrated that my foot would not allow me to help in the lead. However, another big effort, we hoped, would take us there.

We all decided to take a rest day, reach the North Col, go for a one-day reconnaissance up the ridge and then return to Base Camp for a rest, food and further acclimatisation.

> I'm feeling better during this rest day than I have done for ages, but as usual, I'm worried about my health – little aches and pains. I know I'm always nervous, but I can't remember if it's usually this much. It's so difficult to compare my fears and per-formances, past, present and future. One isn't the same when one tackles successive climbs. All the sto-ries, the fears, past experiences and future unknowns, roll in and fall over each other in a mixture of opti-mism and fear. Looking back, Everest was quite a straightforward affair for me, in that my ambition was very simple and clear headed. Also, I feel older and more vulnerable than I did on the Changabang trip in '76, when there was only Joe and me. Then, being just two generated a barrier of intensity that kept a lot of fears out, and either risks were easier to take then or I was less aware of dangers. Also, the rock was firm granite! Now we're forecasting, health and weather permitting, to reach the top in the first week of May. I hope so.

Ang Phurba and Nima Tenzing arrived with some loads from Base Camp – and some letters. Although they were over a month old, written not long after our departure, we seized our bundles of mail possessively and submerged ourselves in thoughts of home for the rest of the day. I read mine many times and lay down digesting the emotional nourishment, and exchanging snippets of news with the others.

'Why do people always say "send me a card" – I wish they'd write to me instead. I need it more than they do.'

'Look, there's a postcard here from a sixteen-man Czechoslovak expedition trying the West Ridge of Jannu – they've all signed it. They met our mail runner at Ghunsa. Nice of them.'

'I wonder if they've got any spare rope.'

'Well they've got a doctor – we'll be all right there.'

Dawn was icy blue as we shouldered our packs crammed with equipment for the North Col. We manoeuvred for starting positions. 'You and Joe had better go last up the ropes in case any stuff comes down – you've got helmets.'

One after the other, we went over the bergschrund and up the rope. As we gasped upwards we were each too involved in a lonely effort to notice the clouds move around us and the snow rest silently on our clothes – symptoms that steadily deteriorated into the violent crisis of a storm.

Thunder rolled through the sky beyond the ten feet of my vision. The others were crouched together, hanging on an ice screw on the ramp. Powder snow streamed over me, building up on my rucksack, pushing me over, exploring ways behind my goggles and into my mouth and nostrils.

'Pete!' Click. 'What a photo!'

Four of us balanced on the ice, unpacking and packing our rucksacks, tying our sleeping bags to our waists for the only option – retreat and descent. Powder snow swept over our feet; it was like standing in a thin white flood over a concrete weir. Larger snow slides plunged over rock steps and billowed into the air.

'They're not really that dangerous, they just look dangerous.'

'This slope's too steep to allow the build-up for a killer slide.'

We danced down the ropes. We were submitting to the mountain's decision, and I realised I was enjoying myself.

In the evening, back at Camp 2, I crouched inside my sleeping bag with the hood pulled over and one arm, with a biro in my hand, extended out of the top like an antenna into the cold to write:

> It was a failure-day that felt like a success. It's amazing how fast the weather changes on this mountain. Now it's still snowing lightly – and, worryingly, rather wetly. We hope it's not wet enough for the long slope on Twins next to us to build up all night and knock tomorrow morning's breakfast over. We've decided to go down tomorrow to relax and eat at Base Camp. We need a lot of food – we're not eating enough to sustain these carries to over 22,000-feet. Also, we've lost a lot of weight – must have been breaking down muscles to provide energy during the last few days. We've left most of our gear at the high point – down suits, Karrimats and pee-bottles – I miss them now!

It seemed as if the four of us had been together forever. However, the shift system of alternating the leads on the wall, and the close living at Camp 2, had prevented me from talking much to Georges or Joe for a few days. When we were all together it was impossible to talk about each other. As Joe and I descended through the deep snow to Base Camp we gossiped relaxedly and freely – it was a good safety valve to do so; it improved our perspective on ourselves and our performance and helped the scenery move past.

Back at Base Camp after nine days away, we exchanged genuine warm smiles of greeting. Mohan related the world news. Nima Wangdi had brought oranges, bananas and cabbage with the mail.

Kami and Nima Tamang prepared nirvana snacks of eggs and potatoes. All were tastes from another world.

At first the three rest days that stretched ahead were all that existed. An outsider, listening to us chatting, happily and excitedly, might have thought we had reached the summit. Coming down to the security of Base Camp helped us realise how much under constant pressure and on edge we had been on the mountain. Beneath

the wind-rattled tarpaulin of the kitchen shelter we reminded ourselves not to tense with every sound outside. Sudden noises were
no threat here. Georges entertained us, his arms sweeping and eyes
glittering with enthusiasm, with an animated monologue about
guiding and crystal and mineral hunting in the Mont Blanc range. We
were away from the warfare for three days – and three days have a beginning, a middle and an end. The first night our happiness was total.

It was a long evening, and when I walked across the grass to my
tent I remembered how ill I had been in this place before. Now I
could walk almost properly, and was no longer weak with stomach
illness. I had become more interested in reading, writing, climbing,
in everything. The air was heavy with oxygen, and I slept peaceful-
ly. Joe's morning groan from the next tent, and a cup of tea, brought
the new day in.

> Yesterday all was relief to be down here – now the
> mountain looms back into my thoughts. I wonder
> what lies before us – a lightning push for the summit,
> past a blur of rock and snow? But that won't give
> time for the feeling of 'home' up there, so necessary
> for confidence.

For three hours we chatted outside my tent in the sunshine – looking up and across at the storm-plastered mountain, talking out our
hopes and fears, united by the same predicament. None of us knew
if we were physically capable of reaching the summit. Even the two
continental super-athletes who had climbed Everest without oxygen equipment the year before had suffered hallucinations and
double vision. Would our lungs collapse, would our brains swell inside our skulls and make us faint, would the blood in our legs clot?
Would our hearts palpitate? Would we suffer permanent brain
damage and never think or talk the same again? Once up there,
would we be able to make it back down again?

The distances high on the mountain seemed vast. From Schneider's
map we calculated that the 5,000-foot altitude difference between the
North Col and the summit was spread over two and a quarter miles of

North Ridge. We flicked through the books and photographs of the mountain, looking from them to the mountain and back.

'Bauer, he's the bloke to learn from. Look what he did with those Munich men in 1929 and 1931 on the North East Spur. *The Alpine Journal* said it was the greatest achievement ever: "a feat unparalleled in the annals … " etc.'

'A lot of fanatics, they were. They were still fighting the First World War. He just about says they climbed to avenge the humiliation of the Treaty of Versailles. Listen to what Bauer says here: " … stern, warlike disciplined spirit … a circle of men who have become one to the death."'

'I hope we don't have to be that intense.'

'They used snow-holes big enough for eight men and reckoned they could carry loads up to 8,000 metres at half-European-Alps speed.'

'They didn't get that high, though.'

'I hope we do. Wouldn't it be fantastic if we climbed it and were back down here in ten days' time?'

'A bit improbable, though.'

'It's a pity it was a Saturday when we got turned back from the North Col. According to Nima's Tibetan calendar, if the weather is bad on a Saturday it will be bad for a week.'

'In Pakistan they say the same thing about Fridays.'

'Look, we've still got to reach the North Col and we haven't enough rope to do it.'

We had forgotten our geometry lessons. We had brought with us a thousand metres of rope, and Erwin Schneider had told us that the West Wall was nearly a thousand metres high. It had taken us a long time to realise that since the wall was not absolutely vertical, and our route was not completely direct, it was inevitable that we would run out of rope.

'I don't fancy using any of these grotty bits of string around Base Camp.'

'What about the Slovaks on Jannu, then? They might lend us some.' 'That's a good four-day round trip to their Base Camp.'

'Ang Phurba might nip across if we ask him nicely.'

Ang Phurba agreed to trot down to Ghunsa and up to the Base Camp of the Slovak Jannu expedition, to try and borrow some. We sent a humble begging letter – and a fruit cake as a peace offering. He returned two days later, carrying 400 feet of rope and a tin of vodka, and justifiably demanding a day's rest.

On the K2 expedition I had sent a lot of postcards inscribed 'Only 9,000 feet to go!' Four days later we had abandoned the climb. Now we had no newspaper contact demanding a supply of regular pot-warming reports to remind a public about our adventure. I decided only to write to Hilary and my parents until I had something positive to report.

Our sleep became deeper, with fewer remembered dreams, until it was time to return to the mountain.

We returned to Camp 2 in the brilliance of the morning. We were fitter, with clearer thoughts and hearty appetites. It seemed as if we had never left. In the afternoon the mist came down and we lay in our tents, shouting out our pulse rates at thirty-second intervals:

'37.'

'41.'

'47.'

'47!'

'You two aren't very fit.'

'I'm reading pornography.'

'I've got a hangover from the vodka.'

At four-thirty in the morning our defences were low against the grim realities of the day. Georges had been complaining of stomach cramps during the walk up. He was still not feeling well and had not slept. Joe had a headache and was sleepless also. I felt frustrated and impatient. 'Well, if you weren't sleeping you should have taken a sleeping pill like me,' I said.

'You're not as alert if you take drugs,' said Doug.

'Are you all going to stop every time someone has a bad night?' I said.

'You've no sympathy when someone else is ill,' snapped Joe.

We decided to postpone the move another day. I lamented the lost time in my diary:

I've never been on such a frustrating stop-go expedition. We've already had more rest days than Joe
and I had on the entire Changabang trip. It's misty
and very still outside, and we're back exactly where
we were a week ago. I want to get up there and to get
to grips with the problem, one way or another, because time, strength, supplies and good weather all
slip away. Georges oscillates in his Latin way, like a
yo-yo. Joe calls him a butterfly. Now it's his liver or
gall bladder. I dish out pills and eventually he de-
cides on a course of Septrin. Suddenly Tigger is
back bouncing optimistically about, which irritates
throbbing-head Joe more, and is a bit tactless.

On 28 April Doug, Georges, Joe, Ang Phurba and Nima Tenzing
and I set off in a line up the fixed ropes on the wall, intending to establish a camp on the North Col. Doug and Georges moved up
quickly with light loads, and by late morning Georges was fighting
up an overhanging chimney that split the rocks below the final
snow slope. Meanwhile, the Sherpas were having difficulty jumaring the tension traverse and vertical step of the halfway rock barrier
that Doug had first led. Nima had to give up and go down; Joe and
I divided his load between us. Then Ang Phurba became stuck for
an hour. By 1.00 p.m. I was two thirds of the way up the wall and
400-feet below Doug and Georges, who were now hauling their
sacks up the chimney.

Suddenly Joe shouted and I looked up at a sky scattered with
falling rocks. I dodged sideways but as the rocks exploded around
me my left forearm was smashed just above the wrist. I felt as if I
had been hit by a bullet. Overcome with fright, pain and rage,
I wanted to fire back and shrieked with the thought I was crippled.
In a state of shock, I eased off my two gloves and saw a depressing
swelling and gash. Blood dripped on to the snow. Joe came down
and filled with sympathy when he saw the mangled damage. He
had managed to duck under an overhang. One of the rocks had
missed Ang Phurba's head by a few inches. Joe related a detailed

story of how he had once broken four bones in his wrist when he tumbled off Three Pebble Slab at Froggatt, and how his wrist had looked exactly like mine.

'I couldn't feel a thing for ten minutes. Then the pain came.'

'This doesn't seem to be my trip, I wonder what I've done wrong,' I said.

'You must have sinned,' said Joe. 'Perhaps it was going to New Guinea with a bird.'

'It's almost as if the rocks were pushed on purpose,' I said. 'They couldn't have been aimed better.'

'It was carelessness.'

'The clumsy idiots could have killed all three of us. When you get up there, tell whoever knocked the rocks off, from me, tell them, tell them ... ' I turned in anger and abseiled, one-handed, down the ropes. I crunched so furiously into the ice that one of my crampons came off. As I strapped it back on I took deep breaths and told myself to calm down. It started to snow. At the bottom of the ropes I met Nima Tenzing, waiting for Ang Phurba to return. When he saw my wrist, he shook his head and said it was better to have a broken wrist than a broken head. I walked to Camp 2 alone and doctored myself.

During the night I woke, imagining arterial contusions and poisoning, and changed the dressings on my wrist. I spent the following day lying in the tunnel tent, reading and writing, plucking at the tangle of the present.

> Dawn: Nima, next door, is muttering 'Om Mani Padme Hum' over the roar of the stove. Ang Phurba wakes up to the brew. He was very tired last night and seems so this morning too. He has a sore throat, and stiff limbs from all the hard ice of yesterday – 'harder than the South West Face of Everest,' he said.
>
> The western sky is unusually dark, with a thin light on Wedge Peak ... Now it's thundering and snowing heavily, straight down with no wind. The noise of falling séracs pinches awake my 'irrational' fear of

avalanches. The others only reached the col in darkness and a snowstorm last night. They still had quite a way to go when I last saw them. I wonder (with half concern, because they're quite capable of looking after themselves) how they're faring today – whether they'll come down or sit it out. If the camp's good they'll stick it out I expect. I wish in a way Joe had come back down with me yesterday – it's far more fun to chat to someone, though I feel quite cheerful. I made a lot of noise when I was hit – like a child – and feel embarrassed about it now. I've been 'in the wars' this trip, as Gran would say. 'It's all in the lap of the gods', to quote Doug. Perhaps I'm cracking up, but I do wonder about superstitions, fate patterns. I'm amazed – perhaps a bit shocked – at my own determination to get up this climb. It seems to go on and on, and I long to get it over with. We've only had five days' climbing in the last two weeks. Day after day passes, and a breakthrough must come.

Mid-day: The Sherpas knock snow off their tent. It's linked by a guyline to mine, and makes a startling booming noise, which wakes me up. These Kangch storms do seem short-lived. I fell asleep whilst this morning's storm was raging and now I wake to calm. Even the choughs are back. I've redressed the cut on my wrist again, and it feels slightly better – or perhaps it's because the air is warmer … I saw figures on the col a while ago, through the binoculars. I wish I was there with them, looking over into Sikkim, I hope they don't plan to go for the summit before I get up there tomorrow.

5.15: Thunder returned in long rolls and sharp cracks. This place wears on my nerves. It's snowing for the fourth time today, piling deep on the glacier. To think we had a month's perfect weather on Everest in '75! Half an hour ago I exchanged waves with a figure on the col – at least I could tell through the binoculars that he was waving, though I doubt if he could see me. I've sorted our loads for tomorrow.

Dusk: It's stopped snowing and some stars and a misty crescent moon are shining, but lightning still flashes over Kangchenjunga.

It snowed all the next day. Followed by Ang Phurba and Nima Tenzing, I went back up the familiar ropes and over the landmarks of 3,000 feet of mixed ice and rock, pulling with one hand, determined not to turn back this time. Powder avalanches poured over us, and one of them concealed a rock, which hit Nima Tenzing and injured his back. Nima insisted that we continue, and that he was capable of going back down alone. He tied off his load to a piton and descended.

I heard voices in the mist above. Doug and Georges were coming down to pick up some equipment that they had left below the final slope. They had not guessed we would come back up in such bad weather, and had been clearing loose rocks.

The wall was littered with abandoned stuff-sacks and gear left in the forays and about-turns of the previous two weeks. Georges' chimney was desperately strenuous, but the last slope fell back to forty-five degrees. The Slovak rope was strung down it, and I clipped in. I counted my steps from one to twenty-five, and then rested my head on my ice axe and gasped for breath. I was determined not to let Ang Phurba catch me up, to keep him out of sight in the mist. The rope was tied to a large boulder. I stood on top of the rock and the wind met my face. The wall was below me. I hope I don't have to come up there again, I thought.

11   ORDEAL BY STORM

30 April–5 May 1979

I followed the tracks into Sikkim. For thirty feet across the broad swathe of its saddle, the col was blasted by the westerly wind. Then the snow became deep and powdery, the light warmed my face, and the wind died as suddenly as it had lived. The sun burnt through the clouds, catching a teeming sky full of swaying points of light like the spray from some distant waterfall. Although there was no view that afternoon, the change of angle and the prospect of company were enough recompense after the loneliness of the long distance jumar.

'Hey up, youth, come inside – there's some hot orange ready for you.'

I sipped the drink gratefully – I had become dehydrated through hours of gasping up the ropes. 'I'd better not finish it all – Ang Phurba's coming up soon with a load.'

Two tunnel tents were dug into a trench in the slope, sixty feet down on the other side of the col. They looked well settled, like two larvae who had wriggled there to hibernate.

'You'd better move in with Georges,' said Doug. 'We're all organised in here.'

'I'm glad you didn't go without me,' I said.

'The weather's been too bad to think of it. How's your wrist?' asked Joe. He had a headache and explained that he had been out-manoeuvred the night they reached the col. 'I was the last to arrive and was greeted by 'Where are you going to sleep?' We only got one tent up and I had a bad night all scrunched up at the back of it.

I've had a headache ever since. Yes, I've tried everything – Fortral, Panadol, Codeine, sleeping pills – the lot. Nothing'll shift it. Doug found this place. Good eh?' Then Joe closed his eyes and replied only in monosyllables.

Ang Phurba arrived and looked at the camp site with a nod of approval 'You go from here to the summit?' he asked. He then un-packed his load, drank, and went back down the wall to Camp 2, leaving the four of us alone on the North Col.

The tents were linked together by a sleeve entrance. We took it in turns to cook, carefully handing food and drinks between us like astronauts passing precious materials between lunar modules in space.

'It's lovely and relaxed here after all those noises at Camp 2,' I said.

There was a sharp cracking from inside the slope. 'It's O.K., does that all the time,' said Georges. 'You see we're camped on a sérac. I think we're slowly moving down into Sikkim, but we'll be O.K. for the short time we're here. It's a good reason to climb quickly.' At least it was a change to worry about toppling over rather than being hit from above by rocks and avalanches.

Daylight left us to the sound of our own breathing and the creaking of the slope. 'Things are looking up,' I wrote in my diary. 'It's great to be here.'

The sun arrived early, for we had moved from the west to the east side of the mountain. The condensation on the inside of the tents crackled off in sheets.

'It's really good outside,' said Doug.

Excitedly, I followed him out to photograph the morning. The dawn wind across the col splashed my face with cold. To the west the upper cwm of the Kangchenjunga Glacier, with the tiny dot of Camp 2, was still in darkness. Wedge Peak had lost its thrusting ag-gression and sank below us into the earth. Seventy miles away the Kangshung Face of Everest glowed with yellow light. To the east, towards the rising sun, I could see the white glaciers, brown mo-raines, low cloud and a blur of peaks in Sikkim; stretching down directly behind us was the many-fluted east side of the North Col, attempted to within a few hundred feet of our camp by Reggie Cooke in 1937. Also rising out of Sikkim was the North East Spur of Kangchenjunga, which joined the North Ridge high above our heads at 25,390 feet. This long spur was crested by many suspended towers of ice – obstacles which three expeditions had struggled across – the Germans in 1929 and 1931, and the successful Indian expedition in 1977.

Joe rarely articulated his suffering – he just lay in his own quiet gloom. No one suggested that we postpone the attempt until he recovered and, without a word of complaint, he announced he was going down because his headache was still severe.

'He's the only true hard man amongst us,' said Doug.

After Joe had gone the snakes and ladders pattern of our attempts was continuing. Most of the steep, difficult climbing was, we hoped, behind us. We were now poised to discover if, as Freshfield and Dyhrenfurth had foretold, the North Col was the technical key to the riddle of the North Ridge. The three of us remaining changed our clothing for higher altitudes. We had already replaced our conventional double boots of leather and fur with special, space-age ski boots of plastic and foam. These were lighter and warmer, though too cumbersome for steep climbing. Plastic boots had been used in Himalayan climbing since 1975, enabling small teams to go high without oxygen equipment and return unscathed by frostbite. However, the revolutionary importance of these boots had received little publicity, and we, like most climbers, had been cautious and conservative about such a radical change of equipment. Now we were convinced. We took off our fibre pile suits and put on looser-fitting, one-piece down suits topped by windsuits; and then packed our sacks with hardware. After a couple of oatmeal biscuits and a drink of tea each, we were ready for our first steps on to the North Ridge and for the upper part of the mountain.

'You be the guide today, Georges, you're the snow and ice man. I'm too tired from yesterday,' I said.

Doug agreed, and Georges was raring to go. Georges came from the guiding tradition of Argentière – his father was a guide, and his grandfather on his mother's side was the famous guide Georges

Charlet, brother of the even more celebrated Armand Charlet. These men were reputed infallible gods of their profession, whose mountaineering judgments were accepted without question by lesser mortals in the French Alps. When Georges was surging with confidence, as on that morning, shouting 'Let's go for eet', we smiled 'Charlet a dit', and followed willingly.

Georges kicked up the ridge, like an eager dog on a lead. His climbing style was alive, light and energetic, and contrasted with Doug's strong, solid, purposeful movements. Fortunately, the strong wind maintained good cramponing snow, and our progress was rapid, despite the altitude. We steered well clear of the large drooping cornices that overhung Sikkim, and threaded our way around rock pinnacles. Occasional patches of hard, rippled ice mirrored the white light of the sky.

'How about stopping for something to eat, Georges?' He took a lot of persuading, so Doug and I sat down on a convenient knoll and opened a tin of kippers. When the rope brought Georges to a stop, he realised he had no alternative but to pause with us.

We were just in the lee of the ridge, so could enjoy the view. 'We're nearly as high as the main Twins Peak,' I said. 'It looks really straightforward from the North Col, only a couple of hours.'

'In the wrong direction,' said Georges.

'There's Siniolchu,' said Doug, 'and that must be Chomolhari way over there in the distance. The pre-war trips all walked past that, then all the way across the Tibetan Plateau to Everest.' With an expansive sweep of his arm, he described the great arc of the route around us.

To the north we could see for the first time the gentle lines of the purple, snow-streaked drumlin-shaped hills of Tibet – a distant, deserted world of austere calm compared to the young, assertive Himalayan giants nearby. Perhaps, as Freshfield had fancied when he saw Tibet from the Jongsong La, those unknown, unnamed hills were within the horizon of Lhasa itself, and the imagination could leap, using them as stepping stones, to the golden terraces of Potala, the palace of the Dalai Lama.

Above us, the North Ridge steepened into a rock buttress 600 feet high: to our left this stretched around above dangerous-looking slopes of deep powder snow to the North East Spur. To our right the buttress increased in size to become the wall between the second and third terraces of the North West Face of Kangchenjunga. The Germans had seen the snowy side of this feature, and called it 'der Zuckerhut' – the sugar loaf. Its avalanche-prone slopes had turned them back in 1931 at a height of 25,260 feet. From the angle of our viewpoint, the buttress looked more like that of a heavily defended castle – so we changed its original name. We hoped that from where we were we would be able to climb the Castle by what appeared to be the weakest point in its defences, a steep arrowhead of snow that split the buttress, capped by a hundred-foot rock step. To reach the foot of the couloir we traversed diagonally away from the crest of the ridge and out of the wind to a small depression underneath the buttress. There we left our loads of food and equipment, estimating our height as 24,400 feet. We had climbed 1,800 feet from the North Col – a good morning's work and exciting progress after the days of struggle for every inch on the wall below the North Col.

Georges led us all down at a cracking pace. I envied his total confidence but, now we were unladen, Doug and I could just keep up with him. Our speed became urgent as the wind increased into a blizzard and snow hurtled across the ridge and into Sikkim. It was impossible to see further than a few feet, and we followed our crampon marks of the morning, determined not to stray on to a cornice. We reached the tents of the North Col camp – Camp 3 – by two in the afternoon, after descending from the Castle in under an hour.

Lying back in camp, we discussed tactics all afternoon, trying to identify the different weather patterns of this higher altitude. At dusk I wrote:

> The wind is whipping over the North Col, and the
> mountain above is ever-changing in the turbulence.
> No matter how brilliant the morning is, the weather
> has always deteriorated by mid-day. Throughout the

whole trip, we've not yet had a 'summit day' of all sun and no wind. Weather permitting, we may 'go for eet' tomorrow, and dig in beneath the Castle. On the upper part, above the Castle, the weather will be critical. If it's calm I think we have a good chance. We've sorted out gear and food which, including the stuff we've left up there, should be enough for a four- or five-day round trip. I think I was dehydrated last night. It's a losing struggle to try and get six pints of fluid a day and anywhere near the minimum 3,000 calories inside us.

In the morning, whilst Doug and Georges were packing up one of the tents to take with us, I went down the West Wall for a short distance and drew up some of the Slovak rope for us to fix through the Castle. At 8.00 a.m. we all set off up the North Ridge. My turn to lead was long overdue, so I went first. Sometimes the wind was so fierce we had to stop as it gusted. At the toe of the Castle, a lot of snow had drifted around the corner into the shelter of Sikkim, and it took a long time to break trail for the last 200 yards to our proposed site for Camp 4.

The snow slope that split the Castle curved around beneath the buttress in a wind scoop, and it was through the ridge so formed that we started digging. It was 10.30 a.m. when we began to carve holes, fifteen feet apart, on opposite sides of the ridge. Doug and I were both convinced of the need for a snow cave at this height to use as a stable base for forays higher up, and Georges soon agreed as he became involved in the digging, calling it the Mont Blanc Tunnel.

'You'd never work this hard for anyone else,' said Doug, shovelling soft snow rhythmically into Sikkim.

'I always liked den-building as a kid,' I said.

By one in the afternoon, we had met in the middle and shaken hands. 'Where's the champagne?' yelled Georges. An hour later we had enlarged the hole into a magnificent grotto. We slid inside and closed out the view through the entrance with large blocks of snow.

In the excitement of the digging we had forgotten to put our windsuits on top of our down suits, and by the time we were inside the cave we were wet with snow and perspiration. It took a long time to warm up. We were tired. The altitude made us feel heavy and all movement was an effort. Doug was positioned at the back of the cave, and when he lit the stove it went out because of the lack of oxygen. He was reading *Journey to Ixtalan* by Carlos Castenada, underlining parts in red and clutching it like a Fundamentalist with his Bible.

'Preparing for the journey, youth,' he said.

I suspected the other two were being lazy and that I was being out-manoeuvred – they probably felt the same. Georges seemed to be ordering me about, lying in the middle and telling me to seal the draught, and then demanding brews at 10.00 p.m. and 3.00 a.m. Then Doug suggested that we had one at 5.00 a.m. Although I knew how important it was for us to take plenty of fluids, I was convinced I'd spent all the night melting ice over the stove. Starting with a few handfuls of snow, each pan of water took an hour to prepare.

In the morning, when we broke out through the entrance, we could see the dome of 23,460 feet, Nepal Peak, soloed by Erwin Schneider in 1930 from its other side. The weather looked encouragingly settled.

It was easier to prepare ourselves in the cave for the day's climbing than it had been in the cramped tents lower down. We were sealed and protected in a constant temperature and tomb-like silence from the weather outside. Here there was no frozen condensation to knock into our sleeping bags, or a groundsheet to spike with our crampons. We wriggled out into the daylight fully armoured to 'do battle with the elephants', as someone said.

'How about you leading, Doug?' I suggested, trying out his mock gruff but effective way of giving suggestions. Georges and I followed him from the hole and along the little ridge until it merged into the snow slope. We moved together, holding the ropes in coils between us.

I was very worried about the state of the snow and I sensed that

Georges was too. Doug was too far in front for me to make out his thoughts. I hacked into the slope, searching for changes in resistance. Large cup crystals of depth hoar lay beneath the surface – ice crust like ball-bearings of instability. After Georges and I had crept apprehensively upwards for 200 feet, we shouted up to Doug to belay. A film clicked through my mind, showing us all sloughing off into Sikkim. Just standing on the slope, waiting, I felt helplessly committed with the other two. I started hating the predicament, and then hating climbing, utterly and in general, and wishing myself out of it.

A hundred and eighty feet below the top of the Castle Doug belayed to an ice screw, to which Georges and I added a deadman snow anchor. Neither placement could be trusted. Above us, the icy slope steepened to sixty degrees. Doug plodded up until, ten feet below the fifty-foot rock step that crowned the slope, he placed another ice screw and shouted down, reassuring us that it was secure. Immediately I began to relax, and joined him to hold his rope whilst he steadily bridged his way up a groove in the rock. The ring of a rock piton, and a tape sling dropped over a spike, were welcome news that Doug was lacing us back on to the mountain, and signalled the end of my nervousness. After an hour the soles of his boots disappeared on to the top of the Castle. I clambered up to join him, relishing the feel of the warm, rough rock.

'Well done, Doug, I'm glad you led that.' Georges followed close on my heels.

'I don't feel quite myself.'

'Neither do I.'

'I don't understand it, we should be O.K. We've only come about 600 feet.'

'Still, we're at 25,000 feet now.'

I screwed up my eyes, trying to ward off the dizziness. The concentration of the climbing below had protected us from the altitude. We staggered towards a large rock, where we left a cache of equipment. Then we walked 200 feet across easy angled ice and rocks until the great snow and scree terrace was before us and we could glimpse the summit triangle through the wind and cloud that buffeted us.

'It doesn't look too far.'

We slid back down, fixing ropes to within a hundred feet of the snow cave. Now we only had two climbing ropes left. The descent took only half an hour, and we were back in the cave at one in the afternoon. When we had first come to this place, it had seemed the wildest, most desolate, most remote spot in the world. Now, within a few hours, it became home. Later it would mean life itself to us.

'I don't like that wind up there, it's worrying.'

'Those towering clouds seem to boil up from Sikkim during the morning until they knock their heads against the westerlies. Then all the turbulence starts.'

The ridge above our heads was the battle zone.

Although I wasn't hungry, I forced food down. We were eating very little, yet we were burning many calories during the day. I felt very sleepy and spent a comfortable afternoon and night resisting Georges' pressure to do the cooking, and thinking of the summit. At last we were going to try for it.

The morning of 4 May started late with a stupid, wordless confrontation, after we'd stated our positions. Doug had already said 'I've cooked every bloody meal on this trip.'

I'd replied, 'You had to because you always chose the place with the most room.'

Now I wasn't going to light the stove after my lengthy session two nights previously. Georges felt self-righteously that he'd cooked the day before. I waited until Doug told Georges to light the stove. I felt very silly. It was 7.30 a.m. by the time we were ready to leave, and a long day stretched before us. We set out for the summit.

By 9.10 a.m. we were on top of the Castle. We picked up the equipment we had left the day before and hobbled awkwardly in our ski boots and crampons across the loose stones. At first I was amazed at our progress – that we could actually walk at such an altitude. Features I remembered from binoculars and photographs glided towards me as I panted past, a detached, living figure on those images. I could see the blue tarpaulin of Pangpema Base Camp, far below, and occasionally could glimpse Camp 2 beneath my feet. We traversed beneath the lines of crags of Point 25,390 feet, where the North East Spur joined the North Ridge.

'Those crags look like Stanage from here,' shouted Doug.

Then we walked into the path of the westerlies.

The winds were gusting across the Great Snow and Scree Terrace at sixty to seventy miles per hour. The rope between us flapped wildly in the air and caught around our ankles and ski sticks and snagged on boulders and ice crustations. Our hoods and balaclavas whipped across our faces. Frequently we slumped kneeling to the ground, bracing ourselves against sudden, furious volleys of splintering ice and snow. The blowing, stinging cloud began to imprison our vision to the rock and ice at our feet – we could have imagined ourselves wintering on an Arctic plateau, were it not for our bizarre, bulky, muffling ice-clad oversuits and our lungs tolling 25,700 feet. We were aiming for the Croissant – a large crescent-shaped buttress at the foot of the steep 2,000-foot summit triangle. The easiest way to the summit seemed to the right of it; but that lay directly in the path of the wind. We stopped and tried to discuss. We knew that our only chance of surviving the night would be somehow to escape from the wind. The snow was so hard-packed that our axes, saws and shovels could never have built shelter before we succumbed to the cold. Our experience of Camps 3 and 4 had told us the Sikkim side of the ridge was sheltered. Doug took over the lead and we aimed for a distant notch on the North Ridge, at 26,000 feet, where we hoped to cross into the calm of the other side.

The notch hovered beyond our grasp through the cloud for a long time. Doug was first over. Blinded by spindrift, we almost flew over it – the winds were now blowing continuously at eighty to ninety miles per hour. As I crossed the ridge, I felt my back stabbed by thousands of needles, as if my whole body was disintegrating. The spindrift blinded my goggles. I screamed into the blast 'I can't see. Are you safe? Can I come down?'

'Pull yourself down with your ice axe,' shouted Doug.

On the other side we knelt, dazed, trying to collect our thoughts. Below us the forty-five degree slope curved away into whiteness. Here there was no wind although it was roaring through the notch above our heads. Doug had also suffered agonising shocks of static.

'I didn't know whether to mention it,' he said. 'I thought I was falling apart.'

It was 3.00 p.m. We spent three hours weakly hacking at the ice, until we had excavated a small ledge that was just big enough to take our tunnel tent. Doug did most of the digging and Georges erected the tent. The altitude was debilitating – I felt as if my body was tied down with lead weights. Once inside, we considered the possibilities for the morning. We would attempt to go up. If we tried to rest for a day at 26,000 feet, we would probably weaken and lose the chance of climbing the remaining 1,200 feet to the summit. We fell asleep for a short while and woke with headaches. The stove kept on going out but Doug steadfastly prepared some soup and then a hot water bottle for Georges, who was suffering from the cold. We took a sleeping pill and two aspirins each and relaxed, listening to the wind beating the night above the ridge. We fell asleep to beautiful warm dreams.

I was awakened suddenly by snapping fabric and a world in uproar. 'The wind's changed.'

I looked at my watch. 1.30 a.m. The tent was shaking and pushing against us. I felt enveloped in comfort and willed it to stop, so that I could travel away again into sleep. But soon we were all wide awake. We turned our torches on. The tent was flapping and crackling wildly, throwing frost everywhere – and our lives depended on it. Where had this wind come from? Why? Why? Slowly, the danger sank in. At 2.30 a.m. the centre hoop snapped and we knew we would have to start fighting for our lives. We held on to the hoop in turns as our fingers numbed, trying to stop its jagged ends from ripping the fabric, taking it in turns to throw on our boots and crampons, fumbling with straps. We shouted curt instructions to each other, cold and disciplined, devoid of emotion, going through the motions of survival – detached and playing to the audience of our minds.

'Georges, hold this for a minute!'

Only our eyes showed caged terror, sharing the thought that this was probably the end. My mind was racing. Not much chance of getting out of this. Family, loved ones, friends; if I do get out I'll have terrible frostbite. We haven't even climbed the mountain. If there is a God, then please, please stop this wind. Why should he? Am I strong enough for this? Is this the time? Concentrate on yourself, we must all do that. No time to pray.

Short lulls of a few seconds gave false hopes. Doug looked out. 'The anchors are pulled. We're being blown off the ledge, the whole tent's moved two feet, we'll have to get out fast!' He squirmed outside and held on.

We were within a second of rolling down and down into the stormy darkness. The wind was at hurricane force, tearing strips of fabric off the tent.

'Don't leave the gear, don't abandon.'

Georges and I furiously packed the sleeping bags and wriggled out of the tent. We collapsed it, ripped it open with a knife and pulled the remaining equipment out, and the wind snatched the tent away. Dawn was now struggling out of the streaming cloud, rocks the size of dinner plates whipped up from the ridge, were swinging through the turbulence like meteorites. I could not even kneel on the ledge without being knocked over. Georges, then Doug, disappeared up the slope above, pulling the mad tangle of ropes, trying to claw their way to the notch. They made it on their third attempt, and my rope went tight. A dark shape hurtled past. 'God, no, somebody's fallen.' It was Georges' sack.

I struggled after them, pulled by the ropes, hauling myself through the notch with my ice axe. It was like trying to crawl into a jet engine at full throttle.

We reeled and stumbled across the Great Snow and Scree Terrace in a dream, resisting our bodies' cries to lie down, sleep. There was so much ice on our faces we could barely see. Now was the time we could give up, let go the end of our strength and sink to the earth. If only there was time to sleep. Voices filled my head: 'Must get down.' 'Must get down.' 'Hurry.' 'Hurry.' 'Now is the time mistakes are made.'

But we had been so near to certain death, our fear was dulled. The day before little windslabs of snow had worried us. Now, we took no care, crunching them beneath our feet.

We reached the snow cave at 8.00 a.m. The entrance was buried and Doug shovelled it out. We drank some hot orange juice and tried to thaw out our feet and hands. I swallowed Vaso-dilating pills.

We reached the North Col at 10.20 a.m. and ate some freeze-dried apricots and melted another drink. Georges was becoming snow-blind, and was complaining of dark vision. We dosed him with eye-drops. Our injuries were coming to life and now we could assess them for the first time. Doug had sustained frostbite on the upper joints of four fingers whilst he had held on to the tent in the wind. I had frostbite on a big toe and on my nose. We had been lucky.

We decided to leave our high-altitude equipment and clothing on the North Col and try to reach Base Camp the same day. The ice on the wall had hardened. We scurried down the ropes and ploughed across the glacier from the foot of the wall to Camp 2. Behind us the wind and cloud of the storm swept across the sky with such speed that Kangchenjunga appeared to rotate in the opposite direction. I realised my ankle and wrist were no longer troubling me.

12   BEFORE DAWN

5–14 May 1979

'I thought – "Why am I down here rather than up there – dying with you lot?"' Joe was waiting for us at Camp 2, with Ang Phurba. Hot drinks were simmering and he was very glad to see us, talking excitedly: 'The wind was like an express train down here. We thought the whole camp was blowing away – Ang Phurba and I had to hang on to the tents for most of the night. We couldn't sleep. That's why we didn't do a carry up to the col this morning. I knew if you hadn't found shelter last night you'd never have survived.'

'Where's Nima?'

'He's down at Base Camp. We had to take him down with his back injury. I don't know how serious it is. He could walk O.K. though. It's probably just badly bruised. Ang Phurba and I came back up yesterday.'

'How's your headache?'

'Seems fine now. I was really depressed when I came down from the North Col – I felt about an inch high when I arrived here. Looks as if I've got a second chance now. Since my head cleared I've been trying to enthuse Ang Phurba into going for the trip, but he's noncommittal – you know what he's like, super cool. He's brilliant crossing the moraines and coming up the glacier, though – he knows the way like the back of his hand. I just put my feet where he does, and it seems a different walk. He's deceptively fast. We came up in three and a half hours yesterday, all the way from Base Camp. Just try following him down now.'

Crevasses had moved, snow had melted, and the route had changed. The intense vigilance of the descent fell away like scales and I took photographs of the sunset, seeing beauty with a power I had not known earlier during the expedition, and feeling gloriously receptive to everything around me. Joe and Ang Phurba drew ahead through the moraines.

'Get the spuds on,' I shouted. I jumped from boulder to boulder, invigorated by the thought of Base Camp and strengthened by the rush of oxygen. I arrived in the twilight, sweating.

The momentum of our experience kept us talking fast. We sat in the warm firelight of the kitchen shelter. 'I was really scared,' said Georges.

'I've never known a wind like that,' said Doug.

I wanted to forget the ordeal for a while, and changed the subject. 'You should see the inside of the snow cave, Joe, it's revolting. Everyone's gobbed on to the ceiling – the colour changed depending on which fruit juice we'd been drinking. And it got noisy too. You know what Georges' throat gargle sounds like. Give us a gargle, Georges.'

We ate our first meal for two days. It was our Base Camp favourite – egg and potatoes. Doug sipped some whisky to dilate his fingers and passed the bottle round. Kami promised a cake for the next day. Mohan told us the U.K. Election results. 'If we'd got to the top, we could say we'd staged the climb as a protest,' said someone.

The thicker air lay around us like the slow support of warm water. For a few hours, delicious warmth and rest and the smell of wood-smoke, vegetation and damp earth, anaesthetised thoughts, suppressed doubt and banished problems. Our minds were stilled and wide open. I spent the day reading, to draw me out of myself. My wrist was still swollen, one big toe was numb and black under the nail, but my ankle was O.K.! By the late afternoon, I was ready to start writing:

> The quality of our survival is good. All these are surface scars around an inner calm. Memories of the

battle anchor me here in perfect equilibrium against the alternating swell of mountain above and the valley and home below. I, the fortunate man alive today, still have much in common with the man who fought the storm. I am so happy to relax, feeling confident that I can climb the mountain, having survived such a night at 26,000 feet. I now know to what extent our equipment can protect us and what distances we can cover up there. I now know I don't have to be a superman. It was a rich experience – I've learned a lot, and feel a strength flow from it. Perhaps I needed, almost enjoyed it, for this feeling. I have to admit honestly, that I would not have missed it. Out of one of the worst experiences of my life, I've learned again how precious life is – we've a new measure for our lives. The mountain has to make us work, has to be uncertain. Through the effort and the weeks the mountain is seeping into us. Through this communion, I am sure, we shall eventually discover the key, and I am beginning to feel ready for it.

Next day the mail runner, Nima Wangdi, was due.

'Jan writes a bit every day,' said Doug.

'So does Hilary.'

'That sounds like a duty to me,' said Joe.

I almost dreaded letters, and I think Doug did too, in case something had happened, in case they were not happy letters, in case something in them disturbed us from climbing Kangchenjunga. We could hear the wind on the mountain, a faint, far-off murmur which emphasised our shelter. A night's rest revived my aches and pains:

6.10 7 May. I can hear the cackling of the snow cocks and the distant thuds in the kitchen, as morning tea is prepared. There are six inches of snow on the ground, and the sun is shining on Kangchenjunga from the east. The wind doesn't look as bad up there today. The sun will reach here soon, and I look forward to it, because I've woken up feeling tired, chilled and a bit ill. I wonder if that's a wheeze in my lungs. I'm taking deep breaths, willing a full recovery. Perhaps the mail will bounce me back again.

10.30 a.m. The sun is beating down and I'm back in the tent after breakfast, listening to music and sheltering my blistered face which looks as if it needs a skin graft. Doug, Georges and I all agree we feel worse today than yesterday. After a brief lull, all the effort and exhaustion of the last few days have at last caught up with us. We're no longer keyed up and excited by the storm, and all our injuries seem to matter more and they hurt more. A cold burn from my watch on my wrist, and ear-ache have just emerged. Also, I've a sore hip from lying on my side without fat cushioning – my buttocks have been burnt up in energy! Joe seems naturally a bit worried if his headache will return and how he's going to perform higher up, having missed the storm and not having been to 8,000 thousand metres like us. Doug said, 'Yesterday I felt like going back up – today I feel like going home.' He says his fingers are only good enough for one more go, and that it's the quality of the struggle that counts. Now he's been on a lot of trips, and is getting older, reaching the summit does not matter as much as it used to.

I did not want a retreat, not like the violent urge to go away, fly home and forget, that I had felt after the disappointment and tragedy on K2 the previous year. I wanted to recapture the glorious sense of well-being and satisfaction that I had experienced after successful climbs on other expeditions.

I glanced through Charles Evans' book *The Untrodden Peak* – the story of the successful 1955 expedition. I found George Band's photograph, looking down on the Great Snow and Scree Terrace from the summit, 2,000 feet above. I projected out little figures on it, slowly moving upwards. I wrote:

> Never in our climbing careers again, I'm sure, will we be in such a position on such a good new route. Doug has been asking his 'I Ching' for a forecast, but the answers are, as usual, ambiguous but interesting.

At the meal time Georges suggested to Doug and me that we exchanged our diaries, to see what we had written about the storm. We declined. My diary was my confessional and, whilst the mountain was still in our lives, such raw descriptions were unsharable and may have caused arguments. Seen through the blurred memories of three anoxic brains, the truth would have presented three different faces. I wrote:

> After such a crisis, we all inevitably write that which helps our own self-esteem. For example, Doug probably thinks he saved all our lives by hanging on to the tent – and, true enough, I suppose he did. But we have to believe in ourselves, as well, to survive. Also, we were each so much alone in what we had to face in that storm, so whatever story we tell afterwards can only be our own.

The weather was settling:

> Tantalisingly, it's a calm night with a brilliant growing moon and cloudless starry sky. If man's strength really does grow with a full moon, our timing might be right yet. No mail runner came today. I didn't realise how much I was expecting him until he didn't turn up.

159

The next day, 8 May, was the last of our planned three days' rest at Base Camp, before going back up on to the mountain. After breakfast Doug said: 'If the mail doesn't come today, I think we should wait until it does. If anything happens to us up there, they'd like it if we'd read their letters.'

'You morbid bugger,' I said.

'You've got to be ready for it, youth. It's easy to die, and it only affects them.'

'Well, let's just hope he turns up. We've got to get a move on.'

It was a beautiful morning and the usual two split levels of cloud – the still shapes in the cwm, and the wind plume along the North Ridge above the North Col – had both disappeared. After the storm, we had descended the 11,000 feet from the notch to Base Camp in a day, but it would be a long, paced effort of four days, camp by camp, to return.

'It's perfect weather, from here to the summit.'

'Just a few gentle zephyrs to waft around your face and keep you alert,' said Joe. 'I wish it'd been like that three days ago.'

'I wish we were up there now.'

'It's impossible to predict what it'll be like in a few days' time.'

'When it's really bad, it seems to take a week to re-form, to re-settle.'

'I don't think there's a pattern.'

'This is the first "summit day" we've seen up there.'

'It could be the calm spell, starting early.'

'Did you bring the description of where the Indians went up the last bit, Doug?'

'No, it didn't give a lot of details anyway, and we don't want to lose the sense of discovery, do we? I remember they said it would be "nearly impossible" without oxygen.'

'The BBC said that their air-dropping of supplies up to 16,000 feet "wasn't quite cricket".'

'I wouldn't object to a high-altitude helicopter whisking us back up there now.'

'I'm dreading going back up those fixed ropes.'

'It's much more fun above the wall, isn't it!'

The two successful expeditions to climb Kangchenjunga before had placed their summit teams on the top at the end of May: in 1955 Brown and Band had reached the top on 25 May, and Streather and Hardie the following day. In 1977 Prem Chand and Nima Dorje Sherpa had reached the top on 31 May. We had read Charles Evans' reasoning behind the timing of the 1955 expedition:

> Towards mid-May there's a regular change in the pattern of the weather in the mountains of Eastern Nepal: the north westerly winds prevalent in the first half of the year slacken, and there is a short and variable, but fairly dependable spell of fine, still weather before the onset of the south west monsoon at the beginning of June, the monsoon that brings not only heavy snowfalls on the higher slopes, but warmth, which rots the deep snow through and makes it dangerous.

So far, the weather had not shown any predictable patterns, and we suspected that this was an over-simplification.

The settled weather mocked our impatience and after noon we grew tense as we waited for the post.

'Joe, have you still got *The Seven Pillars of Wisdom*?'

'No, Ang Phurba's reading it.'

Ang Phurba often spent a long time inside his tent, reading, and I went over and disturbed him. 'Ang Phurba, have you finished *The Seven Pillars of Wisdom*?'

'Yes.'

'Did you enjoy it?'

'Yes.'

'What was it about?'

'Arabs.'

I couldn't concentrate enough to read more than the first few pages.

We gathered in the kitchen tent as shadows lengthened. 'He must arrive today, it's fifteen days since he left.'

Nima Tenzing, his back injury now recovered, stood on a near-by hilltop, his sharp eyes scanning the horizon. We listened to the BBC World Service – a quiz game, news and a music request pro-gramme. It was almost dark when Nima announced he could see Nima Wangdi coming. Our earlier accusations of 'the laziest man in Nepal' changed within fifteen minutes to friendly greetings for the man we most wanted to see in the world. We snatched the let-ters greedily. I felt awesomely excited, as if I were about to open exam results. A quick scan by the light of the pressure lamp – there was nothing amiss in my private world; but they were a month old. I hardly noticed the meal, and went to my tent to read the let-ters for an hour and a half. Joe put some suitable music on the cas-sette player – 'The tracks of my tears', 'Help me make it through the night' – until Georges complained about the noise. It was a restless, dream-filled night.

We left Base Camp in the cool of the next morning, and arrived at Camp 2 at 9.00 a.m. We wrote our reply letters there, to be sent down with Nima Tenzing and Ang Phurba two days later. The gla-cier had moved and melted during the three days we had been away, and we had to re-pitch the tents. We heated up some pota-toes and rice, pre-cooked at Base Camp, and ate and slept well, feeling relaxed and confident.

At 4.30 a.m. on 10 May, Camp 2 was stirring. There was a strange, calm sky, overcast with wisps of clouds, not cold at all. If it were the Alps these would not be good signs. But here – who could tell?

Ang Phurba was to accompany us to the North Col, carrying a load which included a bottle of oxygen, for emergencies.

When we arrived at the bergschrund at the foot of the wall's fixed ropes, we discovered that the Sherpas had accidentally left two jumars at Base Camp. So we had eight to distribute between five people. Since Doug had frost-nipped fingers, and Ang Phurba was carrying the heaviest load, they both needed two each. After a short argument, Joe, Georges and I drew matches for the remain-ing four. Georges won. We climbed the ropes through the morn-ing and into the early afternoon.

Camp 3 – North Col. Dusk. I'm lying at the front of the tunnel tent brewing up. Fortunately Doug slid one of his jumars down the rope to Joe, to help him climb the steep chimney pitch, and Joe slid it to me after he'd finished with it. That made a big difference to last time, when I only had one jumar and a fresh wrist injury as well. Joe cut his finger quite badly on that pitch, and left the rock covered in blood. He's patched up O.K. now, though. The early morning mist cleared, and it was hot work. It took us all about six hours to reach here, and Ang Phurba went straight back down almost immediately. We all arrived very thirsty. We've only one pan here – we left the other at Camp 4 – so it's a hassle, melting enough snow to rehydrate. We brought Georges' little tunnel tent, to replace the one that disappeared into Sikkim during the storm, and cut a new platform for it. Georges is in it with me. He's asleep and making sighing and grunting noises. A fine spray of snow falls constantly on the camp from the wind over the North Col. This tent is not as sheltered as the other, and occasional gusts of spindrift remind me of last week's epic. The plan is to go up to the Camp 4 snow cave tomorrow. Because of the wind, there doesn't seem much possibility of shelter above that, so we've accepted Georges' suggestion to leave tomorrow midnight and make a single night/day 4,000-foot push to the summit. 'To follow through the night the moving moon' – was it Byron who said that? I reckon we've got enough supplies for ten days if necessary (including some bread from Base Camp). Like last time, we've all agreed – we don't want to come up that wall again! As for the mountain above, who knows? I'm sure we're capable of climbing it, but one bad weather setback could do us in so much we'd have to go all the way down (groan) again. What was Gide's paradoxical truth – that man's happiness lies not in freedom but in the acceptance of a duty? Well, we're all doing this as a sort of duty now, but I feel more disciplined than happy about it. I'm longing for civilisation, pints of Robbies mild in The Swan, the lads, Leysin, everything.

At four-thirty the next morning I made the first brew, Doug took over and made a second, and we were soon ready. Doug and Joe climbed on to the ridge first, and Georges and I followed. The sky was a deep blue and the intense wind plucked at our faces which were still tender from the storm. Our legs were tired from the previous days' pull and push up to the North Col, and it took us all morning to reach the snow cave of Camp 4.

4.00 p.m. 11 May. That wind is awful. It whizzes from all directions and during a gust you have to brace yourself this way, and then that way, gasping with the altitude. I let my clothing protect me, my body fight it, and my mind wander. Confused strings of thoughts whilst climbing and resting at this altitude are not unpleasant – the mind fastens illogically on event, place, person. I'm looking forward to safer living and pleasures down below. We're all lying in the snow-hole now. It has shrunk since we were last here, and we're packed together like sardines. We had to do quite a lot of enlarging to get the four of us in. Above our heads are the hachured hacking lines of the first excavation. I stare at them in front of my face – it's like being imprisoned in a disused mine. Georges has just done a sustained cooking session and wants us all to know about it! It's a problem to keep toes warm in here. We've discussed leaving at midnight for the big push, but none of us feels confident because of the wind and our fatigue. So we'll take a rest/wait day here – we've got enough food and it's Joe's birthday tomorrow. He'd forgotten till Doug reminded him! Although it's a deep-freeze, it's better than camping. This climb is keeping us guessing right till the end. It's calm outside the snow-hole, but it's impossible to know what the wind is doing on the ridge above us without going there. Did we imagine that good day, three days ago, when we looked up from Base Camp? All the others are snoozing here in the fridge.

The next day we did not move. I kept looking at my watch, waiting for the time to pass.

3.10 p.m. 12 May. A day in the void, and birthdays mean nothing up here. We've had plenty of time to worry about the weather, legs and lungs. We woke with headaches, which cleared when we enlarged the entrance to the snow-hole. We staggered out for some sunbathing this morning – it seemed a perfect, calm day. Below us were the peaks and clouds of Sikkim. We aired our gear until fear of dropping things and spindrift drove us back in. Once more we've no idea what the weather is doing, it seems to change every half hour. I don't know if we'll have the strength to make another attempt. It's all a great unknown. I wonder if other climbs have such uncertainty – I can't remember. It would be good if we could see the summit, to psyche up, but it's out of sight. I hope it's the best plan to miss a night's sleep, to try for 4,000 feet in one go. We'll see. I think wistfully of the lovely snoozes we had on Everest, using oxygen cylinders. It's like in a submarine, 'On the Beach' in here. It's very cramped, and I feel irritable. But in my mind I see times ahead – not having done it, having done it.

Between seven-thirty and one-thirty that night we took turns to crawl out of the tunnel entrance to the cave, and to scan the sky for signs of settling weather. The light of the moon was blocked by scurrying clouds of powder snow. Eventually we decided to stay for another day, and tried to sleep.

As the second day progressed, the idea of staying there much longer began to be more painful than the prospect of another summit attempt in bad weather. Somehow the plan to leave at midnight was brought back more and more.

> 2.35 p.m. 13 May. I didn't want to climb Kangch on the 13th anyway! But as the weather turned out this morning, we'd have been O.K. going. It's all rather soul-destroying and we're even more irritable than yesterday. Joe is managing, with Doug, to avoid any cooking. Joe seems worried about up top – less self-assured than usual. Or perhaps he's just being quiet. No one's saying much. The ceiling is slowly coming down and we're lying on the border of sleep, often crossing it. I don't think we have the will to stay here another day, getting on each other's nerves. This un-ease outweighs our fear of another storm. We'll just have to take pot luck. Not long now and we'll know.

We crammed a freeze-dried meal inside us and filled two bottles with water to take inside our down suits, protected from freezing. At 5.30 p.m., against all our better judgment, we decided to go.

'The weather couldn't be more inauspicious,' said Doug.

There were three levels of cloud below us, beside us and above, and a strong wind was blowing mad maypoles of spindrift along the surface of the snow slope that split the Castle. At dusk, the lower clouds of valley and sky began to fuse slowly into a continual greyness. The rope had become iced up and, flung by the wind, had snagged across the ice wall seventy feet above the snow cave. Joe, Doug and I stamped our feet in the entrance to the cave, looking at the soles of Georges' cramponed boots as he traversed airily across the wall to free it. It was a bold burst of energy. 'I think it's the start of one of those days,' he said, when we grouped together at the top of the Castle. It was 8.00 p.m. and dark clouds were gathering around our heads. The moon appeared briefly, but soon hid behind flurries of snow and refused to reappear. We had miscalculated, for it was now sliding along a course behind the mountain. We switched on our head torches. I put on a white surgeon's mask, to stop the blowing ice chips from encrusting my face, and to warm the air I breathed.

'The wind's not as strong as last time,' I shouted.

'We should make it if it doesn't get any worse,' said Doug.

Our head torches flickering, we trudged on, wobbling awkwardly over the broken ground. Every few minutes we leant into the wind on our ski sticks, gasping for breath. As we crossed the screes my left crampon came off three times. Doug, to whom I was tied, waited patiently as my clumsily mitted hands fiddled with the straps. The other two disappeared into the darkness.

We found them sheltering behind a large boulder, heating a pan of orange juice. I almost said 'Where are the others?' During that night voyage across the Great Snow and Scree Terrace, we all felt that our team was bigger than it was, that we were a large group.

'The weather's cleared on worse nights than this,' I said.

'Let's go for eet,' said Georges.

Our thick protective clothing was working well, distancing us from our situation. Doug produced a crampon spanner. 'See if you can fix it, youth. Get it right.' After much adjustment I changed the pattern of the lacing and the crampon was secured. We trudged on.

The dark shape of the Croissant appeared occasionally through patches of mist, lit by stars, but the summit triangle was covered by constant cloud, and the moon was lost behind the ridge. Our head torches cut a swathe into the moving whiteness. The weather seemed to be deteriorating, but to what extent we judged differently. The darkness, altitude and weather combined to blur the distinction between our minds and the mountain. We were wandering in a mind-landscape, like sleepwalkers.

On a mountain, four is never an easy number for discussion, and decisions are difficult at midnight, at 26,000 feet in the teeth of the wind. Was the weather worsening? Should we stop here and try to bivouac? We could not agree and confusion resulted. Georges was streaming forward, unaware that doubt was seeping into the ranks behind. Doug started digging into a snow bank, and Joe joined in. I said I thought the snow was too hard and wind-packed, and that it would take too long. To persuade Joe I shouted 'I've got more experience snow-holing.'

'Well, you go and find a better place, then.'

I went over to Doug. 'Will you untie from the rope? I'm going to try higher up.'

Joe untied from Georges as I moved away. I exchanged some shouts with Doug, feeling embittered about the disagreement with Joe. They soon disappeared behind me as I followed the dim shape of Georges into the storm, towing the empty rope.

The slope steepened beneath my axe and boots. I kicked upwards, twelve paces at a time, unable to match Georges' speed, trying to glimpse his light through the sweeping mist. Georges had reached the rocks of the Croissant, and was following their edge. He stopped at the first sign of a hole. I caught up with him. We chopped an entrance and slid inside the bergschrund, out of the wind.

The yellow light and narrow space brought us sharply back to the present.

'I knew someone was following me but I didn't realise it was you,' he said. He lit the stove and sheltered it with his gloved hands from the cold draught that flowed beneath the surface between the ice and rock.

I started to enlarge the hole, using my feet and axe, trying to keep warm and make the sense of a home out of the chaos of the night. It was 12.45 a.m.

The summit filled Georges' head. 'We must not stop here. It is bad to stop at this altitude. We must go now, make or break, for the summit. There will not be another time.'

I was pulled along in the wake of his enthusiasm. It seemed easier and more positive to agree to move than to insist on staying.

Georges had the momentum and I took the opportunity to hang on to it.

However, it was reassuring to know that we had found a sheltered burrow to retreat to.

Georges wriggled out of the hole and I followed him into the night. We hugged the edge of the rocks. My mind clung to a few simple thoughts, 'This is it', 'After this I can go home', 'The Summit'. I couldn't remember the topography, except that we were to aim vaguely for two gullies that would lead on to a long diagonal snow ramp that reached up to the pinnacles of the West Ridge, nearly 2,000 feet above the Croissant. I left my ski stick in the steepening slope and pulled my axe from my holster before Georges did, lacking his confidence on the wind-packed snow.

Georges started traversing rightwards. 'We're on the Ramp,' he shouted. The sky cleared for a few seconds, and we saw the Pinnacles in the deceitful grey light of the moon. 'Twenty minutes away,' shouted Georges. They had looked near, but not, I thought, as near as that. Georges thought we had climbed one of the gullies. I did not think we had.

Rocks barred our upward progress. 'It's the wrong way, Georges – at least it is for tonight.'

I led two ropelengths to the right. The slab of snow I was climbing on felt hollow and unstable and my head torch revealed a maze of slabs of rock and snow. I was lost. 'Always trust your own judgment, Pete,' I repeated to myself. I screamed into the wind 'Georges, we're far too low. We should go back to the cave and wait for the others and for daylight!'

Georges joined me. 'We mustn't lose the height. We've gained three or four hundred metres, we're so near,' he said.

'Let's wait for dawn, then,' I said. 'It's about an hour away.'

It was a cold hour. We kicked out a little ledge and stamped and shook our chilling feet and clapped our numbing hands, hoping that visibility would improve and that the weather would change with the dawn. As the sky lightened, the cloud that blew around us thickened. A voice started singing in my head that this was folly. I hoped Georges was hearing the same.

'Let's go down,' he said.

'What, down to the Croissant bergschrund?'

'No, down!' Then he changed his mind. 'We'll wait in the bergschrund until the sun comes.'

We plunged down through the storm, surprised at our speed, for the angles of night had eased with the light of dawn.

Back inside the bergschrund we tried to melt some snow. The fuel was fading so we changed cylinders. The stove seal leaked with the intense cold, so we threw the cylinder away and chewed nuts. Georges shook my hand, saying 'It's been enough for me, to have been a few hundred feet from the summit.' He went outside. I dug and chopped the hole, building a springboard for a future try.

Georges shouted in to me. 'The others are coming. Come outside.'

'How far are they away?'

'About twenty minutes below us, coming up.'

'I'll stay inside and work on this ceiling.'

I heard Georges saying 'We've just been a few hundred feet from the summit.' Doug's voice sounded cold and angry. I shouted up arguments from the hole, but the snow muffled my words. Doug lowered himself in, unhappy that the team had split up and reacting from hours of concern about us.

'When we saw only Georges just now, we thought you'd been rolled away by the wind. This is a team effort. We must always stick together on this trip, all four of us, and not go sneaking off for the top.'

I explained how I understood the confusions of the night.

'It was a good effort anyway,' said Doug.

Joe and Georges joined us. Attempting to be objective, we discussed whether the bergschrund was a better shelter than the one Joe and Doug had carved out during the night. At least it was higher up. Outside, visibility was no better, and the decision was down.

We dumped some equipment and the ropes, our faces caked with ice, and tottered back across the Great Scree Terrace in the windy dawn. I was the last one to leave the bergschrund, but had such a strong feeling that others were behind me that I stopped and looked around.

A lot of snow had fallen during the night. We returned to the Camp 4 snow cave a lot tireder and weaker, and having been not much higher than when we had left.

13 SOFTLY TO THE UNTRODDEN SUMMIT

14–16 May 1979

Like monstrous red, dead worms, we lay in our sleeping bags, trying to rest in the snow cave – exhausted, set-faced and rarely speaking, our tongues like leather and our minds floating. Our strength was ebbing away. Outside the snow hissed and sifted. It took a long time to extricate my pen and diary, and hunch myself up to try to write some sense into the situation. It was my last entry:

> 3.00 p.m. 14 May. I'm not feeling very coherent – in fact I'm totally spaced out after our night wandering around in the blizzard. We could not have chosen a worse night for our 'lightning' attempt. The weather on this mountain is bloody awful and I want to come home. But I also want to climb Kangch. The problem is, how much energy one expends in a night like last night – we're much tireder now than after the tent strike storm. Every time we have less bounce, less resilience, less energy. But so near yet so far … Everyone is exhausted, grim, and monosyllabic. I know we are deteriorating, but cannot tell how much our judgment is becoming impaired. Georges says he's had enough and is going to Base Camp tomorrow. 'Fewer mouths to feed' is one of my less sympathetic reactions. We are too high for pity. We'll probably go down to the North Col and pick up some food, and then the day after

tomorrow go back up to the Croissant where we have found a bergschrund (it needs enlarging). Then we'll make the next (third) summit attempt on the 17th. If only it had been good weather last night. Now we'll probably be quite satisfied if we reach the Pinnacles on the West Ridge (the point where the '55 expedition reached the ridge from the other side). The top of Kangch is open to discussion. I seem to go O.K. at high altitude, but cough like everyone else when I get back ... It's quite a calm day now outside the cave after being cloudy and blustery. We always seem to hit this weather wrong.

I spent the afternoon tending the stove – I thought if I did a long cooking stint I could rest self-righteously for a while, and escape from the long tension-ridden hassles about whose turn it was next. I prepared tea, beef soup, shrimp creole, and then melted some water to fill a bottle. I felt irritated every time someone asked 'What time is it?' for my watch was in my pocket. To reach the stove I had to lean across Georges, which hurt my bad wrist.

Our conversations flared and dwindled and the little jokes amongst us had died. I wondered how determined the others were – it was impossible to assess objectively. Joe was focusing himself entirely on recovery, never offering to cook or brew-up, just lying down, cocooned, sleeping and resting, accepting all offerings. He said little, except that he wanted two days' rest. I hoped he was not weakening, because I trusted his judgment implicitly, and felt there could be something invincible about our combination.

Doug was at the back of the cave, nursing his frost-nipped fingers, saying more than anyone. He was tiring mentally with the constant re-covering of ground between camps, which he found boring and negative. Most of all, his family worries obsessed him, and he longed to be home with his wife and three children by his birthday on the 29th. I could not assess this worry, its stature was beyond me. He was on the verge of giving up the climb, and said he certainly would not have more than one more go, although he agreed it would be a pity to leave, when so near, for want of 'a ha'penny-worth of salt'. I admired the way he was trying to persuade Georges to stick with us – I hadn't the energy to argue.

All that appeared of Georges was a noise and a nose stretching from the circular hole that was the tightly-drawn hood of his sleeping bag. He seemed isolated and withdrawn, as if he were missing communication with men of his own language. The freeze-dried meals nauseated him, and he refused all food. He was going down, and mentioned parallels with routes in the Mont Blanc range that one completes without actually continuing to a summit. He was satisfied, and I respected the firmness of his decision. Perhaps he knew himself better than we did, and had the courage to act on that self-knowledge.

I did not want to leave the mountain until we had climbed it. The summit was still my obsession. Our two attempts at 26,000 feet in blizzards had given me confidence. I felt our weather problems were because we were still too early in the season, and that we should use the food we had left at the North Col in anticipation of the ten days' settled weather before the monsoon that Charles Evans' book had predicted would arrive.

The next day dawned so blue and calm that at first I resented it. The storm had spent its energies and the sky promised stability. Doug announced that he had received a revelation during the night, as clear as if it had been written. He knew he must have a go for the summit, and that he must not go down. Joe and I said nothing. Doug proposed forcefully that we left that morning. I bit back the comment 'What would happen if we all had to obey our own different dreams?' – for I knew he was right. The discovery of a third Gaz cylinder clinched the decision, for it meant that we did not have to return to the North Col to re-stock. I agreed to go, regretting having spent so much energy cooking the previous day.

Doug made a final plea to Georges: 'Do you feel like sharing our adventure?' he asked. 'Do you want to have another try with us?'

'I agree with the concept, using the weather, but I haven't the juice,' said Georges. He hurriedly packed his equipment and set off down, quickly disappearing beneath the convex curve of the North Ridge.

Some of our equipment was still icy from the previous attempt, so we started to prepare on the little ledge outside the snow-hole, in the sunshine. Spindrift soon drove us back inside. We packed slowly, at the same pace as our minds were adjusting to the idea of another upwards move. At 8.30 a.m. we were ready, and relieved to see the tiny dot of Georges reappear on the North Col. The sky remained free of clouds.

It was Joe's turn to break trail through the Castle, but he was still reluctant to leave. After kicking six steps at a time up to the foot of the fixed rope, he stopped and shouted that he was going too slowly and needed a day's rest. Doug went up to encourage him, and then took over the lead. I waited for them to gain more height, before starting, so that we would spread our weight over the dubious slope. I hoped that we weren't taking on too much after so little rest from the all-night effort.

When Doug reached the Castle he stuck his head over the top and shouted 'There's hardly any wind.'

Joe and I joined him, and it was true. Now, after all the hesitations, doubts, errors and setbacks, there was, suddenly, a discovery. The air was unbelievably calm – so calm we talked in half whispers, as if not wanting to disturb a sleeping storm. It was as if the earth had now decided to help us.

'Highest cairned footpath in the world, youth, twenty-five to twenty-six thousand feet,' said Doug. He was full of energy and built a string of cairns a hundred yards apart across the Great Snow and Scree Terrace. If stories about high-altitude brain damage were true, we might need them when we descended, as emphatic signposts of deliverance to hallucinating minds.

Occasional clouds towered up from below and blew across the terrace, but we sensed it was just an afternoon bluster, and the sky remained blue above us. We were soloing, for we had left our two ropes above, at the bergschrund the day before. Now we were unencumbered and free of the tangled procedures they imposed.

Doug was first to reach the cave at 2.30 p.m. and I, then Joe, arrived at half-hour intervals after him. We each chose a corner inside the bergschrund to work at with spade, saw and ice axe. There was no waste disposal problem, because the gap between ice and rock plunged deep into the mountain. I tried to order the progression of my sawing and slicing, but my oxygen-starved mind was distracted by instructions from imaginary Irishmen and Welshmen. After two hours we had cleared enough space for the three of us to curl down and rest; I managed to book the middle, and Joe was manoeuvred to below the entrance. Using karabiners as clothes pegs, we hung a sheet of aluminium foil from a rope to reduce the draught.

I crawled outside. The mountain was shaking its head clear of the sea of afternoon clouds. Particles of ice were dancing down the snow runnels of the summit triangle, glimmering in the fading light of the disappearing sun. We had nothing to fear from the weather. However, 2,000 feet of unknown snow above us could hold unpleasant surprises. I cut some blocks of snow and, as I dropped back inside, I slid them across the entrance of the hole – like the hatch of a submarine.

'Freeze-dried turkey, I'm afraid, Doug.' He overcame his vegetarianism, for there was no alternative on the menu.

We had arranged a code with Georges, that on his return to Pangpema he would listen to the evening weather forecast and light signal bonfires if the forecast was good; one if it was encouraging, two if it was very good. But once we were inside, we did not want to lose heat, get snow on our clothes or disturb the manhole. We took sleeping pills and lay inert, conserving heat, like tramps sheltering in a wintry city.

Doug suffered from his fingers during the night, and asked for painkillers. Warmly nestled between the other two, I slept well and woke feeling calm. We drank tea and fruit juice and ate a cupful of cereal, then packed our equipment – cameras and films, a small deadman, two ice screws, two rock pitons and 150 feet of rope. We would travel light, and not take emergency equipment, but trust to speed to take us to the summit and back that day. Through gaps between the blocks of the entrance, I could see blue sky. I was the first to worm my way out and announce a perfect day. 'If we can't do it today, we're dummies,' I yelled down excitedly into the muffled world of the hole, an escaped prisoner announcing sunshine to the inmates of a cold, dark dungeon.

I led off at 8.00 a.m. The sunshine touched the slope only thirty feet away, and we moved into it; climbing further to the right than the Croissant – along the line which Georges and I had followed fifty-four hours before. This time, however, the terrain where we had been lost in the vicious night storm seemed to flow past us as we climbed. I managed twenty paces at a time, and the vast area of rocks that barred access to the Ramp grew near surprisingly quickly.

Although we had studied the area through binoculars from Pangpema, I could not remember the topography in such detail as Joe and Doug. When I reached the hollow snow slab that had unnerved me two nights before, I was too far to the left, so Doug took over and led for a hundred feet up the right-hand of two gullies that split the rocks. Then Joe traversed a snow shelf to the left-hand one, which he climbed in two tricky rock pitches. 'My Rock Band,' he grinned.

Because his plastic ski-boots did not fit, Doug was wearing conventional leather and fur boots, and his feet were troubled by the cold. 'Can you do the leading?' he said. 'I'm expending a lot of energy with each step, trying to keep my toes warm.'

Above us, a triangle of snow narrowed into a neck between some rocks, and I led through this to the start of the Ramp.

'Will you stop a few minutes whilst I warm my feet up?' asked Doug.

I needed no persuading to take a rest. Twelve hundred feet above us, looking deceptively near, the Pinnacles on the West Ridge dominated the unbroken thirty-three degree sweep of the Ramp. The way was clear. Our confidence was increasing with the height. Our brains were not exploding, the blood in our legs was not clotting, our hearts and lungs were not palpitating – we just needed to take a few more rests than usual. We were in a good mood.

Joe took over the lead and climbed strongly and steadily through loose and slabby snow. I went to the back and as we moved together we kept the rope stretched between us, in case part of the slope sheered away beneath our feet. My thoughts fell into step behind the others, and I was too involved to worry about the time we were taking. 'At least these tracks will show us the way down, unless they become covered by spindrift. We won't be having another go – we shouldn't need to. We should definitely reach the Pinnacles now. Just keep concentrating. Will I faint if I close my eyes? When will the hallucinations start? I want to climb higher than the Pinnacles. I want to reach the top, to feel inside that I've climbed Kangch.'

Joe reached a curled hollow on a small snow arête, and we stopped there for fifteen minutes whilst Doug took off his boots to warm his feet. Joe unzipped his down suit and held the cold feet against his stomach.

'You're going well, Joe,' I said.

'I'm pleased to hear that,' he answered, 'I thought I was going really slow.'

I looked around to assess our position. We were about 500 feet below the brèche next to the Pinnacles on the West Ridge. We were now higher than all surrounding summits, except Yalung Kang, the West Summit of Kangchenjunga. The slow descent of the summit of 25,919-feet Kangbachen was a vague and distant measure to our progress. The rocks of the Croissant disappeared beneath the steep ground under our feet. The top of the North East Spur looped like a broad white caterpillar on to the North Ridge. The terraced séracs of the North West Face now supported our height, and the séracs of Twins Peak, so feared from below, looked tiny. The soft hills of Tibet were warm red and sunny. The architecture of the Himalayas, which had seemed chaotic and hostile down on the glaciers, now appeared simple and bold. The summit triangle of Kangchenjunga reigned over the vast silence of a world in order. We were now climbing its throne, and all our efforts of the past weeks lay below us, forgotten.

It was my turn. Whilst I had been following Joe, it had been easiest to relinquish my fears about the snow to his decisions. Now I worried about the hollow noise of the wind slab beneath my boots. At first I kicked my feet into it, but this used too much energy and took too much time. I spread my weight on to my feet and hands and scuttled across like a crab to safer snow, pulling the others, unsuspecting, in a sudden burst of activity. A long broken rib of black tourmaline ran down from the brèche, a line of security above an ocean of changing snow. The involvement of my hands and the integration of moves that the rock demanded, drew my mind away from abstract thoughts. I brushed snow from holds and eased my weight from foot to foot, and drew levitation from the joy of the movement. I was in the shadow, and sunlight streaming from the ridge drew me upwards, gasping with excitement and straining against the invisible reins of thin air.

Roofless pillars of fading and re-forming cloud and low dazzling sunlight greeted me. Light moving air touched my face and drew my eyes to the south. This was the point on the West Ridge which Joe Brown and George Band had reached twenty-four years before, and until now no one had been there since that expedition. Through a hole in the cloud below me, I could see the Great Shelf of the Southern Yalung Face, from where Band and Brown had climbed. It looked flat, white and near. If we had known that side of the mountain, we could have considered going down that way, but such knowledge had to be earned.

I was grateful to be alone for a few moments on the other side of the mountain. It was as if my insides, that had been hard, now thawed, and I felt released from the tension of the Ramp. The calm of the afternoon, the warm sun and the rough golden gneiss of the ridge seemed to tell me that I had been there before. The blue shapes were disturbingly familiar and were shimmering and richly humming, like a memory. I clutched the ridge and steadied myself, and then picked up some rocks, gripping them tightly in my hands.

The Ramp had taken six hours to climb. It was 3.30 p.m. and the sun was falling. I took in the rope as Joe climbed up to join me. The southern view appeared in his mirror sunglasses, and lit up a smile. He took in Doug's rope.

Brown and Band had followed the West Ridge. Just below the summit, Joe Brown had climbed a crack in a sheer wall, after turning up his oxygen supply to six litres a minute. However, the day after, Streather and Hardie had avoided this struggle by a traverse on the southern side. This we hoped to find. At 28,000-feet, the slightest unnecessary effort would take a heavy toll on our resources of strength.

'We've got a chance,' I said.

'What time d'you think we ought to turn back?' asked Joe.

'5.15,' I said. 'That'll give us an hour before sunset.'

Doug arrived. 'Hang on, hang on,' he said. 'Just wait ten minutes whilst I take some photos, and then I'll take over for a while.'

We did not know exactly where, or how far away the summit was. Doug, then Joe, then I climbed across little ribs and gullies in the South Face. We were filled with wonder and excitement. Below us, the Great Shelf appeared and disappeared through drifting clouds; Jannu, buttressed and strong soared up to the west, beside the descending sun. To the south east, in Sikkim, great anvil-shaped clouds boiled up.

Doug stopped twice to confirm that we wanted to continue. Then he climbed behind the skyline and reappeared suddenly on top of a large block of rock. 'The top's ten feet away,' he shouted.

I stuck up a thumb, Fantastic! – and followed the rope as quickly as my lungs would allow. It was 5.15 p.m., and there was not a breath of wind.

We straightened up and looked around, our smiles expanding from deep inside us. We stumbled about, taking photographs, shaking our heads, inarticulate, heady with success. 'I should be thinking great things,' I thought. But none came. For a few moments I could hardly speak. For long seconds I felt overwhelmed by the happiness of pure carefree and uninterpreted emptiness, separated from the knowledge that we had yet to descend.

'I've so forgotten myself as to shake hands,' said Doug.

'I'll wait till we get down,' replied Joe. 'No chorus in my head.'

We had been on summits before. We had dreamed of them, for their lure endures for ever and there is no escape, for summits match dreams. But this one we did not touch. The top was ten feet away.

It took three attempts for the delayed trigger-released mechanism on Doug's camera to work. Our frozen smiles came easily.

'The South Summit looks near.'

'That flat-topped mountain must be Kabru. Isn't Jannu a long way below us?'

'I can't believe it.'

'Don't touch the top, Doug, we want to get down again – mustn't upset whatever lives there.'

'I'm trying to climb round the summit – it's too corniced anyway.'

'It's a quarter to six.'

'Come on Doug, stop taking photographs, we're not actors, it's time to start off down.'

'You'll be glad of the copies, Joe.'

'Me? I'm only a shopkeeper!'

As we turned to leave, a large black alpine chough with ragged wings flew from nowhere, flitted above our heads and disappeared. 'One a birth, two a death.' This solitary witness seemed a good omen. We left the summit untrodden, hoping that it would always remain so.

The sky, rock and ice were steeped in red around us. We moved quickly, trying to lose as much height as possible before darkness. We had been allowed to sneak up but would we be allowed to sneak down? I felt strongly that we had to cheat someone, something, for the descent, for our lives. I thought 'Everything I've ever learnt must now help me down. If I relax my discipline slightly, I shall trip and fall.' Flickering storm clouds were dancing towards us from Everest and Makalu. The sunset then reappeared behind them. We raced against the storm and darkness. Now, thicker air combined with our urgency to draw us downwards, and our speed briefly reassured us. I waited at the brèche whilst Doug, then Joe, descended the tourmaline rib. The shadows of the Western Ridge and Summit reached down the summit triangle to the Croissant. The flanks of the North Ridge and the

Twins glowed in the setting sun. The upwards moves of the rock rib were still fresh in my mind, and I reversed them, clinically. We had reached the Ramp. A large black cloud was sweeping across the sky towards us, its skirt torn with orange-grey light.

We lost our earlier tracks in the darkness and spindrift. Doug tumbled over a step in the snow and fell ten feet before skidding to a stop. We put our head torch on, and I went first since, unlike Doug and Joe, I did not wear glasses or contact lenses. Lightning flashed and spread around us, too brief to be a guide. Little nicks in the snow showed me the way, and I kicked into the crust and slab that I had feared earlier. In the dark valley below, at Pangpema, a lone fire winked at us like a chink of light from fires within the earth. They had seen our head torches! They knew we had done it! They were with us! I felt strong.

At 9.00 p.m. we found the entrance to the bergschrund cave. Doug slid in to light the stove, and Joe and I chatted for a while, as excited as the safely landed passengers of a wounded aircraft.

14 DOWN WIND

16 May–2 June 1979

We sipped tea inside the shelter, sealed in for the night, oblivious to the hovering storm outside. Sleeping pills could not dispel the intense cold, and we twitched restlessly through the night. Occasionally Doug groaned, as spasms of pain shot through his body from his frost-damaged fingers. Joe cared for him, feeding him analgesics, whilst I pulled the drawcord of my cowled sleeping bag tight. The cold seeped in through all our protective layers. Our minds clung to the ballast of one thought: we had done it!

In the morning our movements were sluggish.

'5 – The Great Snow and Scree Terrace; 4 – The Castle; 3 – The Ridge, 2 – The Wall; 1 – The Glacier and Séracs,' Joe listed the obstacles we had to descend to Camp 2, to safety.

'Life's simple up here – not much to pack,' said Doug.

We stuffed our sleeping bags into our sacks, fumbled with boots and crampons and tottered out into the cold dawn. We were weak with dehydration and cold, and for many days had eaten little. It was tempting to allow gravity to guide our steps, for our bodies responded feebly to the signals of our minds. In the harsh world of high altitude, a climber must obey his inner conscious voice, for the simple instructions of that voice are his only defence: 'Kick into that slope to break through the windcrust, change the axe over to the other hand, clench those fingers and warm them up, wipe the snow from your glasses, don't trip on that rock with your crampon points, keep going, it's not far now.'

Descending unroped, we drifted apart, but re-grouped many

times to sit out the waves of dizziness that swept over us. It was the worst time.

Doug swung down the ropes that hung down the Castle and reached the snow-hole first. He shovelled out the buried entrance. The ceiling had collapsed to within three feet of the cave floor, but there was enough space for the three of us to lie down beside the stove and melt some snow. We rolled the drink around our mouths before swallowing it – it had the recuperative effect of a miracle-cure.

'Three to go,' said Joe.

The wind had paused only for our summit day. Now it had returned. Its freezing violence pushed our bodies, lashed us with our rucksack straps, and plucked at our woollen hats and down hoods. Coils were whipped from our hands, and the rope seemed imbued with a mad life of its own. Yet this wind came from a blue sky that stretched from us to Everest, and implied no threat. It was a relief to reach the North Col and step from the wind-blasted crust into the deep powder of the sheltered Sikkim side. Here we could talk without shouting.

We drank again, and rooted through the camp-site for food, gathering together our strength and concentration for the 3,000-foot descent of the wall. There was too much equipment to carry down, for heavy loads would make our movements even more cumbersome, and increase the risk. Yet we were loath to abandon it; so we tied it all up in bundles and threw it down the wall.

After two and a half hours on the North Col, we could not afford to rest any longer, for it was mid-afternoon, and there were still two obstacles to descend before nightfall. We set off on the tense repetitive ritual of clipping and unclipping our friction devices, sliding down, ropelength after ropelength.

The wall was melting. The high afternoon temperature heralded the approaching monsoon, but we had been living in freezing air for many days, and the change of temperature caught us by surprise. The wall was falling down around us and crisp snow had turned to watery ice. Great black rocks, loosened by the heat, keeled over and crashed down at the slightest touch of rope or crampon. Water ran freely down the rope and, whenever we could shelter beneath overhangs from falling rocks, we slaked our thirst. Doug, descending first, ripped an anchor from the soggy ice and snow, to be held by the rope above. We tiptoed down, our eyes bright and swivelling with watchful concentration.

Some of the equipment we had thrown down had burst from its containing sacks, and we could see a few tattered remnants hanging irretrievably on the wall. The rest was scattered over a wide area on the glacier. We had arranged for Ang Phurba and Nima Tenzing to come and help us. Two tiny dots had left the tent of Camp 2 when we had started down the wall. However, they were moving painfully slowly, and when we reached the bottom of the ropes they still had a long way to come.

Joe put out his hand. 'You know me, Pete, I've waited till we're down,' he said. He had studiously withheld the gesture since the summit. Even now it came too soon. We quickly discovered why the Sherpas were approaching so slowly.

Normally, half an hour sufficed for us to reach Camp 2. This time half an hour saw us floundering in waist-deep, wet snow, only a few hundred yards from the bottom of the wall. We took off our sacks and crawled, dragging them beside us to distribute the weight. Lightning flared in the west, and large snowflakes fell from the darkening sky, hiding the menace of the séracs that flanked us.

'Best Success-Juice, Sahib?' Nima Tenzing was carrying a kettleful. It was a happy encounter. He and Ang Phurba pressed on to retrieve the gear we had left piled at the foot of the wall. Night fell and we lost their tracks.

The pattern of crevasses had changed. Doug and I yelled abuse at each other. 'Watch that rope, Pete, you're supposed to be a professional guide.'

'Shut up, you middle-aged hippie.'

'You're just a middle-class achiever.'

'Working-class hero.'

Fun was not far away, for we could smell safety. The solitary tent of Camp 2 loomed up, blanketed with snow, and the two Sherpas arrived back simultaneously. They fed us hot sweet tea and a large meal, as we snuggled in the back of the tent, rapturously warm and relaxed, and comforted by the purr of the primus stoves. There was no longer any need for sullen manoeuvrings around the stove. Cooking had been an aversion we shared. But to be cooked for was heaven. We were cosseted like sick children, and had to take no more decisions. Ang Phurba was more chatty than we had known him before.

'Better to have walkie-talkies on mountains like Kangchenjunga,' he said. 'Big problem us knowing what you do.'

In his calm, offhand manner he delivered the latest Himalayan news, gleaned from the transistor radio at Base Camp. Gauri Sankar had been climbed by an American–Nepali expedition, and Ang Phu, one of the most talented of Sherpa mountaineers, and our companion on Everest in 1975, had been killed. We were too tired to absorb the meaning of the news, and it only brushed the surface of our minds before we fell asleep. Outside the tent, the snow stopped falling and a new moon rose for the third time since we had arrived below Kangchenjunga.

We left early, to beat the snow-softening sun, and tantalised by the prospect of a Base Camp breakfast. Doug forged on ahead, and Joe and I chatted inconsequentially. Occasionally we stumbled, learning to walk again on boulders and level ground. The rush of oxygen brought on by our loss of height anaesthetised the weariness of our wasted limbs.

I was apprehensive about Georges' reaction to our success, I need not have worried. He bounded down the moraine to us, carrying fruit juice, and hugged us exuberantly in fond Gallic embraces. He never mentioned any disappointment of his own, and we were never to suggest it. My apprehension was foolish, and my heart warmed to him with affection and respect.

He chattered excitedly: 'How was it? We could see you nearly all day, except when you went behind the ridge to the top. I took many photos through the zoom. The others were really involved, and kept on looking. It was really exciting. Did you see my fires? You missed them the first night? The weather forecast was bad, but I thought what the hell, and lit two, to encourage you! Hey, and there's some girls here. Dawa and her friend. They came up with wood and eggs. They're really cute, it's like they've come from another planet.'

Dawa was there, with her lovely smile, and I hardly dared look at her. A griffon vulture wheeled in as if in a salute above our heads. Mohan and little Nima Tamang greeted us, proudly grinning. Kami had baked a chocolate cake and we quickly drained the bottle of whisky. The meadow of Pangpema was greener than it had been on our previous return. It was as fragrant to our senses as it had been to Freshfield on his arrival there from the Jongsong La, eighty years before. It seemed so long ago since we had seen fresh grass growing in the spring.

After breakfast the following morning, I climbed the hillside behind Base Camp. The dawn light was still low and soft, and the ground was sprinkled with snow. I hoped that the uphill effort would clarify my mind. As I climbed, I disturbed a group of twenty bharal, or Himalayan blue sheep. For half an hour I followed them quickly up the hillside, staying within fifty feet of them, admiring their deft, goat-like movements over the steep ground. The sun arrived and lit their shapes, and they bounded away, to disappear behind a distant spur.

I had climbed nearly 2,000 feet and stopped to sit on a boulder before my mind was blunted with fatigue. My stomach was gurgling, unused to the rush of food since our return. I pondered the inevitable questions that accompany a mountaineering success. Had the mystical experience of reaching the West Ridge been no more than the result of a combination of lack of oxygen, food and water, and perhaps an excess of negative ions in the air? 'That hill, cragged and steep where truth stands.' Mountains do not reveal truth, I decided, but they encourage something to grow inside – something I was not yet able to explain fully. Our adventure had ended, and I tried to sense the birth of a new direction. Wordsworth loved mountains, but wandered most of his life beneath the 1,500-foot contour. He had not needed experience of such violent stimulants, such risk, to shock him into moods of awareness. It seemed silly that the summit was so important, and a near-miss so different.

Had I become over-reliant on these extremes, as Marie the painter had hinted in Paris so many months before?

I was feeling ecstatic, yet did not hope to sustain this ecstasy through my life. I wanted to measure my life through contrasts, and to do that I had to return to 'the other life'. On the mountain, too much inter-personal exploration would have weakened the united front we had tried to hold together for the climb. Antagonisms had never been allowed to become open, and had always been defused at an early stage. However, back in the other life at least people had other preoccupations; it was possible to relax and allow relationships to develop more subtly, without being under constant pressure. That was where the other side of the balance – the true interest of humanity – lay.

Pride, self-esteem and ambition are seldom analysed by the mountaineer, but we all admitted that we were looking forward to a few heady days on our return – to be patted on the back by our mates in the pub, with a pint in hand, no more. The disaster on K2 had left me lost for a year, but now, for a while, my ego was reasserted. I was happy to have emerged unscathed, with only a black toenail and a few numb finger ends. I had gained confidence and learnt much. I thought of future projects in a new light and was dazzled by the possibilities. My fear of high altitudes had been exorcised. Six weeks of effort and acclimatisation had helped us find a key to the summit. Our three forays above 26,000-feet had acclimatised us specifically for great heights.

The morning light had flattened across Kangchenjunga, and I returned to the camp. The night's snow had melted. We had a day to pack before twenty porters arrived from Ghunsa. Georges left, intending to visit the Slovak camp beneath Jannu the next day, to thank them for the rope. With him went Mohan, skipping like a spring lamb and humming with happiness, released from his long Base Camp vigil.

Doug had already filled several large kitbags, marked KHUMBU. He and Georges had permission to attempt three Nepali peaks in the autumn – Kussum Kangguru, Nuptse and Everest – and Ang Phurba was to take the equipment with him to his village near these mountains, before the monsoon stopped flights. Doug's thoughts had transferred quickly to his next project, as if Kang-chenjunga had already been absorbed into his vast Himalayan experience. After my dreamy morning walk I was shocked by his speed, and argued with him, demanding some tents for my autumn expedition to Gauri Sankar.

On the morning of 20 May we walked away from Base Camp. It seemed as if the spell of Kangchenjunga had held us from leaving the mountain for a lifetime. As we waded across the river plain at Lhonak, our thin bare legs made us look like storks. By early afternoon we had reached the edge of the forest above Ghunsa. Our first steps beneath green trees stirred in us a sense of total peace.

'I still can't believe we've climbed that mountain,' said Joe.

We lay down on the grass amid yellow flowers. The milky river below us filled the air with sound and a light wind brushed the treetops, faintly sighing. We closed our eyes, relishing the warm oxygen-enriched air and the scent of the flowers. After many weeks in a barren world of snow and rock, we were in a garden, beautiful and haunting as though pre-visited. We slept deeply until mid-afternoon, and woke refreshed. That sleep was Kangchen-junga's parting gift.

We had left a lot of muscle on the mountain, and our thighs and joints ached as we jolted down through the forest.

Below Ghunsa it was Peer Gynt country, with gloomy mist clinging down the steep, wooded hillsides, and the fire a cosy focal point. Oxygenated elation had worn off, and I was glad of the rest day the porters demanded. Doug was making fun of Joe's icono-clastic nature.

'He's going to love talking about this trip when we get back. I can just see him now in the Moon, hands outsplayed in an earnest blue-eyed expression: "Well there we were at 28,000 feet, just three ordinary johns like us. Anyone could have done it. It all felt really normal."'

When school finished for the afternoon the usual crowds gathered round, and some excitable youths started a water battle around us with old plastic syringes. One of them, escaping from his pursuer, tripped up over the fire and knocked our dinner flying. Kami lost his temper and laid into the culprit with his foot, which started a wild rumpus. It was the first time I had seen a Sherpa lose his temper and go out of control. Usually they erred the other way, and were too polite to say what they thought. Doug looked over his glasses at Kami and admonished his Buddhist conscience severely. The dinner was put on to simmer again, while we enjoyed salivating and watching Kami and little Nima co-ordinate the meal. Nima, our kitchen boy, was one of two young Tamang brothers whom Ang Phurba had adopted in his house in Khumjung. Joe was perceptive about hierarchies and often teased Ang Phurba that he, a member of the Sherpa super-race, exploited Nima like a slave – and Ang Phurba laughed, for he, also, had just read some short stories by James Lester about black slaves in America.

I asked Ang Phurba how he would spend the money he earned during the expedition and he replied immediately 'Yaks.' Material comfort, or moving to Kathmandu where he could exploit the tourist and expedition trade more effectively, didn't interest him. More important was the prestige that a large herd of yaks brings among the Sherpas. Yaks are a time-honoured investment, and it was good to know that the old ways have not yet completely changed. No men of Ang Phurba's village have yet sold their houses and permanently moved to Kathmandu, despite the fact that most of the households contain at least one member sometimes engaged in work connected with mountaineering and tourism, and some of the younger men spend as much as eight or nine months of the year away.

Now we were thinking a lot about returning to our friends and families, but the Sherpas didn't seem worried at all. Long absences are commonplace to them, and they know that news is not expected of them until they turn up unexpectedly to announce their own return. Only Kami talked about going home, because he had to help his father organise a festival in Namche Bazaar.

At the bridge at Dobhan, the magical halfway crossing of our return, children were splashing in the river. We stood aside on the narrow trail to let through hundreds of people coming towards us.

We watched, fascinated, as lissome young girls in saris of brilliant reds and blues, and large families of three – perhaps four – generations, all dressed in their finery, walked past. They were going to a wedding and stared back at us blankly. Hindus do not understand foreign tourists. No doubt, to them we were just paisa-wallahs, who had so much money they could travel – not to visit relatives or to attend a wedding, but just to see new things, without knowing anything and leaving their work and family to wander like cows.

When we reached the high ridge, we looked back towards the mountain, but it was hidden by the approaching monsoon. Georges paused to have his future told by a Brahmin soothsayer from a village among the terraced fields far below. Laughing with embarrassment, Mohan translated the questions and answers. Only one answer was correct: 'Did I get to the top of Kangchenjunga?' asked Georges.

The soothsayer said nothing, but raised his hand to the sky and pointed at the tip of the index finger.

We left the Sherpas and the porters a day behind, and pressed on to Hille and Dhankuta. During one long, thirty-mile day we walked continuously, without breaking step. It seemed as if we were 'lung-gom' mystics, following one of the legendary energy meridians of the Himalayas which Doug had described to us during the walk-in.

At Biratnagar airport we weighed ourselves out from the mountain with the concern of boxers after a fight. I had lost nearly two stone.

As we flew to Kathmandu over the gathering monsoon clouds. I pointed the zoom lens of my camera back at the massive bulk of Kangchenjunga, and across at the black prow of an impregnable-looking mountain – Gauri Sankar, 'The Eiger of the Himalayas'. I would return before the summer monsoon was over.

Four days later we were among the rolling green hills of Derbyshire.

15 SUMMER

2 June–18 September 1979

Climbers have a phrase for their need to compensate for all the weeks of deprivation – retraining in the pub. My return from Kangchenjunga coincided happily with the annual Mynydd Climbing Club 'Carnival Crawl'. This event comprised a circular tour of all the eighteen pubs in the district of New Mills, the evening before the town's Carnival Day. The only rules are that you down a drink in each. About twenty members assembled for the occasion, and Hilary and Steve, an American friend, arrived after an eighteen-hour drive from Switzerland, just in time for the start. The crawl begins by crossing the moors above the town, to take in the peripheral 'country' pubs. It was my first exercise since the walk-out from Kangchenjunga. The drinking was spiced with a few games of darts and pool, and I played whatever Blondie records were stocked in the various jukeboxes on the way. Debbie Harry had been our cult figure on Kangchenjunga. Hilary, not having been on such a crawl before, was discovering comers of New Mills she had never dreamed existed. We had not seen each other for a long time, and started as surface-shy strangers, warily circling. However, it did not take long to relax.

Steve started off by not knowing anybody; by halfway he knew all of our group, and by the time he reached the demanding rapid succession of six pubs in Market Street, he was striking up long and involved conversations about Vietnam and the world in general with strangers nobody knew.

'What beautiful people!' he kept on exclaiming, and went to the fish and chip shop to order mushy peas.

It took a couple of days to recover from the evening.

The Kangchenjunga team met one last time, at Joe's shop at Hope, in Derbyshire, to sort out our photographs together. No doubt, in the history of expeditions, ours had been relatively happy, but during that afternoon we achieved a fleeting unity that had been rare during the climb. Talking among ourselves, and with Georges' American wife, Norma, Joe and I realised how much Georges had been suffering from a lack of communication during the climb. Although Georges' English was excellent, he had missed many of the subtleties of humour, discussion and disagreement among the three English – subtleties on well-understood levels, evolved on many expeditions together. Also, I began to understand how Joe and I had often presented a strong complicity on many issues – an unspoken understanding that was a product of our long weeks together on Changabang, and which was invisible to us, but apparently impenetrable to those outside.

We realised that we had not got a usable expedition photograph of the four of us together. We walked past trees, trembling and bowing under the touch of a June breeze, out on to a green meadow. There, we played dandelion clocks whilst Norma clicked away with a couple of cameras. Two landmarks dominate the Hope Valley – a very tall factory chimney near Castleton, and the dark bulk of Mam Tor, the shivering mountain, a summit encircled by the ditchlines, visible from afar, of an old Bronze Age settlement. For photographic background, we chose Mam Tor.

The afterglow from Kangchenjunga was disturbed by the shadow of Gauri Sankar stretching out across the summer. In mid-September I would be going back to Nepal on the Gauri Sankar expedition. I had committed myself to this nearly two years before, whilst I was working for the British Mountaineering Council in Manchester. A letter had arrived announcing that the Nepali authorities were opening the mountain to expeditions. A day later Dennis Gray, the General Secretary of the B.M.C., came into the office and saw the note.

'I might get a trip together to have a go at that,' he said.

'Hard luck, I've already sent a telegram,' I said.

It had seemed wise to join forces. A few days after my return from Kangchenjunga I met Dennis Gray and the other two members, Tim Leach and John Barry, to discuss our expedition. It was still not clear which route the American–Nepali expedition had climbed that spring (the news which Ang Phurba had announced during our descent from Kangchenjunga). However, it did not matter, for there were many challenging new routes to do on the mountain. We reaffirmed our intention of going, and agreed to write off for more information and photographs.

Fortunately, the other three members of the expedition seemed prepared to do most of the work. Tim Leach, an architectural student, had the largest job, in organising the equipment. The wheels were in motion, and as yet I was only partially turning with them. I had difficulty in appearing enthusiastic about the whole new project, for Kangchenjunga had left me exhausted and sated at the same time. I was drained of the physical and mental energy for any more prolonged effort and worried that by going to Gauri Sankar I might be pushing things too far. It was the first time I had committed myself to a double-Himalayan-season year. Yet I felt I could not back out, and trusted that feeling. I had three months' grace for rejuvenation, and appreciated the summer with the intensity of a soldier home on leave. Not that I could afford to be idle. Earning some money again was an urgent priority, so I returned to Leysin where Hilary had got a temporary job at a local hospital. My foot and wrist were still weak and so she introduced me to a Canadian physiotherapist who had worked for the Canadian Olympic team, and whose eyes glittered when I told her my problems.

'It's ages since I've worked on an athlete,' she drooled.

After two weeks with her I pronounced myself cured.

Returning to Switzerland offered a change in socialising styles. The bar regulars at the Club Vagabond, where the International School of Mountaineering is based, are mainly Anglo-Saxons, or what the few English there call patronisingly 'colonials' – Australians, New Zealanders, South Africans, Canadians and Americans.

Before he was killed, my predecessor as Director of the climbing school, Dougal Haston, wrote a novel, *Calculated Risk*, based on Leysin, which abounds with descriptions of the Vagabond's 'beautiful people' – all in their mid-twenties and good-looking, cosmopolitan, promiscuous and boozy; without the cry of a child, the quaver of an old-age pensioner or the stern voice of work and responsibility within earshot. The real situation is not quite so playful. Nevertheless, the happy social atmosphere, the wide variety of people, good music and cheap beer make the bar a more relaxed haven than the rather austere Swiss bistros.

While I was away on Kangchenjunga I had been appointed President of the Association of British Mountain Guides, so on my return found myself in the thick of the impassioned on-going argument about the conditions of Britain becoming a full member of the International Union of Mountain Guides. This had been accepted in principle two years before, but the prejudice against us was strong.

'In my village a child touches and begins to understand snow as soon as he can walk, he has a feel for mountains from an early age – but all your guides were born in cities.'

'The English? But they *hire* guides. They can't become guides themselves!'

Beneath all these objections was an undercurrent of tribal and trading protectionism – a suspicion that, once the gates were opened, barbaric hordes of unkempt British, out for loot, would stream in from the north and steal all the clients.

I attended the summer meeting of the International Union which coincided with the annual fête of all the guides in the Swiss canton of Valais, at Bettemeralp, a village high above Brig in the Rhone Valley. On the Sunday morning the guides attended an open air mass, and the priest blessed the banners of all the different sections. The music of the long alpenhorns, the grey uniforms of the guides and the white robes of the priest, the sunlit mountains and meadow, all combined to give a special harmony. The ritual and commitment reminded me of Sherpas being blessed by a lama before going on an expedition.

British mountain guides in the Alps have a valuable friend in Madame Joan Pralong, the post-mistress at Arolla. She is, by origin, a Geordie who married a Swiss eighteen years ago. Although not an active climber herself, she has a passion for mountains and mountaineering, and believes in the dictum 'Mountains may divide peoples, but they unite mountaineers.' She saw immediately the problems of misunderstandings between the British and Alpine guides, and masterminded a number of casually relaxed meetings between British and Swiss mountaineers. It was at these get-togethers that I first met André Georges from La Sage, the great nephew of Joseph Georges, the famous alpine guide and companion of I.A. Richards and Dorothy Pilley, and Denis Bertholet from Verbier. Denis had been a member of the first expedition to attempt Gauri Sankar in 1954, and he lent me a number of invaluable photographs of the mountain.

In early July I suddenly became leader of our expedition. I received a letter from Dennis Gray, explaining that he was having to drop out owing to financial and work pressures. It was a sad loss, for Dennis had led an expedition to the mountain in 1964 that had nearly reached the summit, and for many years Gauri Sankar had been a personal ambition. Now with only two months to go, I had to find his replacement. Fortunately, a local Swiss guide of about my age from Leysin offered to come along. Guy Neithardt frequented the Club Vagabond, had climbed with Dougal Haston and worked for the climbing school. He spoke English with a northern accent – learnt, he said, 'in bars' – was tolerant of the idiosyncrasies of British mountaineers and appreciated their sense of humour.

Like most Swiss, Guy had a strong loyalty to his village and I had learnt much from him about what it meant to be a 'Leysenoud'. His joining us meant that, apart from a small expedition John Barry had been on to India, I was the only member of the team with any Himalayan experience. This, I hoped, would be a good thing, because we could approach the mountain without too many preconceptions, and it would be a refreshing change for me to climb with talented alpine technicians.

A letter from Al Read, the joint leader of the American–Nepali spring expedition to Gauri Sankar, enthused me further:

> I can imagine how you feel about our success on Gauri Sankar. We were very fortunate to have made it! It is an incredible mountain and certainly another route by you will be a very worthwhile endeavour.

Al went on to describe how his expedition had climbed the West Face direct to the North Summit. This meant that the South Summit and the West Ridge up to it, which had been the route his expedition had originally contemplated, was still unclimbed. Al listed its difficulties, but thought it 'might be worth a go'.

When I was fourteen, I had travelled to Manchester to hear my first mountaineering lecture entitled 'Gauri Sankar, the Eiger of the Himalayas'. Don Whillans had described how their 1964 expedition was plagued by Tibetan bandits and how the Japanese in 1959 had been robbed down to their underpants. The incomprehensibly vast size of the mountain and the complex topography of the area around it had fascinated me. They had toiled for weeks through dense leech-infested jungle and across the lower spurs of the mountain's ridges, before only just failing to climb the North Face.

Vivid recollections of that lecture began to link hands with a recurring memory – of being on the summit ridge of Kangchenjunga. Once a mountaineer has climbed so high, for the rest of his life he dreams of returning. I no longer needed to indulge, rest, sleep and forget. Mentally I was ready for the mountains again. But when I went rock climbing in one of the Leysin quarries, I was shocked at my weakness and consequent lack of confidence. Simple problems I had solved many times previously were scary. The first time I took two clients from the climbing school up the Tour d'Aï, one of the spectacular limestone towers high above Leysin, I made a mistake that was due to carelessness rather than weakness, however. I took my boots off at the foot of the South

West Face to change from shorts into breeches. One of my boots toppled forwards and bounced 600 feet down the scree, towards Leysin. It was a long hop to retrieve it, but it would have bounced even further if it had dropped in the Himalayas.

Each week I left Leysin with one or two clients to climb in different areas. I was surprised to find that north, east and south, within two or three hours' drive, it was possible to escape the crowds. Here there was a 'Hello' contour, below which the crowds of passers-by averted their eyes, but above which mountaineers and walkers were few, and greeted each other cheerfully. I was filling out my mental picture of the characters of different mountains, their ridges, faces and hidden cwms. We never covered the same ground twice. I was fitting together the jigsaw of their valleys and passes, delighting in 'connected knowledge'. The maps of Switzerland became alive, and I was building a structure of memories and associations that helped me feel more and more at home.

On a succession of climbs, your senses are continually sharpened by moving quickly between two different worlds; the tension and isolation of the climb, and the gregarious comfort of safety, friends and beer in the huts and valleys. The emotions of departure and return, which are separated by long stretches of time on an expedition, are – in the Alps – compressed within a single day.

Towards the end of my alpine summer the peace of mind I had regained in the mountains was shattered by a phone call from my mother in England, to tell me that an exploratory operation on my father had discovered a tumour on his pancreas.

Travellers always take it for granted that nothing will change at home while they are away. Home is the reassuring place where there is always love and shelter, without obligations – always trusted to be stable, so terrifying when it changes. First came shock and despair, and then I clung to disbelief. My father was only fifty-nine. There was a tradition of longevity in the family, all my grandparents had lived well into their eighties, and one Gran was still a lively eighty-seven. Surely the disease would not be fatal?

A few days later Hilary and I drove to my parents' home in Bramhall on the Cheshire Plain. We visited my father in hospital, and he seemed cheerful, smiling bravely and trusting of the medical care he was receiving. Afterwards with my mother, we subjected the utterances of physicians and surgeons to intense analysis, at times basing future hopes and fears on nuances of expression. I had always distrusted miracles, but now my father's life was hedged, I believed in them.

One of the most advanced cancer treatment clinics in the world, the Christie, is in Manchester, and my father was to start fortnightly treatment there with the latest American drugs. He came home from hospital. He was restless. I spoke to him as he paced around the room, as if being relentlessly stalked.

'I suppose you know from your climbing what it's like to be gripped?' he said.

I tried to comfort him, but realised I didn't know, and had never learnt. He never expressed darker thoughts than that. I could only try to imagine how his illness erected a barrier between him and the healthy world.

The organisation for Gauri Sankar now became a remote point of reference for me; an emptiness. My responsibilities divided me, and I went mechanically through the motions of preparation. If I went to Gauri Sankar, I determined to climb the mountain quickly and safely, and come back home again as soon as possible.

Hilary had to fly back to her job in Leysin, in time for the start of the autumn term at the American School. During a few afternoons I went rock-climbing on gritstone crags of the Peak District – Baldstones, Gardoms and Stanage. Gritstone is an old comforter. The crowds are one of its charms, for they soon break up as you recognise the groups amongst them. Easy friendships are renewed and made – local friends, and friends from Leeds, Sheffield, Birmingham and London. And gritstone routes never change – the same holds and moves and problems are always there, to be quickly remembered. On the gritstone edges there are no tempests to transform the landscape, no slopes to avalanche nor splintering rocks to fall. My university climbing club at Nottingham used to hold competitions around pub tables – someone started to read the description of one of Stanage's 400, fifty-foot-high routes, and you scored if you were the first to rec-ognise it. Some climbers got the right answer after the first three or four words.

The American climber Yvon Chouinard once remarked that 'all climbers are a product of their first few climbs' and it is true that a person who learns his climbing on small but difficult crags may take up big-wall climbing or become an alpinist, or an expedition mountaineer, but his first love will always be free climbing on the crags. I have never lost a yearning to revisit gritstone. Stretching, reaching, pulling, pushing, it is the best exercise in the world.

I climbed into the evenings. The wind softly combed the moors, and clouds paced slowly, alternating light and colour from bright sunlight to black storm – until the sun finally set in a red blaze. By late August, the green in the valleys below was tired, but the rock was always warm.

I returned to Switzerland for the first week of September, to fin-ish writing some articles and to drive a carload of equipment and food for Guy to take to Kathmandu – he was flying a few days lat-er than the other three of us, since he was finishing his final course to qualify as a guide. At the Swiss frontier, the customs demand-ed that I empty the car and carry all the stuff across to a building to be weighed. I lost my temper and told the customs men they could keep it and eat it. They reassured me that the money would be repaid if the food and gear left the country, but they would not let me in until I had paid about £100 duty. When I arrived in Leysin, I parked the car outside my apartment and received a parking ticket. I moved the car, and someone inside another cha-let threatened to call the police because I was using their parking space. The next day I was summoned to the police station for a different reason.

Whilst I had been away, a false and misleading article about my climbing school had appeared in a Valais newspaper, saying I was certifying Swiss and foreign guides. I had, in fact, just run an alp-ine training course for one British guide; it would have been illegal for me to certify anyone. However, two Swiss climbing school directors had canvassed a wide protest, and triggered off the remorseless wheels of bureaucratic inquiry. The legitimacy of my work permit and my right to run a climbing school was being questioned. I felt threatened and mildly paranoid after these brushes with authority, which jarred with the settled peace I had found in Leysin – where the friends I had made and my love for the surrounding mountains justified my feeling at home.

The political problems of my work in Switzerland were not helped by dogs back in England snapping at the tail of the Gauri Sankar expedition. Ken Wilson, former editor of *Mountain Magazine* and self-appointed guardian of the moral conscience of British mountaineering and its politics, has a fiery, outspoken manner which regularly entertains all those not under attack. As a member of the Mount Everest Foundation Management Committee, which was supporting the trip, he had criticised our expedition as being too weak for the difficulties of the mountain. When John Barry, the director of Plas-y-Brenin Mountain Centre, joined the team, Ken had spoken as a member of Plas-y-Brenin Management Committee, and said that the centre could not afford John's absence in the Himalayas. When Dennis Gray dropped out, and I invited Guy Neithardt, Ken reverted to his Everest Foundation role and criticised its subsidy of foreigners.

Now John Barry was coming under heavy pressure from a number of sides not to go with us and fifteen days before we were due to leave, he sent me a telegram resigning from the expedition. It took a day on the telephone to England, canvassing support and playing on John's conscience until he decided to stick to his guns and come with us.

During the final week before our departure, I received a prize at a reception in London for my book *The Shining Mountain*. My father was determined not to miss the occasion, despite his illness, and with my mother he arrived on the train from Manchester. I felt sadly proud of him. Hilary also flew over for the day. Our relationship had had many tense moments during the summer, for I had had little time to share with her, little time for the pauses, the constant exchanges of thought that are essential if love is to progress. It was hard, being apart, for we changed apart. I was condemning her to another long and worrying wait, constantly checking the post box. She had strength, and said goodbye without crying or smiling.

During the final days I lived two lives. My house in New Mills was filled with chaos as John and Tim arrived with food and equipment to be packed. The telephone rang incessantly. Then I would leave the Gauri Sankar expedition in New Mills and visit my mother and father, talk with them, and relax. I reassured myself that they were both loved members of a community, surrounded by the warmth of friends and I knew that my brother would be travelling regularly from his home in London to see them.

When Tim, John and I flew from Heathrow, I trusted faintly that things would sort themselves out and that the expedition would make sense once we saw the mountain and arrived at its foot. But I was filled with aching guilt. I knew that I had not been honest with myself, that I had avoided three questions: 'Will he die?' 'Will he die whilst I am away?' 'Should I go?'

I was haunted by the sight of my parents at their front door, waving goodbye, after I had spent the afternoon in the garden, picking apples.

PART 3

GAURI SANKAR

16   FIRST TIME

19 September–8 October 1979

Gauri Sankar has deep religious significance for both Hindus and Buddhists. Sankar (the North Summit) is the Hindu god Shiva, married to the goddess Gauri (the South Summit). The Buddhist Rolwaling Sherpas living south of the mountain can only see the South Summit and call it Jomo Tseringma. Throughout Buddhist Lamaism, to as far away as Sikkim, Tseringma is considered the most holy mountain of the Sherpas.

In 1971 a small group of Norwegians visited the village of Beding in the Rolwaling Valley below the mountain and suggested to the inhabitants that they should petition the authorities in Kathmandu for their peak to be protected from 'conquests' and big expeditions. The gesture, they felt, of leaving the upper few feet of a mountain such as Kangchenjunga untrodden, was not enough. *Mountain Magazine* printed a photograph of a Rolwaling villager signing the petition with his thumbprint. Better than any words this picture spoke that the protest was heartfelt, a significant gesture from such a normally tolerant people.

The Norwegians were among the founders of an increasingly influential school of thought in the seventies called *Friluftsliv*, which called for a less competitive attitude to climbing and a more environmentally sensitive approach to the mountains. They drew parallels between what had happened in the Alps over the last hundred and thirty years and what they could already see happening in parts of Nepal over thirty years.

The inviolate summits of Gauri Sankar were an ideal symbol

of the principles and beliefs that the Norwegians wished to protect, because they were not only important in the religion of the surrounding peoples, they were also a world-famous challenge to mountaineers. Gauri and Sankar were two of the last unclimbed 7,000-metre summits in the Himalayas. The spectacular profile of the mountain was prominent from the plains south of the Himalayan chain, and all photographs of it showed razor-sharp ridges, loose vertical rock faces and avalanche-swept gullies. Hence, the mountain was well-known among the world's mountaineers as a 'last unsolved problem' of high-altitude climbing, and more than forty expeditions had applied for permission to climb it. A number of illegal attempts had been made, including one of Japanese origin, which was stopped by Nepali authorities in the autumn of 1973.

There was a great deal of hesitation before Gauri Sankar was once more added to the 'permitted' list along with forty-seven other peaks, late in 1977. For some time it had been uncertain whether the mountain was in Nepal. The 1960 Nepal-Tibet/China agreement generally followed the watershed. However, a map published in 1968 and researched by Erwin Schneider showed the North Summit firmly in Tibet. It was only early in 1979 that the Chinese conceded this northerly loop of high-altitude territory including both summits to Nepal, whilst retaining all the northern and eastern ridges and approaches firmly in Tibet.

The government of Nepal stipulated that at least two Nepalis be members of the expedition to make the first ascent, one of whom was to be included in the summit team.

Al Read's position in Kathmandu, as President of Mountain Travel Nepal, enabled him to submit the first successful application under the new regulations. Owing to Gauri Sankar's significance, he composed the expedition of five Nepali Sherpas and five Americans. As co-leader, he selected my Everest companion, Pertemba Sherpa. In the spring of 1979, the expedition duly climbed the mountain, and an American and a Sherpa left the higher, Northern, Summit decisively trodden.

Once the North Summit had been climbed, the joint conditions ceased to apply. However, we wanted to include a Sherpa in our autumn attempt, so that the spirit of the co-operative effort with the Nepalis could be maintained. A Sherpa could help us to climb the mountain in a manner as sensitive and respectful as possible to its religious significance. Our lightweight expedition, we hoped, would leave little mark on the mountain.

At the Sherpa Co-operative building in Kathmandu, Tim, John and I met members of a Norwegian expedition, among whom was Nils Faarland, one of the original exponents of *Friluftsliv*. He was tall, a brown crew-cut accentuating a slightly mournful expression, carefully dressed in breeches, a fawn anorak and silk scarf, which contrasted with our tee-shirts and denim shorts.

Nils asked that we did not tread the top of the South Summit, beyond the point at which we could reasonably say we had climbed the mountain. The Norwegians were going to attempt another holy mountain – Numbur. He confessed they had only discovered its special status when the preparations for the expedition were long under way. Didn't he feel guilty about attempting a sacred summit, we asked?

Nils spoke English slowly and carefully, as if dictating a statement: 'Yes, I do, I wish I had known. But it gives us a good incentive to carry out this expedition in the best possible way, in an alternative style. We have only natural fibre equipment – we have no nylon clothing, and very little steel or aluminium. We want to get away from the techno-culture, and use equipment that is the least harmful to nature and at the same time durable and suitable to our purpose. The gap between man and nature is getting wider, and we want a reunion.'

'Haven't you got nylon ropes?'

'Yes; we had hoped to bring silk ropes, but it was not possible. Maybe for the future.'

'Have you had much stuff specially made?'

'No, we have bought it all from the shops at retail prices. In this way we can stay out of "the circus". It is wrong for manufacturers to keep on generating new models, just to keep their sales competitive, and to use expeditions to the Himalayas to promote their products.'

'Must have cost you a bloody fortune!'

'Fortunately, our leader, Arne Naess, works in shipping and he deals in money. So we can forget about money and concentrate on more important things. I have talked with many lamas about what we should do. They say that, to respect a special sacred mountain, we should not attack the mountain aggressively, but we should get the monasteries near the mountain to bless the expedition and should bring ourselves closer to and live with the mountain with good thoughts and an open mind, and think of our tents as transportable *gompas*.'

'How do they decide which mountains are sacred, then?'

'That's a big question. Better to say that once all nature – rivers, seas, forests – was sacred, but now only some mountains remain unpolluted. Usually, special sacred mountains are covered with permanent ice and snow, and have double peaks. But more important than shape, you recognise a sacred mountain by the feelings it evokes – strength, fear or joy.'

'Nobody in Kathmandu's mentioned to us yet that Gauri Sankar's sacred.'

'It depends very much how strongly man is attached to his original culture. Many Hindus and Sherpas, in particular those who have had long contact with people from our culture through technical assistance projects and tourist feeding, have been so affected by Western attitudes — which are cut off from nature – that they deny the existence of sacred mountains altogether.'

Nils continued to talk, emphatically. When we parted we caught a taxi.

'I prefer to walk, and not to use such machines,' said Nils.

'I wonder if he walked here from Norway,' said John, after we had left.

'I bet he goes to the dentist when he's got a toothache,' I said. 'Imagine what he'd be like if he got his teeth into one of the real, no-holds-barred personality sellers like Messner.'

'Bloody nutcase.'

'It must be costing them a bloody fortune, staying in single rooms at the Yak and Yeti.'

This was an opulent Hilton-style hotel; we were staying at the Himalayan View. It was the cheapest place we could find with a shower.

'What a name for a hotel,' said John, 'you can see bugger-all.'

We continued to discuss Nils, sniggering uncomfortably.

'He's wide open to piss-take.'

But he had impressed us.

'You've got to hand it to the lad,' said John. 'He certainly believes what he says.'

Our capacity for spiritual self-questioning was exhausted, we wanted to discuss the more prosaic details of our expedition, and also we were in need of light entertainment.

'Council of War,' recommended John.

'Decisioning to be made over a beer,' I announced.

'Right oh, Skip.'

We went to the rooftop restaurant of the Yellow Pagoda and, sipping Nepali beer, watched the sun set over the city.

'These Nepali birds are gorgeous,' commented John. 'Only five feet high, but four foot six inches of that is SMILE.'

We stepped into the metal cage of the hotel's lift. I was apprehensive. 'I bet this is a relic from the Rana Dynasty, a real museum piece,' I said. I went on to explain the theoretical action to take if a wire snaps and a lift were to lose control. 'You jump up and down, and so you have a fifty-fifty chance of being in the air when it hits the ground – if you're in the air, you only fall a few feet.'

Intrigued by this suggestion, John started leaping up and down as the lift started moving. It madly bounced about like a puppet on the string.

'Stop it John, you only do that in an emergency!'

One hundred feet above the ground the lift shuddered to a stop. Our heads were level with one of the floors, peeping through the grille.

'Now look what you've done – you've probably jerked the wire off the cog,' I said.

We started shouting for help. Scores of pairs of legs appeared from nowhere, jabbering excitedly in Nepali and milling around in front of our noses. Fear in my eyes, I bridged across the walls of the cage, holding myself in the air and anticipating the downwards plummet. Tim seemed puzzled by my nervousness; John was amused by it and laughed from the back of his throat. An hour later a mechanic arrived, solved the mysteries of the jamming and winched us to safety. We descended by the stairs.

'You were really scared,' said Tim.

I felt ashamed, as if I had failed the test of some adolescent ritual.

We spent our first few days in Kathmandu on a seemingly endless administration circuit – British Embassy, visas, trekking permits, insurance, sorting equipment and communications. Our preparations were simplified by delegation. Our Sherpa sirdar and fifth member of the team was Pemba Lama, who had been on the 1975 Everest trip, as well as seven other Himalayan expeditions. Pemba's help made shopping simple; we planned with him what food and equipment we needed, gave him some money and he disappeared into the bazaar and bought it.

As our foreman, Pemba was entrusted with the recruiting of the Sherpa cook and cook boy to accompany us. However, I did not like the cook – he seemed shifty. I trusted my first impressions, for you can often read a Sherpa's character on his face. So I complained.

'This is the most important job of the expedition, Pemba.'

It transpired that Pemba's choice had been pressured, either by family or outside interests. All was resolved the next day, when Pemba introduced us to our new cook, Dawa.

'What happened to the last one, Pemba?'

'Unfortunately he is sick and cannot come,' was the grinning reply.

Pemba was tall and well built, and the expanse of his wide smile was broken by a gold-capped tooth, a relic from a motorbike accident. Sherpas generally climb for money, and not enjoyment, but Mike Cheney had told us that Pemba was different, that he was an ambitious mountaineer, and Mike asked us if we would, if possible, allow Pemba to accompany us to the summit. Pemba was keen to live up to this reputation, and he was fully aware that the prestige of being an accomplished mountaineer was helping him in his career. Pemba's family was a lowland clan of Sherpas, from Solu, contrasting with the Khumbu Sherpas, such as Ang Phurba and Nima Tenzing, who lived at higher altitudes. Like many of the modern generation of Sherpas, Pemba retained his house in his home valley, but rented rooms in the heart of Kathmandu – where he invited us to meet his wife and eat lunch. We threaded our way through a warren of alleys and courtyards, into a corridor and up some twisting stairs. In a corner were a Buddhist altar and butter lamps, and a sophisticated cassette player with many tapes of Western music.

Like all Sherpas, Pemba was an astute, intuitive and cheerful fleecer of expedition finance. 'Joining money', 'deposits', 'advances'; he tried to bargain for them all. Nils had touched our consciences, and we paid for holy rice, coloured prayer flags and a contribution towards a Kathmandu monastery, where a lama had blessed our expedition. Then our liaison officer, a Hindu sub-inspector in the Kathmandu police force, joined in the demands for equipment and advances. His name was Sankar Pradan – the same as the mountain we were going to attempt. Throughout these negotiations, Mike Cheney played an inter-mediary role. His position was invidious – as an employee of the Sherpa Co-operative, he had to represent the interests of the Sherpas and see that we employed as many of them as possible; and as an Englishman, Mike had to be careful he did not abuse our trust in him. Small and thin, with a large hooked nose and baggy military shorts, Mike was an ex-Darjeeling tea planter. He had never worked in England. He was one of that perennial group of Englishmen and women who are born with a hunger and nostalgia that can only be set at rest in the East. Nepal had absorbed him completely.

Sankar was demanding that we give him a tent.

'Don't pull rank on me, mate,' said John.

'John used to be a captain,' I explained.

Sankar told us that though his pay as a lieutenant in the Kathmandu police force was only twenty-one rupees a day – about seventy pence – which was the same as we would be paying our porters during the approach march, he was not begging. It was in the regulations. We sought the arbitration of the Ministry of Tourism at our expedition briefing. Yes, we would have to buy a tent for him.

At the Ministry of Tourism, we met Arne Naess, 'the man who deals in money', the leader of the Norwegian Numbur expedition. A dynamic, wiry, forty-two-year-old, based in London, Arne seemed more in tune with the British climbing mentality – and humour – than Nils. His expedition's 2,900 kilos of baggage was stuck in Delhi, and he was about to fly back to sort it out.

Our expedition was poised to depart. We booked a bus, and piled all our equipment into it, followed by fresh vegetables, our Sherpa team, and numerous other, unidentifiable hangers-on, out for the free ride to Barahbise where we planned to recruit our porters. We appeared to have more cassettes (forty-two) than any item of climbing equipment, including pitons and karabiners.

'What a sight!' exclaimed John. 'All held together with string, straps, hope and a lot of luck.'

Sankar arrived, garlanded with flowers of farewell by his wife and relations. The friends of Dawa, the cook, had been plying him with chang all morning, and he was drunk and panicking about lost equipment. This endeared him to John, who recognised the symptoms.

'Only time Sherpa can't help himself is when drunk,' said Pemba.

All was ready.

However, Guy had not arrived. He had been due the previous day, 24 September, but had not arrived then or on this morning's flight from Delhi. Tim offered to go to Barahbise and back with Pemba, and we asked the Sherpas to hold the porters there until our arrival.

'If I'd been Tim's age I'd have gone,' said John as the bus

clattered away, 'but I don't fancy twelve hours on a bus in this heat.' He turned to Sankar. 'Belay the last pipe, Lieutenant.'

Embarrassed by the change of plan after all the formalities of farewell, Sankar reluctantly went home.

Kathmandu days drifted into each other ... time, precious time. John was appointed chief Guy-collector, and armed with a brief description of Guy and primed with some basic French, taxied to the airport twice a day in the hope that Guy would arrive.

I had first met John during a mountain guide's test on Ben Nevis in February 1977. Unlike other soldiers I had met in the mountains, he had determinedly and quickly proved that he was a keen and able amateur climber. Nevertheless, he was proud of his soldiering background. We had long arguments about the moral value of physical courage. I placed courage on the lowest rung of virtues. I argued that, anyway, the grey areas of daily city life offered more challenges to courage than the glamorous and black and white problems of mountains or the battlefield, and that courage was often just a euphemism for a mixture of anger, pride, stubbornness and physical strength. Although John had since left the Royal Marines to become director of Plas-y-Brenin, he had not lost his strong commitment to idealistic warrior virtues – the readiness to sacrifice oneself in the service of a common cause, disciplined submissions to rank order of the group, a veto on showing fear in the face of danger and, above all, a very strong bond of friendship and trust between men.

John loved to make me cringe with his military parlance. 'Right oh Skip,' he said, whenever I suggested anything, and when I asked his opinion, he replied: 'What do I think? I don't', or 'Awaiting orders, Skip. I need to be briefed.'

Much to his disappointment, the only orders he received from me were a few mutters. It was a humorous change from the taboo on recognising leadership roles on Kangchenjunga. We discussed endlessly the nuances of difference between 'friendship' and 'solidarity'. John – and Tim – were horrified at my stories of the high-altitude manoeuvring on Kangchenjunga and other expeditions. I realised I had been on too many expeditions with the same people. This time I had to start from the beginning.

As we wandered around, John and I chattered so much that Tim could not get a word in. I had been the same age when I went to the Hindu Kush in 1972, and remembered vividly my shock on seeing an Asian slum for the first time. I projected these memories of my earlier self on to him. But Tim kept his own counsel. He seemed not to be quite on our humour wavelength – or was he above it?

Guy was not on the morning flight of 27 September. We all went to the airport in the afternoon. The Norwegians were there. All their baggage had arrived, and the customs were charging them £4,000 duty.

'Why didn't you under-value it all?' I asked.

They were sadly resigned to this 'contribution to the king'. Again, Guy did not arrive. In our conversations he was assuming the role of Arch-demon, and the others were beginning to question my choice of the team. We decided on an emergency plan to replace a minimum of the ropes and tents he was bringing by a quick shopping spree, and to leave without him the following mid-day.

'Flexibility – one of the principles of war,' said John.

As we left the airport, just as we were getting into a taxi to return to the town, we saw Gauri Sankar for the first time. One hundred and thirty miles away, the mountain glowed in the setting sun. 'Absolutely fantastic!' Our spirits soared.

I understood why Gauri Sankar was thought for so long to be the highest mountain in the world, and why it was confused with Everest, which is out of sight, far to the east. For us, its magnificence was a summons. For me, that sight of Gauri Sankar was a turning point, it gave me confidence.

The following morning John telephoned from the airport. 'Guy's arrived. Yes, we've flannelled all the gear through, and for nothing. Bullshit beats brains every time. He's had a trip of Homeric proportions that makes our journey out seem a journey to paradise. Fire in Bombay airport, delays, diversions, the whole works. I've never been so pleased to see someone I've never met in my whole life – this is the seventh time I've been here. He's shattered – but he speaks perfect English!'

The team was together at last. Guy's feet had hardly touched the ground before he was loaded into the Sherpa Co-operative Land Rover, along with Tim, John, Pemba, Sankar and myself. We drove north for three hours, along the road built from Kathmandu to the Tibetan frontier after the signing, in April 1960, of the Treaty of Peace and Friendship between Nepal and China.

Barahbise was the last outpost of beer country. We savoured the last drops. Two middle-aged American ladies were there, heavy with make-up and jewellery, sipping Coca-Cola.

'Quite a change, Barahbise from New York,' quipped John cheerfully. They had been to the Tibetan border in a taxi, and were only staying in Nepal a few days before leaving for Bali.

The forty porters were about to desert, having waited for four days, but we only smiled when their foreman, the Nykay, came to complain. All past problems were irrelevant. The Nykay was a Sherpa from the Rolwaling Valley, and wore a flat Chinese cap with the sinister air of a Far Eastern guerrilla. Our tents were pitched, the porters' loads were ready, and Dawa brought us a mug of tea. He had the cook tent organised like a well-drilled section – John's ultimate accolade.

In the morning Pemba tied pieces of purple string around our necks. 'From lama, Kathmandu. His blessing – don't move it,' he explained. Pemba's father was a lama at Junbesi monastery and this gave authority to his instructions. The day was hot and steep, and our sweat ran freely with the dye, staining our tee-shirts an alarming blood colour.

'I've never been with such a funny-shaped team of lads,' I said.

'The big, the tall, the short and the thin,' said John.

'John's big and short, Guy's tall and thin, Tim's thin and short, and I'm normal,' I said.

We argued as we walked.

John and Guy tried to carry porters' loads. As they staggered about, eyes bulging and necks juddering with the strain, a small boy aged about nine walked past beneath a similarly enormous load.

'That can't be doing him any good.'

'I think we should ask the Nykay to pay him off.'

Then four barefoot girls walked past carrying loads. 'I don't know how they do it,' said John. 'Seeing them would make women's libbers shut-up.'

Guy was still dazed by his journey. 'I have no idea where I am,' he said. 'It's as if I've parachuted somewhere in Asia.' We showed him our position on the map.

Pemba and Sankar started a 'these porters and the people of this place are robbers' scare, and we split up among our caravan to keep a watchful eye on our belongings.

'Don't group together, lads, if they throw a grenade it'll get all of us,' barked John.

We climbed 3,000 feet from rice terraces, through jungle to rhododendrons and, on 30 September, we crested a ridge, in a cool mist, and celebrated with glasses of rakshi or millet spirit, renowned for its taste of vinegar and dirty dish cloth.

I had been slotted into the role of the expedition's hypochondriac. Much to John's merriment, I fastidiously avoided all wriggling fauna, and the contamination of dubious food and water. In reply, I teased him for his absentmindedness and clumsiness. He had burnt a hole in a tent with a candle, lost his watch, and forgotten to bring from North Wales the soups, binoculars, two tents and detailed notes about the walk-in.

'No wonder you married someone who could look after you!' I taunted. Conversations with John had the cut, thrust and parry of a sword fight as we tried to penetrate the armour of each other's pretences. One morning the barracking went too far and became physical.

I was toiling up a steep muddy slope behind John. He came across a snake, sleeping on the path, and quickly flicked it at me with his umbrella. The snake wrapped around my leg and I danced about until I had shaken it clear. I was furious, and hit John as hard as I could with my ski stick.

'There're poisonous pit vipers around here.'

'It wasn't poisonous, I could tell from the shape of its mouth,' said Guy.

'My last trip was nearly ruined by thoughtlessness like that,' I yelled. 'How, how … ' I searched my mind for the epithet … 'how childish, how unprofessional.'

The others all snorted with laughter as I stalked off, sulking for over an hour. I did not play the fussy hypochondriac again, and John did not throw any more snakes.

For nearly a whole day we walked along a rough road linking the Kathmandu-Tibet road in the west with the village of Jiri in the east. The road had been begun two years previously, as a Swiss Aid project, and was now half-finished. We marvelled at thousands and thousands of terraces – vivid monsoon greens etched over the foothills below, their ripples accentuated by pale, slanting sunlight. Rice was evidently thriving up to the 6,000-foot contour – rice that had been planted in June, before the monsoon. Tall, chalet-like houses dotted the slopes, contrasting sharply with the poverty we had witnessed during the previous days. But what was the cost of this apparent prosperity?

These hill sides below – and above us, implied the most serious and dramatic erosion problem in the world. Nepal's midlands were once covered with forests, but in the last twenty-five years over half of the land has been cleared to provide fuel and more space to grow food for the rapidly-expanding population. Meanwhile, in the Bay of Bengal, an island of 40,000 square miles of silt is building up from the washed-away soil of Nepal. In his deeply-concerned book, *Stones of Silence*, George Schaller noted with despair:

> The biggest export of Nepal is soil, some sixty billion tons being carried by its rivers down into India each year. Nepal will soon be derelict unless it protects its watersheds. Once man has destroyed what the mountains have offered, the forest and the soil, there is no reprieve.

We left the road at the town of Charikot. Youths in Western clothes tried to persuade us to photograph the local dwarf, and their sniggering contrasted with the fresh-faced cheekiness of the children who left their sloping football pitch to practise their English, surrounding us at the evening's camp-site at Dolokha: 'How are you?' 'Where are you going?' 'We are very hungry, you give us rupees.' I had camped there in 1975, on my way to Everest, and recalled the same conversations then.

Village life was nearing the climax of the ten-day most important national festival of Nepal – called, among many other names, the Durja Puja, or Dassera. High wooden swings with fibre ropes were the main holiday attraction. We had passed many of them beside the trail, and watched young men, including our porters, propelled skywards energetically and competitively, hooting with laughter. Whenever there was an opportunity, we also had a go. The swings were so popular that watching children rarely had a chance to ride!

That evening the sounds of drums and trumpets, cymbals and gongs, floated up the hillside. Sankar explained the Hindu significance of the festival, which celebrates the rescue of the goddess Durga from the clutches of the demon buffalo Mahisasoor. On the tenth day, after nine days of praying, the God Rama kills the demon, and good triumphs over evil.

'I, also, have seen the Hindu movies in Kathmandu,' laughed Pemba.

I could not decide if his laughter was from embarrassment at our interest; from thinking that Westerners and his generation of Sherpas should know better than to listen to such old-fashioned superstitions; or from a belief that religion doesn't necessarily have to be serious.

'I hear that Gauri Sankar is a very sacred mountain,' I mentioned to Sankar.

He looked up sharply. 'Who told you that?' he asked.

The following morning we stepped along the cobbled street of Dolokha, sheltering beneath our brightly coloured golfing umbrellas.

'This is the day of the year all people wash and change their clothes,' said Sankar. He himself was, as usual, dressed immaculately with neatly combed and parted hair. Through doorways we saw women scrubbing and sweeping. Naked children splashed around and kneaded their clothes in water troughs. Everyone had flower petals and coloured rice on their foreheads. The unhurried, purposeful activity carried on as we walked throughout the village. We could have been invisible. We followed Sankar to the temple. Mist swept around us, and the buildings dripped with moisture. We passed brightly painted lion statues.

'This temple is for the god of courage – he rides on the lions,' said Sankar.

'We'll need some of that,' said John.

An old man with long hair was sitting cross-legged on a small enclosed platform of smooth, red, hardened mud, tinkling two hand-bells, chanting prayers and staring, in a trance. Sankar offered to daub me with rice, but instinctively I refused. Guy wrote in his diary:

> We leave this place. Everything is strange. Pete confides in us with an open smile, but he is not at peace. Nobody feels at ease. Have yesterday evening's stories of divinities affected us? At Pete's request, everyone inspects whether the good-luck string is still around his neck. Ouf! So one doesn't risk the anger of the gods. One can take that how one wants, but still the atmosphere was odd. I can't stop thinking that a group of people, all in a religious trance, emit something. Are these vibes communicated to us, or is it just our imaginations that are working too hard?

We dropped swiftly 3,000 knee-jarring feet to the Bhote Kosi – 'the river that rises in Tibet', which we were to follow. Within the space of two hours the change in country was startling. We watched with delight a troop of monkeys swinging through the trees. John wished his little boy, Bounce, could see them. We camped that night at Pikhutu in a meadow of sand and grass beside the river.

A couple came in at dusk from a village an hour away up the hillside, carrying a baby with terrible boiling-water burns over his head, neck and chest, at least thirty per cent of his body. We asked when this happened – four days ago. His pulse was fast, breathing difficult and he had taken no food or drink since the accident. He was only just alive. John ripped some cloth from his sleeping bag liner to cover the child, who opened his eyes briefly in the torchlight. We gave them 200 rupees and urged them to go to the hospital – though we knew it was three days' walk away. How could they have done nothing for four days? They thought everything would be closed for the festival. We stared incredulous at their helplessness and seeming lack of concern. Why had none of the locals moved a finger to help? Perhaps they did not realise the seriousness of the child's condition. Or did they just accept death more readily than we? The parents walked off into the night with their son. None of us had the heart to talk. We turned aside, each to his own tent and his own thoughts.

Our eyes, blinkered by days of mist, opened wide next morning to see Gauri Sankar astride the gap at the end of the valley. A cloud smoked between its two summits. The West Ridge, our chosen route, curved across the view, a giant 'S' shape, tipped forward on its side. The mountain's features, picked out by the morning sunlight, slotted into our minds that were already imprinted by our well-thumbed file of photographs. 'A climber's nightmare'; 'Deeply notched, as if bitten by a disgruntled giant' ... I fought off other people's descriptions of the mountain. Perhaps I would only be able to understand its form from this distance. A climber approaches each mountain virtually blind, and has to learn to see as if for the first time. I looked at it through half-closed eyes, struggling to perceive the symbolical power of the double peaks. A pair of horns. The goddess's lap where the eye comes naturally to rest like the lap of horned Isis, upon which the pharaohs sat; the nurturing, fertile, birth-giving mountain.

The sight of the mountain triggered off an hour's animated discussion about the route, and about the importance of acclimatisation.

Pemba was very talkative compared to Ang Phurba. He chipped in with 'tourist herding' stories, including some lewd gossip about the unashamed washing habits of French girls on treks. His descriptions, delivered with ribald humour, were so vivid that we peered around every river bend, expecting to see nubile Parisiennes, merrily splashing each other.

Although he was less excitable and his English was slower, Guy did not usually miss as much of the conversation as Georges had done on Kangchenjunga. But when the three 'Anglais' drifted into the inevitably recurring topic of rock climbs in Britain we did not think how much it excluded and irritated Guy.

The rock climbing discussions also highlighted our different attitudes. Since I had begun going on a succession of expeditions, I felt I was losing touch with hard technical climbing and its animated move-by-move analysis. I was aghast when Tim said that routes like Right Wall and Citadel were 'all right'. We used to tease him about his descriptive vocabulary and the way he divided the quality of life into five tiers: 'superb', 'magic', 'all right', 'rubbish' and 'crap'. The eight years' difference between us was a climbing generation, and to me Tim seemed very youthful in his black and white judgments. But there is a lot of no-nonsense Yorkshireman about him and no one could do the routes he has done, like soloing the North Faces of the Grand Charmoz, Les Droites and the Super Couloir, without having his own strengths and self-confidence. At least he was coming out of his early silence and learning to answer and abuse us back, and he asked me many questions about 'going professional'. To him life seemed clear – one climb after another.

It was a relief to have turned north, away from the crowded foothills and the busy east-west route. On 4 October John looked up from the map. 'Base Camp's fifteen miles and 10,000 feet up. We're in for some scrambling, lads!'

During the previous few days an occasional leech had fastened on to us. The porters called them *tsuga* – a menacing noise, like an emphatic sucker. Now, the jungle was swarming with the enemy. Hundreds of them dropped from trees, latched on to us as we brushed against leaves, and caught hold of our shoes. Unseen, and unfelt, they humped about, through lace-holes, underneath socks, up our legs and, on reaching the warmest, juiciest places, injected anaesthetic, anti-coagulant, and sucked our blood. Every few minutes we stopped to fight them off. The leech-deterrent textbooks recommend flames or salt. Usually we just gargled screams and flicked them off. The record number repulsed on one foot was over twenty. The leeches recognised John as a fitting opponent in their plunder, and his feet became sieves of pouring blood. At lunchtime we fled to a boulder in the river, from where we could see them approaching without cover, waving their terminal suckers like scanning radar. Guy never had a chance to smoke his Gauloises. As soon as he lit one it was passed between us, a burning brand of leech destruction.

As we gained height, we climbed out of enemy territory. Hanging on the opposite wall of the Bhote Kosi, we saw the opening of the Rolwaling Valley – 'The furrow made by a plough' – and the home of the Rongsherwa Khambas, who celebrated the sanctity of Tseringma. The first expeditions to attempt Gauri Sankar – the Franco-Swiss under Raymond Lambert in 1954, the British led by Alf Gregory in 1955, and the Japanese in 1959 – all approached the mountain up this valley. Beyond it, to the east, there was a route over a high pass, the 18,745-foot Teshi Lapcha, to the Sherpa town of Namche Bazaar in the Khumbu district below Everest. A traditional route of trade and migration between Rolwaling and Khumbu, in recent years it has also been frequently crossed by groups of tourist trekkers.

We were climbing into a hanging valley, even more abrupt than the Rolwaling. Beside the steep track, the Bhote Kosi plunged over falls and rumbled through boulder-choked pools. Then the ground flattened. We had reached Lamobagar – the open ground.

The first building was the whitewashed police station, next to another one marked 'Customs'. The authorities were waiting for us. Our trekking permits were seriously inspected and a message that we had arrived was sent in Morse to Kathmandu.

We had a tea party, Nepali style, on two lines of chairs facing each other. One of the policemen stood aside, loosely holding a rifle.

'Lee Enfield 303,' identified John, snapping a film into his camera as if he were loading one. 'They were used in the First World War – really accurate.'

We asked the questions. No, few Westerners had ever been there – apart from the Americans in the spring. Yes, there was still some trade with Tibet, mainly for salt, butter and tea; but now the old traditions of deals between individuals were not legally allowed, and the people did not like negotiating with impersonal Chinese officials in the Tibetan villages. No, 8,000 feet was too low for yaks, but the villagers kept goats, cows and shaggy cow-yak mongrels. Yes, of course there were many Sherpas, Rongsherwa Khambas, and Tibetan refugees in Lamobagar, over half of the 250 population – they lived on the other side of the river plain half a mile away around a *gompa*. It looked a hard life. With a mixture of awe and superiority, like officers of the American cavalry surveying an Indian reservation, the police pointed at distant clusters of grey stone houses.

We camped in no man's land, halfway between the Hindus and the Buddhists. Tim and Guy paid off the Barahbise porters and Pemba and Nykay started to negotiate for a new set from the village. At dusk John and I set off to investigate the sound of a drum. We walked into a small courtyard in front of the *gompa*.

About twenty girls in Tibetan dress were jumping around, laughing and giggling. If it had started as a dance, it had deteriorated into a rough game of 'hop and knockdown'. A bearded lama in his mid-thirties jumped up and guided us into the front room of the *gompa*, where about fifteen men were dishing out chang from an enormous tub. I think they had been drinking it all day, and they were determined to induce us into the same grinning state.

'Great, an ale up,' said John. 'Enough to convert me to Buddhism.'

We squatted down and they plied us with chang, continually filling our bowls up as we sipped – such is the custom. By the time Guy and Tim arrived we were mellowed and lightly happy. Next to me was an old Tibetan, wrinkled and dishevelled, with long pigtails and a few whiskers. He was most intrigued by my hairy legs. On my other side was a sad youth with big teeth. He spoke a few words of English and seemed to want to travel with us, to escape, for us to open a door for him to the outside world. But he did not even have the will to join us as a porter. He turned out to be the village loafer, and an 'asker' – demanding an umbrella, film and cigarettes.

Guy conversed with a mother and daughter, much to everyone's hilarity – the girl wanted to work as a porter, the mother wanted to know if Guy was married. Guy referred the first request to Pemba, and politely declined any implications of the second.

We dashed back to the tents in the darkness and pouring rain.

Despite the chang-induced euphoria, the meeting with the youth had depressed me. He reflected the decline the community had undergone since the days of flourishing trade with Tibet – a decline that was a raw contrast to the hope and enterprise I had seen in the Tibetan community at Hille in the spring.

There was no sign of the festivities when we returned to the *gompa* the following morning. Another of Lamobagar's four lamas, a smiling little man, opened the inner doors with a large and ancient spring lock, and showed us inside. On top of an altar there were three Buddhas, lit by a huge enclosed candle in a container. Pemba prostrated himself before the Buddhas and took some of the wick from the candle. Round the painted walls were pigeon-holes full of sacred books. The lama touched our heads with one in blessing before unwrapping its protective cloth. The book was about six inches thick and loose-leaved, composed of long narrow strips of paper each about two feet long and six inches wide, printed in Tibetan letter-press. Pemba could not read Tibetan, but his Sherpa vernacular was sufficient to communicate our questions. The lama did not know how old the books were, but they were there in his grandfather's time. Each little strip of fabric hanging from a book indicated that someone had read it all.

The lama recommended prudence in what we were going to do and told us our Base Camp must be a holy place, and we must not kill animals there.

The village houses were scattered among huge boulders. Another lama approached us, shuffling. I wondered whether they were prayers he was muttering, or memories of better times that no one cared to listen to. He was of a different sect, and on Pemba's advice we gave him money too. Prayer flags, invoking the benevolence of mountain gods, were strewn above a bridge, and they fluttered with the swing of the wires as we crossed. Although they were faded and torn, the flags still worked, said the Sherpas. The sunshine crept down the vegetated hillside, and on to an old man who was trembling with the early-morning cold. He was supporting himself with a hand on the shoulder of a small boy. They both watched silently as we turned up the Rongshar Gorge. Many Sherpas believe that it was through this gorge that their ancestors migrated into Nepal 500 years ago, after travelling 1,250 miles from the Khams Region of Eastern Tibet. According to legend, they were shown their new home in a dream. We were now walking towards the land of their spiritual and ethnic origin.

The river was older than the mountains. It maintained its channel from the highest plateau in the world as the Himalayas began to rise during the Eocene, fifty million years ago. The great canyon of the Rongshar still deepens as the mountains continue to lift.

The footpath was rarely frequented, but still survived the encroaching vegetation, threading muddily and improbably across the precipices above the shadowed gorge. We met a father and son, returning with the trade of Chinese plastic shoes and Tibetan butter from the north. I envied the comradeship that must have grown between them, over the days and nights of their lonely journey.

The path dipped steeply to the river. To the north east, another gorge joined the Rongshar – the Kang Chu. This torrent drained a finger of land that projected into Tibet – land that was only ceded to Nepal in the 1961 bargaining. In this valley lies the village of Lapche (La-Rimpoche, or 'precious hill'), the hallowed birthplace of Jetsun Mila Repa, a wandering lama poet and saint who lived in the eleventh century, and taught by parables and song. Mila Repa was one of the Bodhisatvas, a reincarnation of Buddha, who lived under rocks and in caves, where the faithful still go to see his footprints. It is said that he converted Tseringma, the goddess of long life, to Buddhism.

The early Everest expeditions approached the mountain from the north, as for them Nepal was the forbidden land. Both the 1921 and the 1924 Everest expeditions descended the Rongshar Gorge as far as the Nepal frontier. A.F.R. Wollaston, who relinquished his New Guinea ambitions for the lure of Himalayan exploration, reported in 1921 that the locals were 'a friendly and good-tempered people, much given to religion.' Thirty years later, in 1951, another Everest reconnaissance party had descended the gorge. Eric Shipton and Mike Ward had become lost whilst exploring the northern side of the watershed. Then one of their Sherpas said he could recognise the northerly opening of the Rongshar as he used the route when smuggling horses. 'At once the geography of the region became clear,' said Shipton. The group had no permission to be in Tibet, so they travelled at night to avoid detection. Even so, they were chased back into Nepal by Tibetans waving swords.

According to Erwin Schneider's 1968 map, the border followed one of the Rongshar's tributaries, the Chumalagu Chu. We stopped at the confluence, before climbing up this valley towards Gauri Sankar. It was here, at 7,200 feet, that Dennis Gray's 1964 expedition was abandoned by its porters. They were forced to establish their Base Camp in this area – probably the lowest base camp ever used by a Himalayan expedition.

The peaceful atmosphere of the Rongshar had changed since Wollaston's remarks. Dennis and his team had to call in twelve Nepali soldiers to protect the camp, when it was threatened by armed Tibetan bandits – robbers who, according to Don Whillans, 'are not too particular about their choice of victims. National reputations, climbing clubs, permits, mean nothing to those lads; if you've got something, they want it!' We asked the Nykay about robbers, and he reassured us that the last problems had been five years before – the Nepali and the Chinese authorities now had a firm grip on the area. He related gleefully the story of the 1959 attack on the other side of the mountain, and pranced about miming Japanese climbers and Sherpas brandishing ice axes and fencing with Tibetans on horseback.

Gray and Whillans and their small team had spent weeks

hacking through the undergrowth of the Chumalagu Chu, and ferrying loads towards the mountain. 'It was,' said Dennis, 'some of the thickest jungle in the world.' They had marked their route with red paint – some of which was still visible. As we started to duck through the jungle, these marks – combined with the traces of the American–Nepali expedition of the spring and the knowledge of our porters, most of whom had carried for that expedition – helped our routefinding.

'We're on the Tibetan side of the river,' I said to Sankar, pointing at the map.

'If we're in Tibet, then we must go back,' he said.

'I think the map's wrong, then.'

The porters shouted, hooted and whistled as they ducked through the steep mossy undergrowth on the sides of the colossal gorge. Everyone slipped and slid on the greasy black soil of the bamboo thickets. Bamboo is a solid plant, and a secure, if sharp, handhold. There were some dangerous sections across the muddy cliffs above the river, and we split up and anchored ourselves, helping the porters across as they struggled with their thirty-kilo loads. They thanked us with their eyes. The roaring of the water was so loud that we could not speak without yelling.

At dusk we crowded beneath the kitchen tarpaulin suspended from tree branches to wait for the meal, preferring the communal warmth of the fire to the isolation of our tents.

'I wonder why Ang Rinzi prefers to bring the food around to us?'

'I don't think it's a religious reason – it's because they don't want us to see what variety of food they are cooking, or how many people we're feeding.'

'What's sizzling in that pressure cooker? I bet we don't get any.'

'Must be feeding about fourteen people.'

'We'll make a stand for some of *their* chili and potatoes tonight.'

The Sherpas cushioned us. On my earlier expeditions we did all the cooking and hiring and firing of porters. Now we were overseers with only a vague idea of what was going on. Were we, as Jung says, living in bottles of Western air, protected from our travels by objectivity, causality and all the other intellectual apparatus?

Pemba and Sankar had tried to use the porters' flints but without success – they were townies like us.

Upon popular request, John told us some of his favourite stories: 'The Two Hundred Thousand Ton Punch', 'The Man Who Went Out to Buy a Packet of Cigarettes and Ended Up in Peru', 'The Punch-up at the Courmayeur Disco', and 'The Day I Ambushed a Pig'.

'You've got to be an Irishman to talk like that,' I said. 'You won't be able to bullshit your way up this route you know.'

'It doesn't matter if these stories aren't true,' said Guy, 'it is the way they ought to have been.'

'All my stories are true,' said John. 'Just wait till I get back from this trip; I'll have a few more!' John had the gift of making everyone laugh.

Stars scattered across the sky, above a frail mesh of interlacing twigs, and we peered at their white brightness through the interstices of the plaiting. John expressed simple wonder at them all. Guy countered with a reel of boggling facts and figures, describing the size of the universe.

'That's the cosmology lesson over for tonight,' he said.

'Isn't John naively endearing?' I said patronisingly. Endearing – we finished the evening trying to explain the word to Guy.

Throughout the approach march we had been worried that the regular afternoon rainfall would be falling as thick snow on the upper reaches of the route. At dawn we peered worriedly at the snow-covered distant mountainside above the jungle, hoping that the covering was light, and would melt with the early-morning sun. We knew that the barefooted porters would never carry through snow, and were rushing them up towards Base Camp before any long period of bad weather with major storms blew in. We crossed the river with some logs and ropes, and continued the ascent through gnarled and stunted trees swathed in bearded lichens which made the air glow green. The sphagnum covered the stones with a thick carpet and we had to kick in up to our ankles. But the jungle cleared with altitude and we were able to make camp on a small open bluff amid the rhododendrons. When the clouds opened a brief window the view 5,000 feet down into the Rongshar Gorge was breathtaking.

'*Un pays de loups!*' said Guy.

We no longer had to stoop through rhododendron shrubbery. We walked upon open slopes of stunted juniper. Then steep alpine meadows reared up into broken rocks. The mist came down; and the route zigzagged intricately up cliffs. We were now at home, in mountain country. We talked mountaineering politics. Only our deepening breathing told us we were reaching 16,000 feet.

'Base Camp,' announced Pemba, after consulting one of the Lamobagar porters. We hurried about, muffled figures erecting tents. The falling snow surrounded us with a white, moving void. There was nothing to see.

17 KNIGHT MOVES

9–26 October 1979

I awoke with a start, to a thunderous booming. Pemba was knocking and shaking the snow from my tent and daylight filtered through the fabric as he cleared it.

'The Americans also had bad weather,' he said in a matter-of-fact tone. 'The first few times a mountain has bad weather. Then, after many people have come, the god goes away and the weather is good.'

Outside, the cold light of dawn revealed mist and whiteness. The snow continued to fall. Pemba and the other Sherpas began to prepare a ritual, with a meaning sunk deep in time.

The pattern of the earliest rituals has always been for man to make an offering and, by giving, to achieve a receptive and aware state so as to become part of the interplay between himself, the earth and sky and the gods. When Buddhism came to Tibet in the seventh century, it was absorbed by the resident animist faith of many gods – the B'on religion. Today, the Sherpa religion, Tibetan Lamaism, is a thick mixture of the old animism, manifesting itself in mysticism, magic and demonolatry, overlaid by a layer of Buddhism.

The earliest myth of the founding of Tibetan civilisation concerns the building of the Samyang monastery, the first Buddhist monastery in Tibet. The people, so the tale goes, worked very hard every day building the monastery, but every night evil demons came and destroyed their work. The people were making no progress at all, so they asked the Guru Rimpoche what to do.

The Guru said it was no wonder they were having trouble, they weren't making the gods happy, only spending a lot of money. When he taught them how to perform an offering ritual, the gods helped the people build the monastery, not only keeping away the demons, but also carrying the heavy things and working while the people slept, so that the building was completed in a very short time.

The ceremony held at Base Camp on 10 October, before we set foot on Gauri Sankar, followed the basic pattern of a Tibetan Buddhist ritual. Pemba had arranged a garland of little flags on a string between two poles and an altar was built just outside the kitchen shelter, consisting of a flat rock surrounded by four vertical stones with a little butter on the point of each. We all sheltered from the snow beneath umbrellas while herbs were thrown on a plate of burning embers on the altar. Behind it was a large tray of offerings – some rice, chocolate, nuts, a cup of milk, bits of cheese, a can of beer and a bottle of whisky. The Sherpas sang, throwing rice and spirit in the air as further gestures of invitation and welcome. This wining and dining of the gods was to make them more friendly and obliging towards us and to encourage them to struggle against the malevolent demons of the area.

Two porters stayed to keep us supplied with wood. One of them, Pemba Sherpa, was a lama and read the appropriate Tibetan text for Tseringma, throwing fistfuls of rice in the fire. He also soaked a juniper sprig in milk and whisky and sprayed the fire with it. The ceremony lasted half an hour. Towards the end he put a small piece of juniper in the palms of our hands with a taste of whisky which we had to lick up. Finally Sankar, our liaison officer, raised the Nepali flag and led an unsure rendering of the Nepali national anthem. Although a Hindu, he had taken part without self-consciousness.

At the end of the ceremony the mist suddenly tore apart and a ray of sunlight poured through a rent in the cloud. The rainbow colours of the prayer flags shimmered in the diagonal light and the rocky promontory of our Base Camp became a glowing island amid boiling cloud.

The weather was so bad, and the fleeting clearing was so dramatic, it did seem that we'd angered, and then momentarily pleased someone. Emotionally, the ceremony was valuable.

The shafts of sunshine encouraged us upwards. After the ceremony was over we started up the snout of the glacier, to make a reconnaissance. According to Schneider's map and Al Read's information, Gauri Sankar was separated from Base Camp by a ridge a thousand feet above us. The Americans had approached their West Face route by abseiling down the other side from a notch on the ridge.

However, we had taken a risk, climbing 8,800 feet out of the Rongshar Gorge in three days to Base Camp at 16,000 feet; our rapid approach had been against all the acclimatisation rules of 'taking it easy'. The spring expedition had taken six days over the same distance. Now we determined to spend at least a week acclimatising to our new height. Guy was enjoying every minute now he was 'above the height of Mont Blanc'. He was still fresh from his three-week Swiss guide's course and was climbing steadily, whilst a residue of acclimatisation had stayed with me from Kangchenjunga. When John had come to the Himalayas before, a headache had grounded him at Base Camp for a week, but this time he found the rapid gain of altitude over the previous days tiring but not debilitating.

Like seasickness, altitude sickness strikes unpredictably. As we kicked up the heavy snow Tim was moving slowly, vomiting occasionally, but forcing himself upward.

We crossed a slender snow bridge above a deep crevasse. The mist had closed in soon after we left Base Camp, as if Tseringma's appeasement had only brought a brief respite. Now wind blew thick snow around us. The snow levelled out and dark rocks signposted a ridge. The altimeter read 17,000 feet. Wind met our faces from a new direction and static electricity buzzed in the air. But where was the notch? Rocks and snow tilted in confusing directions and opinions differed. We huddled around the map and compass, and split up to make fifty-foot forays in the gathering blizzard. No clues made sense.

'We'll have to wait for a good day,' I said.

'Acclimatisation training,' said John.

We plunged back down our line of tracks to Base Camp. The light was fading, and the tents were smothered in snow. The 150 multi-coloured prayer flags stretched high above the ice-hewn rock and rubble were unaffected, a garland of greeting and protection. The prospect of the climb's uncertainty was awesome and we still had not even seen the mountain.

We were in the middle of a two-day storm. If the snow had fallen earlier, we would have been stranded far below Base Camp. That night snow piled deep around us, only to melt in the warm morning air. John was flooded out of his tent. 'I'm going to call this Camp Niagara,' he announced.

I spent the day reading and sleeping. Beneath the shelter of the kitchen tarpaulin, John and Guy sorted fifteen days' food to take on to the mountain. Occasionally someone hurried between tents, well wrapped and bundled up beneath the falling snow. The sounds of the kitchen, and conversations, were muffled by the heavy stillness. The two wood porters huddled all day around the fire. Tim did not emerge.

At sunset the clouds began to move in horizontal plumes in the valley below us. Jagged peaks were etched beneath the Milky Way, beyond the black depths of the Rongshar Gorge. Our tents were poised on the edge of space. We stooped into them and lit candles to keep out the cold night.

'Pete, get your camera.' Dawn brought a rush of excitement. We could not see the mountain we had come to climb, but we could see its angular shape. The two summits of Gauri Sankar announced themselves as two vast, beaming shadows silhouetted across miles of morning air.

'God, it looks enormous.'

'And steep.'

After a quick breakfast, we shouldered our first loads, to establish our cache at the foot of the West Ridge. The sun came rolling on to us as we broke trail up the glacier, breathing purpose into our cold climbs. Its dazzling splendour bared the bones of the mountain and provided the missing clues to our earlier confusion.

The ridge was bifurcated, and we had to cross a spur and traverse to the Notch. At last the mountain stood before us, and we lay down our sacks and straightened up to look at it. Pemba scrambled confidently to the summit of a nearby rock pinnacle for a better view.

When the first Sherpa peoples passed Gauri Sankar on their journey from Eastern Tibet, the mountain was already alive in their imaginations. When they saw the mountain itself the old worship of the goddess that they brought with them was intensified.

> The goddess Tseringma has a beautiful, well-shaped white body, the colour of which is reflected in the mountain snow. She has a light, slender face like the moon, three eyes and shining snakelike blue-black hair that has been arranged high and is decorated by a ruby. In her ears hang beautiful earrings and in her hands she holds a vase of eternal youth and a prayer wheel, with jewellery that is more precious than those belonging to any human being or god. She wears a thin, soft, tight clothing, and sits straight on a lion of very light colour.[1]

In the present century, even the taciturn Lancastrian Don Whillans, was to remark as he turned back from Gauri Sankar: 'It's a lady.'

We were daring to touch the untouchable. The mountain did not fall back in cloud-swept terraces of vast distance like Kangchenjunga, it curved across our vision with a massive strong presence, stretching around to touch us at one of the tips of its horseshoe. Huge tentacles of ice dripped down from the summit snow caps.

We pointed and swept knowledgeably with our hands, asserting ourselves despite our insignificance, as climbers are wont to do when nervous.

1. From an original Tibetan Lamaist text, quoted by F.W. Funke in his *Religiöses Leben der Sherpa*, 1969.

'This must be the point which Clough and Whillans reached in '64, before they went back down and traversed round at a lower level to the North West Ridge.'

'The American route looks steep.'

'Yes, but we're seeing it head on, and they said it was a lot more feasible than our ridge.'

'A bloody good effort.'

'Lambert walked around the mountain in '54, and said it was impossible everywhere above 18,000 feet.'

'Well, that's been proved wrong since.'

'Our ridge looks a long way round.'

'It's knife-edged for a long way.'

We cut the West Ridge up into pieces, for our hearts were not yet big enough to absorb its scale. The expansive, overwhelming vision of the mountain threatened to flood us with exhilaration and awe – feelings that were easiest to control by treating our presumption as a job of work to be done. First we would descend 300 feet from the Notch on to the Tseringma Glacier that flowed out of the arms of the horseshoe into Tibet, and would follow the glacier beneath this low arm of the West Ridge to place an advance camp almost at the same height as us, from where the ridge rose steeply for 2,500 feet towards an ice-cream cone of a summit – Point 19,800 feet. After this sharp cone the ridge looped horizontally for about a kilometre, rose again into another horizontal section and finally buttressed a rock wall beneath the plateau of the South Summit. According to Schneider's map, the route was over four kilometres long from the start of the difficulties. And then, if we had the energy, there was the traverse to the North Summit.

'It's simple,' announced John, 'just get on the ridge and keep on it to the top. Tim can do the rock steps, Guy the elegant ice arêtes, you can do the plods, Pete, and I'll do the bits in between. It's in the bag. All we've got to do now is climb it.'

We tied a couple of ropes together and slid on to the glacier to begin the long traverse. Fresh snow lay deep, and airlocks boomed a protest at our disturbing steps. 'Trespassers will be avalanched' thundered the shaking surface. We glanced at Guy for reassurance.

'The angle is slight, it won't go,' he said.

The sight of the mountain above our heads gave us the excuse to stop, gasping with the altitude, and gaze.

We marked our tracks with prayer flags on bamboo poles, and cached our loads on regaining the ridge at a gentle dome of snow. Clouds moved around us and it was snowing as we returned to Base Camp. The day's purpose had been accomplished, and we were relaxed and happy. We had started.

These beasts of burden days melted into each other. Three times we repeated the pattern of the first day, carrying loads up to the Notch, down the abseil and then across the Tseringma Glacier to dump food, fuel, tents, ropes and equipment on an ever-increasing pile. The afternoon snows and night winds brushed over the surface, illuminated by distant lightning, stippling our tracks until the glaciers became innumerable virgin ripples of snow. In the morning we broke trail again.

On the second day Guy stayed at Base Camp, nursing a cold before it became any worse. John was always in a lively, argumentative mood at breakfast time. That day the topic started with Apartheid, Rhodesia and Colonialism. Then it degenerated into a vivid description of the night's bowel movements.

'You're just trying to shock me.'

'That's not shock, it's prudery.'

John was suffering from diarrhoea, and I reached the cache of equipment at the foot of the West Ridge before him. I went back down to help him with his load, but he insisted on refusing the gesture, despite my taunting him as a *Boy's Own* hero.

We all had different styles of determination. No one seemed to play the high-altitude manoeuvring game on this expedition – and with only one player the game collapses. On other expeditions I had not encountered the self-sacrificial quality that John had, and was encouraged when occasionally his off-guard comments hinted that he was weakening.

'Must say, my strong ethical feelings about using porters or Sherpas evaporate a bit every day when I carry one of these loads,' he said.

Our team needed a leader; this I discovered when the others agreed to my tactics, and did what I suggested. However, this was a new role for me.

I was uncertain what to do about Tim. He still had not come with us since the reconnaissance in the blizzard, rarely emerged from his tent and was eating little. Yet whenever we asked him how he was, he always replied chirpily 'Much better, I'll be with you tomorrow.'

Sankar had felt very ill when we had first arrived, and we had decided to take him down to Lamobagar, when he suddenly recovered. We assumed that Tim was just taking a little longer.

The clouds boiled up from the jungles of Nepal at about eleven in the morning, and hampered our attempts to reconnoitre the ridge. The first difficulties of the ridge were four rock towers, stacked on top of each other – or so we thought. On the third day Guy and I emptied our loads and went for a scramble to discover a 400-foot-deep gash between us and the first tower. We returned on the fourth day with John and wandered around down snow slopes and rocks, failing to resolve the best way down into the gash. Nevertheless, we decided that the next day, 16 October, we would leave Base Camp for the last time and make a final carry to our load dump, and there establish an Advance Camp.

We had spent a lot of time discussing Tim's condition. Now we had to do something. On his brief appearances he had been looking ghastly, only nibbling, saying nothing, head in hands and we had resolved to take him down when we returned from our final carry. At dinner time, John went to see him. He returned with serious news.

'He doesn't know what time of day it is, whether it's light or dark, or even that we've been up the hill today.'

We decided to give him some of the emergency bottle of oxygen we had brought with us. But we could not find it. The bottle had not been seen since Kathmandu, where it must have been stolen.

Snowfall prohibited movement in the darkness. Through the night John checked to make sure that Tim was not slipping into unconsciousness. Immediately at first light, the following morning

John and Pemba Sherpa, the wood porter, set off to help Tim down. Pemba Lama, Dawa and I started after them as soon as we had packed tents and food, and Guy had prepared a first-aid kit for me to take down, and gone over how to inject Lasix intravenously. He remained at Base Camp with Ang Rinzi and Sankar.

As I descended I was hoping, 'He's been so stubborn, if only his stubbornness can pull him through now.' More oxygen, loss of altitude, was the only cure for cerebral oedema. The self-reproach that accompanies tragedy was creeping in, 'If only I had insisted he went down before.'

Tim was lying inert in his blue fibre pile suit, beside a stream. John was standing over him, in the sunlight. I stopped on the slope above, my heart sinking with futility. John read the question in my eyes, and stuck his thumb up.

'He's just resting,' he whispered. 'He's incredibly weak, but I think he's going to be all right. It'll be a slow business – he's been vomiting and falling down a lot. He can hardly walk, but refuses to let me carry him – understandably.'

After eight hours, we were all nearly 4,000 feet lower down, at the Rhododendron Camp. Tim was resting in his tent, and was starting to smile at John's cheerful banter. John and I relaxed beside the fire, our conversation released by the slackening of tension. We had had a fright. As the sparks flew upwards into the evening air, topics came and went inside our heads, and we talked as idly as two housewives over a fence.

The next morning John and Pemba set off back up to Base Camp, to start on the route with Guy. Before he left, John spoke to Tim gently, like a father. That afternoon I wrote in my diary:

> We got Tim down just in time. Now he's talking
> more, and starting to feel disappointed. He's waking
> up to what happened to him. He took a lot of per-
> suading this morning, and firm words. It's even
> harder to take disappointment at that age, you just
> don't see round a predicament. He's eaten some-
> thing at last, though, and is reading *The Ginger Man*,

so he must be perking up – haven't noticed him read before. He doesn't want to write his career off as a high-altitude climber and wants to go back up again. Yet he's so weak he hasn't moved from his tent all day.

'When I put as much effort into something as I have into this trip, I don't give up,' he said.

Warm, reassuring letters arrived with Jetha, the mail runner, the following day. Tim was recovering quickly. On the morning of 19 October, I set off upwards from the Rhododendron Camp. I exacted a promise from Tim not to move anywhere for at least four days, and left him in the care of Dawa, the two wood porters and Sankar, who had come down to help. I walked up the 4,100 feet to Base Camp in under three hours, feeling fit and perfectly acclimatised.

Ang Rinzi, the kitchen boy, was alone at the camp, and pleased to have some company. He handed me a letter:

To: P.D.B.
From: J.B.
You will need to bring:
a) cup
b) spoon
c) soup bowl/plate
d) mattresses as req'd
e) inner tent
f) water bottle
g) J.B.'s foam and Guy's bidet
h) vibrator
i) cans of beer
j) kitchen sink

I think we have everything else – a mighty big think that. The Vango tent was hugely unpopular with them what had to carry it! You could be lucky to get a night in it. Hope all was well below. See you. John.

John, Pemba and Guy had left Base Camp the previous morning. I could see the remnants on the ground of the farewell ceremony – the burnt juniper, the holy rice scattered towards the mountain. I packed my sack, preparing to follow them. Ang Rinzi pointed at the numerous cat tracks in the snow – he didn't want to be left alone with lynxes. I reassured him that Pemba Sherpa was to come up and stay the following day. Base Camp was a bleak place.

I set off, keen to find out what was happening on the mountain. The silence was only broken by my breathing and the crunching of my boots on the snow. Crossing the Notch was the final transition to a life of ice and rock, dominated by the West Ridge.

They did not hear my arrival above the roar of the stove, until I zipped open the tent door. 'Ay up, lads. Where's the brew, then?'

'Come into the galley, mate.'

I crouched inside. 'Seven letters for you, Guy – looks like five are from Helen. You beat me by three, and John, I'm sorry, there are not any for you.'

'I think I forgot to tell Kath we were having a mail runner,' he said.

'You're not in the jungle now, you know.' The letters were the last voices from home before the mountain.

John and Guy had split up and found two ways to the icy col at the bottom of the gash. Next day we would start up the first tower. The weather was settled, and high above, the West Ridge wrapped around us, filling a 200-degree sweep across the night sky.

Pemba was on breakfast duty. The day started before the sun arrived, with the stove lighting – the taps of the pump followed by a soft purring. As snow melted in the pan, Pemba chanted prayers. The smell of burning incense stick drifted to the rest of us in our sleeping bags – a reminder of the mountain waiting outside.

It was a day full of contradictions, false starts, misleading clues and wrong turns. John and Guy went first, and Pemba and I followed carrying rope and equipment. Several traverses, diagonal ascents, gullies, rock steps and rope throwings later we were all on top of the first tower, having reached it by different ways and having left the snow slopes criss-crossed with tracks.

'Looks as if a rabbit warren's come out to play,' I taunted the day's leaders. Pemba and I dumped our loads beneath the second tower and returned to Advance Camp to put a brew on. Guy continued directly up the wall of the second tower:

> It rises up and I have to take off my crampons. I climb steep almost holdless snow-covered rock for a long way, feeling clumsy in my big double boots, and get a good handjam, which allows me to put in a piton with the other hand. But what's the point in continuing? There must be an easier way. It would be desperate to carry loads up here. I abseil a hundred feet back to John. It is late, and night has fallen when we reach the Advance Camp, shattered.

Dinner was ready when they arrived, a cheerful meal in the snug social unit of the Vango tent, Swiss, Irish, English and Sherpa freely insulting each other.

Guy described how next day five ropelengths circumnavigated the problem.

> John is in front today and climbs 'comme un chef' – after a long traverse on the north side of the ridge, he goes straight up in the direction of the summit of this enormous second tower, up 350 feet of rockslabs covered in powder snow. A short storm blows in, and the hail bounces down the slope and over us. John reaches the top and shouts with excitement: 'It's unbelievably exposed up here.' As we return in the blizzard, we misunderstand each other and accidentally let go of a rope, which disappears down the slope. We rejoin Pete, who is sheltering from the storm in a rocky niche, waiting for us. John just runs down the ropes. Then there are long 'easy' bits where it's necessary to concentrate very carefully. I tell myself that, after all, 'Je suis guide', and there is no need to fail.

I arrive last at the col in the gash and think 'They could have waited.' I lose my temper. Oh blow these bloody English, I'll get along all right by myself. The storm has passed, and the sunset is extraordinary. In fact, they are both waiting for me on the other side of the col. Good. We return together. It's my turn to be porter tomorrow.

That evening, I wrote my own verdict on the day in my diary:

This ridge is a *long way*. Point 19,800 feet, the ice-cream cone, still looks days away. It's becoming clear that there's a lot of hard work and time ahead of us on this climb. To be gone through day by day. Our movement is positive, upward, and we must sustain it.

John wrote:

Some difficult climbing and always this enormous ridge ahead. We hardly seem to make any progress even after an exhausting day's work. Great fun coming down the fixed ropes at night. Fantastic views – all very exciting, but the main feeling is one of effort. Don't like to be defeatist, but I think it is perhaps more than four men can chew. Suspect Pete feels the same. Still keep plodding on.

The summit of the second tower was perfectly flat. 'Good place for a camp-site,' I said.

'A mite short on space, and long on exposure,' said John.

As we started to climb the third tower, we looked back to see that the second tower leaned drunkenly to the south, with a gravity-defying tilt.

'Like the Leaning Tower of Pisa,' said John. 'If we camp there, it'll boast the world's most precipitous lavatory.'

The south side of the ridge was sun-toasted and ice-free – a pleasant change from the cold shadow and powder snow up which we had come.

'Watch that rock, John!'

Two hundred feet of scrambling up piles of loose blocks balanced at forty-five degrees on the sunny side took us to the top of the third tower.

We stood on the rocky, airy crest of the ridge beneath the fourth rock tower. 'You don't mind if I have a go at leading, John?'

'You sure you can manage?' he grinned.

I tiptoed across the friable wafer rock of the south side of the tower, trying to distribute my weight, tapping my feet on to the largest holds, and touching finely balanced rocks until they tumbled into the void. The afternoon sun roasted my back. I hung on a piton and belayed. This was what I really enjoyed. Not humping loads of food and fuel and letting my mind wander – but pure, exploratory climbing, so demanding as to absorb concentration completely, mind controlling body, shrinking the world to the rock in front of my face, pinning my thoughts to here and now.

'You'll have to lead through, John – you should be able to handle it, the rock looks more solid above me.'

'Just leave the technical stuff to me, Skip.'

John launched himself over a bulge and climbed quickly up a shallow groove in the wall.

'Watch out!' I ducked as the shadow of a large rock fell past me.

'Should be better now. Fantastic climbing,' John did not pause until he reached the top of the tower, a hundred feet higher up. He sailed back into view, sliding down the rope to land beside me. We were both pleased.

'The ridge seems to fall back a bit up there,' he said.

'Didn't you put any runners in?'

'Hadn't got any.' We waved to Guy, tall and perfectly balanced on the top of the third tower.

We grouped together on the second tower. 'There's no way I'm going to sleep in a tent on here,' said Guy. 'It's not a camp-site, it's a … "nid d'aigle."' And so it became – not Camp 1, but 'The Eagle's Nest'.

Guy had also had an enjoyable day. 'It's so different, being alone,' he said, 'and in the middle of the Himalayas! I'd have felt I had wings if it hadn't been for the heavy sack – oh, and that rope we dropped yesterday, it'd got snagged and I soloed down to get it. I tied on to it and climbed back up. Really strange – I felt as if I was being belayed by an invisible second.'

Pemba had been down to Base Camp to pick up some paraffin and nylon tape. He returned with disquieting news. Pemba Sherpa, the wood porter, had not come up from the Rhododendron Camp as arranged to keep Ang Rinzi company. Yet the tents were still visible far below at the Rhododendron Camp. Perhaps something had happened? And Ang Rinzi was becoming very anxious, alone with increasingly bold snow cats.

A rest day announced itself before anyone articulated the idea. Nobody wanted to get up, and we snuggled into our sleeping bags until it was too late to go on to the mountain. I felt that deliciously guilty sense of a reprieve, like when you hear rain on the roof of an alpine hut in the early morning and you know you don't have to get up. Then the sun came.

'Sun sun sun here it comes.'

The Vango tent was our community centre. Over breakfast we flicked through the photograph file endlessly analysing, discussing and digesting the problem. We were trying to learn, to divine the mountain by trial, error and experience, so that we could climb it, safely, surely, sanely. Our minds wandered over the possibilities. We had made mistakes, would make more, but there was a saying 'The shortest way between two places is three sides of a square.'

'I'm glad I haven't my reputation to think of,' said John. 'What euphemism are you going to think up to call our tactics, Pete? 'Modified' alpine? 'Capsule-style'? You will notice, Guy, that these useful expressions, democratically selected by our leader, embrace a wide range of ethical weaknesses in an ever-degenerating spiral towards traditional Himalayan strategies.' John blathered on, his barracking undermined by his complicity in the enterprise.

We counted the gear – seventeen ropes, thirty karabiners,

twenty-five rock pegs, fifteen ice screws, four deadman snow anchors, three lightweight tents.

'O.K. John, you're good at arithmetic, how are we going to fix two and a half thousand feet of rope along a ridge that's over two miles long?'

It was, in Royal Marine parlance, a 'make-and-mend' day. We clowned around, modelling food and equipment for suppliers who had asked for photographs of their products in action. On the mountain we would have other things to think about. We picked randomly, like free-range hens, at little tasks. We aired our sleeping bags and clothing in the sunshine, sewed and repaired, cut nylon into slings and sharpened crampons. As we were learning about the mountain, so our equipment began to feel part of ourselves. At high altitude there are few clues in the survival game, and it is important not to miss them. Only in rare moments could we allow ourselves to love the mountain. Love requires a relaxed flow of communication, and we would have to be too wary for that.

I could not accept that our footsteps, as the Sherpas seemed to believe, would pollute the mountain. 'Tseringma, we are one of the earth's species, so why can we not tread here? … ' I stopped the prayer, laughing at myself. What was I talking about? It was, after all, only a mountain!

'A brilliant idea, this rest day,' said Guy. An intimate, reassuring ritual, it had the mental therapy of a spring clean. We stoked up with food and drink and crawled back into our sleeping bags to dream of the view from the summit. The 'weekend' was over.

During the night the world below returned to gnaw at me. I awoke composing endless letters about mountain training disputes, the climbing school, my parents and Tim. Pemba had left during the rest day to pick up some more freeze-dried food and to keep Ang Rinzi company at Base Camp. In the early morning, he returned – with Ang Rinzi! Pemba broke the news – Tim and the rest of the expedition had packed up and left the Rhododendron Camp. Pemba had not seen any sign of them. Perhaps Tim had suddenly deteriorated and had to go down. Ang Rinzi would not stay with the snow cats any longer, and so he had brought him up. Had he made the right decision, he asked?

We discussed the problem for over an hour and, as we talked, another dilemma was emerging. John voiced his concern about his job — it was now becoming obvious that the climb would take much longer than we had thought, and that he would not be back in time for a crucial management committee meeting on 13 November. The fact that he had not received any news, and his wife was pregnant, was also beginning to trouble him.

I was angry. 'Look John, we've all got our own worries. Why did you leave it till now before remembering your responsibilities and stopping us all in our tracks? Don't have a black Irish mood and throw this guilt trip on us now. Ten days, fourteen days, what's the difference? Expeditions are like marriage, you have to stick with them, for better or for worse! We're spending far too much time bothering about things that have nothing to do with climbing the mountain – the Tim problem, your problem, they're all just energy drains, and we need all the energy we've got to get up the hill.'

Eventually we evolved a master plan – next day Pemba would escort Ang Rinzi down the mountain until they discovered Tim's fate, and then arrange an extra mail run to carry an apologetic telegram from John.

We returned to the mountain with relief, as if fleeing from the moral problems of another planet, a different reality. Guy and I moved up to the Nid d'Aigle, and John drew satisfaction from carrying an enormous load in support and helping us scrape off a patch of snow on which to pitch the tent. 'I really enjoy hard work,' he said before going back down, 'but fancy coming thousands of miles to dig a hole.'

A child spends hours absorbed in play, building dens and dugouts in trees and mud. The climber constructs his new home high on the mountain, and quickly settles in. Below our perch on the fantastic parapet of the Nid d'Aigle, the sun threw strangely clipped shadows across the southern face, and Guy and I smiled like children. He cooked spaghetti bolognese and we talked about Dougal, the hero of his youth, about Everest, about our ridge. We almost forgot where we were.

The next day was perfect. Above the fourth and last rock tower the ridge leant back. Guy seemed designed for ridge climbing. With the seemingly careless poise of a gymnast, he balanced up rocky arêtes, uniform coils of white rope in one hand, the other balanced nonchalantly on rugosities. His studied grace and precision matched the photographic poses in French books on mountaineering technique.

'Let's see how far we can get.'

We were travelling light. We climbed pitch after pitch, elated with the altitude and the sun's warmth. The new springboard of the Nid d'Aigle had released intense energy from within us and we felt that we could climb upward forever. But the declining sun reminded us to return to shelter. We had climbed a thousand feet of new ground.

We soloed downwards. Far below us, on the white glacier, a pageant of tiny black specks moved backwards and forwards, enacting a mysterious drama to us. Now two orange tents glowed on the Nid d'Aigle. John was ensconced there, and when we arrived he unfolded the plot.

'I was just about to leave Advance Camp this morning when guess who hoved into sight but Tim, bent double under an enormous sack and eyes set fast on the summit. He seemed right as rain, if a bit pale about the gills. He carried a light load with me up to here – he's really improved, moving slowly, but otherwise O.K. Says he'll do another carry – he's staying at Advance Camp. Seems really impressed with the mountain – it's the first time he's seen it. Pemba and Ang Rinzi have gone back to Base Camp. Oh and Guy, you know that down suit you gave to Pemba? He hasn't got it with him – he flogged it in Kathmandu.' We crammed into one of the tents and cooked and chatted into the evening.

'Your turn as rope boy tomorrow, Pete?'

'Yes, Captain.'

Guy and John climbed through the morning to the previous day's high point whilst I fixed ropes and anchor points on the way.

When I caught up with them, John was hanging on to steep ice, fifty feet above Guy, his whole weight balanced on the front points of his crampons, and his enormous calf muscles bulging out of his gaiters.

'Dancer's legs these, mate. Just point me at this hill. No problem. Great ice.' A large chunk fell away as John brandished his axe, and hit Guy in the mouth. Blood dripped from the wound on to the snow. We crouched into the slope, wary of further missiles.

Two hundred feet above, a granite overhang jutted out into the sky. For us it was an important landmark, the day's 'project'. Many days before, Guy had seen this from the glacier, and espied a tiny ribbon of snow that cut across it. Now he claimed ownership of this ledge, and we christened it the 'Vire Neithardt'. Pitons sang into the firm rock and we followed John as he edged across.

'What can you see around the corner, John?'

'Fantastic, it's snow, it's the ice-cream cone. Just a snowplod to the point from here, have a look yourself.'

The sun had come through the cloud, the wind had dropped and the rock was golden. The vastness of Tibet to the north was in darkness. We plunged back down into the shimmering mist. Imperceptibly, by degrees, the climb had come alive.

27 October–4 November 1979

A jagged, milk-white crystal guarded nearly two miles of the ridge. It floated in the air, tethered insubstantially to rocky buttresses, a fragile spire of arrested harmony. Thin shadowy lines and narrow flutings glowed for an instant, then faded. The shifting light helped us to glimpse a hint of its variety but not even the thickest cloud or the darkest night could disguise its shape.

At last we were climbing pure ice and snow. I crouched beneath the roof of the final overhang, watching showers of ice cascade improbably from far out above my head, falling clear through the air for hundreds of feet. The roof blocked news of John's progress, and the only measure was an occasional pull for more rope. Then the rope tugged for me to follow.

John was astride the ridge, gripping it between his knees as if holding the mane of a great bucking white horse.

'Haven't got a belay. I've hacked a bit off the cornice and feel fairly secure,' he announced.

John seemed unperturbed, whereas the exposure unnerved me. The new airy situation demanded mental adjustment. The giddy drop screamed into my head 'Don't fall.' Was this classic hubris? Were we over-reaching ourselves? We were black flies, crawling on to a white paper origami – except that we had no suckers on our hands and feet, just a few inches of driven steel suspended us above the void.

'You're in a morbid mood today,' said John. 'You seem obsessed with thoughts of death.'

'Just a mild attack of jitters,' I confessed. 'The snow seems a bit sloppy and loose, and I don't like the look of those cornices.' I climbed above him, carving steps and smashing the cornice down into the depths of the North Face of the ridge. I uncovered a small rock from beneath the snow, and spent half an hour tapping a wobbly piton into an icy crack. We had no ropes left to fix. 'It'll be the big pull up tomorrow,' I said.

John stormed into the lead again. There was no protection. 'Exciting stuff this,' he yelled.

The only marks of his passing were a few crampon scrapes on the surface. I followed him, chopping steps.

'You may as well lead to the top,' I said. 'I'll consolidate a pathway.'

We could look across at the next section of the West Ridge. It looped a long way down the other side of Point 19,800 feet to a heavily corniced horizontal section half-a-mile long.

After 400 feet we stopped, for we could go no higher. 'I'll just lick the tip of the ice-cream,' said John. He pushed his head through the summit and looked around. 'Amazing place, incredible drop on all sides – but it's a hell of a long way! What do you think?'

My mind choked at the sight of the endless sweep of the ridge – it was too long to absorb. We were both depressed.

'Was Changabang like this?' he asked.

The Changabang climb had been just as exposed, and just as much hard work, but every ropelength gained height and there had not been this constant danger of cornices and poor belays.

'Going down and then horizontal all that way is going to sap us,' I said.

'Guy dismissed it as one hour – maybe two – step-cutting,' grinned John. 'I wonder what he'll say when he sees it – Nom de Dieu!'

'Hacking out a camp-site'll have to come first.'

'It's gripping enough standing here.'

It had been a long day wound with tension and a taste of things to come.

We met Guy on the way down. He was coolly starting up the arête towards us, carrying a heavy load. His poise looked characteristically nonchalant. 'What a sensation! All alone above a sea of cloud!' He greeted us smiling with enthusiasm, carved a slot and left his load and descended with us. During the long abseil, the rope John was sliding down pulled out the piton it was secured to. He managed to jump on to a ledge and keep his balance.

The hazards and decisions of the day time were simple – black and white, compared to the problems that surged back during the hours of night on the Nid d'Aigle. It helped me to turn on my torch and write them down:

> We initially planned just to leave fixed rope on the difficult bits, but now it's becoming clear that a full scale 'capsule' leapfrogging technique running the rope out between camps is the only way we've got a chance of doing the route. Now we're going to have to pull up all the ropes below the Nid d'Aigle – and after tomorrow, all the way below Point 19,800 feet. So I have to decide what to do about Pemba and Tim. If all that mattered was to reach the top, then it would be obvious to ask them to go back to Base Camp. Why?
>
> a) Pemba has just come back up here after two days' holiday at Base Camp – a strained thigh he says. (Why do Sherpas always come up with childlike excuses? After all, he just wanted to chat with his mates.) He seems impetuous, and more at home with a jumar than an ice axe. We can only trust him to carry loads.
>
> b) Our progress is determined by how fast the lead pair can put out ropes over new ground. So far, one man carrying loads has been able to support this progress – and it doesn't look likely that we'll go any faster higher up. It's possible that, with five of us, there will be

some redundancy — one or two passengers.

c) Our food and fuel supply is already sparse, and with two extra mouths along our time will run out more quickly.

d) All these are minor issues compared to Tim's health and ability to acclimatise. Tim cannot have recovered completely, so quickly, after having been so weak. And we are now going so much higher. If he turns ill again, high on the ridge, trying to get him down could kill us all. Of course, the summit isn't the most important thing – our survival is. We cannot justify sending Pemba down now. Guy doesn't think I'm hard enough to make Tim understand, and he's probably right. Tim wouldn't be the same problem if he wasn't so blindly determined. Whatever I say probably won't make much difference to what he does anyway. I'll dash down in the morning to see him. But this isn't war, we're not an army requiring orders – the mountain is still unknown. So perhaps it's best that we're all on it together, wanting to climb it together.

In the morning, Guy and John prepared to go up to establish a camp on Point 19,800 feet, with Pemba in support. A pan of water was knocked over, delaying breakfast, and then Guy burnt his down suit on the stove. He started to mend it laboriously with little pieces of Elastoplast, cursing.

'If it was physically possible on this camp-site,' said John, 'you'd say that Guy had got out of bed on the wrong side this morning.'

I wanted to descend to Advance Camp before Tim moved, so I left them packing.

It was many days since I had touched this ground. Our first probings there had been exploratory, exhausting and uncertain. Now I felt confident, having lately balanced above dizzier heights than these. I was down in an hour.

Tim was sitting in the entrance of the Advance Camp tent, heating up a drink. The inside spoke of ordered independence. Next to him was a load, neatly packed, to carry up to the Nid d'Aigle. Behind him, his sleeping bag and equipment were carefully folded, as if prepared for a kit inspection at Scout Camp. I had intended to tell him how thoughtless he'd been, not sending Pemba Sherpa up; how we'd spent more time talking about him than the climb, and how worried we were that he'd be ill again when we were up on the ridge. But on seeing him, all these intentions died, and it was obvious there was only one solution – he should come with us.

'Glad I got down here before you set off. Can you pack up your personal stuff and I'll help you carry up any food that's left. I'm going to pull the ropes up. Any tea?'

Tim was visibly relieved. 'Magic,' he said.

It took all afternoon to pull up the ropes. As we climbed, it started to snow. We were taking away all the lower rungs to use them higher up the ladder. The physical gesture of commitment was made, and now the concomitant isolation and self-reliance could enter alternately to exhilarate and agitate us. Our momentum would be spurred.

Or so I hoped. Tim and I reached the Nid d'Aigle as Pemba arrived from above, singing cheerfully to himself. 'John and Guy coming down,' he announced.

'What!'

Yes, there they were, swinging down the ropes in the twilight. The sports plan was disrupted. After their late start, Pemba had become stuck for an hour whilst jumaring up the fourth tower. They had divided his load between them, but had arrived on the summit of the point too late to dig a camp-site. Nevertheless, they had uncovered some better anchors on the ridge.

John, Tim and I crammed into one tent. It had been eleven days since we had been together. There was much mocking and laughter. I did not realise how Tim's joining us upset the social balance of the team, as Guy recounted:

> I feel very uneasy. The three British sleep together, and I am installed with Pemba. Nevertheless I go to eat with them, but I feel a complete stranger to all their discussions. To them I am the Swiss guide, to be laughed at. Well, they'll see. I hate being a stranger, put on the side. A very bad calculation on Pete's part. I feel alone against the three of them. It would be good for them to find themselves alone sometimes.

At dawn I tried to stir some action, for once a sergeant major in a dozy barracks. 'Come on Pemba, get a brew on. Come on John, can't you see the whole trip's sliding. We've probably got, I reckon, a one-in-three chance of reaching the South Summit. We've got to make more progress.'

'Snow cat came here last night,' said Pemba, pointing at tiny tracks in the snow around the tents.

'How'd it get up here?'

'Must have come up the south side.'

'If it can climb like that we ought to put a rope around it and get it to lead the rest of the route.'

That night John described the day in his diary:

> Big move to Camp on Point 19,800 feet Guy and I are to occupy so we can only carry our own kit and two ropes each. Has snowed a bit during the night so no tracks and slippery rocks. The other three follow with heavy loads to stock the camp. Arrive at the Point early afternoon, very hot and fairly tired. Pete arrives shortly after, then Tim, then Pemba. Pemba goes back down straight away. We set about hacking a camp-site on this knife point. The map'll have to give it a lower height after we've finished with it! Pete and Tim descend at about 4.00 p.m. Guy and I carry on digging and chopping in snow and ice until 5.30 when just before dark we try the tent for size – it fits! Tie it down with ropes and axes. Sort out gear on the

edge of nowhere and go in tent where somehow we forget there is a 6,000-foot drop immediately outside the door. Calling the camp 'Neuschwanstein' after mad King Ludwig's Bavarian cloud castle. Guy says he keeps on hearing Wagner's 'Lohengrin'. Plenty of food but no tea. You wouldn't believe this camp-site. Gear hanging everywhere. All has to be tied on. I'm on the outside! Will try to push the route along the ridge tomorrow.

Back at the Nid d'Aigle the same night any satisfaction I might have felt with our logical progress received a jolt when Tim staggered me with the assumption we should be going alpine-style beyond Point 19,800 feet. It hurt my pride to have to justify more pedestrian tactics and my defensiveness is evident in my diary entry about Tim:

This feeling that the younger and ambitious, particularly Yorkshire-bred climbing generation are so prickly and opaque, must slot me as an older, done-it-all-not-much-to-learn-now-set-in-my-ways greybeard! When I went to the Hindu Kush in '72, we pushed ourselves so hard we found our limits and only just got away with it. Perhaps Tim would have been best going on a trip with his younger mates, having a few epics, making a few mistakes, surviving and learning his own level that way. The youthful plunge and a measured pace don't seem compatible.

The early morning sun lassoed the turret of Neuschwanstein, nearly 2,000 feet above us, picking out the orange of John and Guy's shelter on the tip. We envied them for the warmth of the sunshine.

Pemba, Tim and I packed up our camp, our fingers stiff with cold.

One of the tent poles slipped out of Pemba's hands, to stop on a ledge 150 feet down the South Face. Although he had just vomit-ed up the kippers he had eaten for breakfast, Tim climbed down unroped to reclaim it, following the tracks of the snow cat.

John and Guy were inside their tent when we arrived with our loads. It was one-thirty in the afternoon. 'What's up, John?' I asked.

Guy was sitting silently in the back of the tent, and I could not see him. John was their spokesman. His face was gloomy with dis-appointment, and he shook his head as he broke the news. 'Thrown a wobbler, I'm afraid. It's unjustifiable, Pete. Guy and I have had a long talk about it. We did a couple of ropelengths. The whole ridge is unstable – I could feel it vibrate when Guy cut a step a ropelength away. There's no security – the nearest rocks are hundreds of feet away. We only had that eight-mil non-stretch rope to climb on too. There are immense double, triple cornices, all just about to fall over. I nearly came down to stop you wasting the effort coming up.'

'Well, we're all here now. We've shifted all the food and gear up, we may as well stay the night,' I said, and did not comment fur-ther. This was not the time for a back-seat driver to voice opinions.

We cut a platform for a second tent, and Tim, Pemba and I in-stalled ourselves. That night, huddled in the corner, I wrote:

> The first night in a new camp is always the worst and has to be well sleeping-pilled, to forget these monster drops on all three sides. It's an amazing place. We have to resign ourselves to the creaks, thumps and groans from the ice. A fast return home now is deliciously appealing, but we must have another look. Tomorrow will prove if they are right. I wish I'd been here to encourage them, but I've wanted the back-up to run smoothly, hence all the hard work but safe support jobs I've given myself during the last two days. Tim is now loving the excitement of our position, and to him retreat is not

a word. His ambition appears cold and hard, and
should give us impetus. But everyone must agree
about the next step. I want success, or justified return.

Guy did not sleep much that night. He was first to break the silence of the morning. 'I have been thinking for many hours, like
before a big route in the Alps,' he said. 'I am not going to give up
two months' work just like that. This is no place for those who are
homesick. This bit of ridge is mine, my problem, and I am going
for it.'

John was stunned by Guy's change of heart, but quickly recovered: 'Guy, I'll never mention your German family origins again,
you're a Frog, through and through.'

After breakfast I descended to the fourth tower to recover the
first six ropes. I looked around, imprinting the ground on my
mind, and anticipating any problems that might arise during descent. Between each ropelength as I came up I left orange nylon
slings around the rockmarkers for our return.

As I climbed back up the ice ridge towards the camp, I saw,
across hundreds of feet of space, the tiny figure of Guy moving
cautiously along the back of the gigantic cream roll of snow.
Between us and below us was the shadowed world of the north
side. And today, certainly, he would reach the security of a clump
of rocks on the ridge – the Red Tower.

The whole team was back together on Neuschwanstein by four
in the afternoon.

'We should have stayed out longer,' said Guy, 'but I persuaded
the others to come back. I thought it would take a long time but
Tim had made a motorway of steps behind us and it only took half
an hour.' He was excited at the day's progress. 'Sometimes my
mouth was dry with fear. At one point John said to lasso the cornice – it was shaped like a mushroom and it worked! Amazing.
We've put a big sling around it, it's a good runner. In another
place, where the ridge was too thin to climb on, I descended down
and up again on the south side; very delicate. Fantastic climbing!'
In his diary he wrote: 'The team is back together again, morale has

increased, and I think we should crack it. My vengeance is complete, upon myself and the others.'

The two tents on Neuschwanstein were pitched almost on top of each other, five feet apart.

'God, you're timid,' mocked John as I twisted more ice screws into the mountain, to tie myself on to that night. He and Guy, in the upper tent were doing all the cooking for the five of us. The dome-shaped tents were much more roomy than the claustrophobic tunnel tents we had used on Kangchenjunga; nevertheless, it was a cosy squeeze for three people. Tim, Pemba and I lay in our tent, waiting to be fed, and listening to the conversation above us.

'Look Guy, you're not in Switzerland now. Why can't you have double standards of hygiene like the rest of us? Clean cutlery, pristine pots, cordon bleu cooking just don't make sense up here. You've used most of the expedition's toilet paper to wipe your Karrimat.'

'Pass me a spoon, John.'

'Here you are, mate.'

'Hey, clean it first, it's got a lump of yesterday's soup on it.'

'I'll chew it off.'

'You, you, you're an animal!'

'Snarl.'

The days had slid into November. Soon the winter winds would arrive to threaten our fragile hold on the ridge. We had not much time.

Tim was by far the best technical climber of the team, to be deployed as a last secret weapon. On 1 November, I held the rope as he took the lead. However, he was not yet attuned to cornice-climbing, and spent three hours traversing steep and difficult ice beneath the ridge, changing his mind, and returning again. Meanwhile Guy, on a load-carrying day, arrived from the back, uncoiled a rope of his own, tied on and soloed along the top of the ridge above us. This helpful gesture had an unspoken but implicit message: 'I told you so.' Then John breezed into view, having spent an enjoyable morning pulling up five ropes from below the other side of Neuschwanstein.

'It's great being on your own for a time, isn't it?' he said. 'I looked across and couldn't see you, so I assumed you were galloping along and would need some more rope – so I brought some. Didn't realise you hadn't actually moved anywhere yet.'

Logistically, the expedition had piled right up behind the front. Needled, I led across a large cornice, my anger having overcome my fear. Guy advised me where to place a deadman anchor. The rope became tangled. I misunderstood him, suspected a patronising tone, and cursed him loudly. Guy said nothing, left his load and sped back along the ropes towards Neuschwanstein. We never discussed the incident. Only John followed me.

At last the ridge had stopped going down, and was starting to loop gently upwards in long, horizontal sections interspersed with short steps. I took the lead again, demolishing the cornice with two-handed blows of my ice axe, and carving a path along the top of the ridge.

'It's all right when you get used to it,' I yelled. 'I don't know what all the fuss is about, my granny could walk along here; it's no worse than the Midi-Plan traverse.'

John arrived and we hung from an ice screw. 'It's not quite how I remember the Midi-Plan,' he said. 'I mean, on the Midi-Plan hundreds of people have already tested the cornice for you. Still, I get the idea now – Piolet Bludgeon – no technique, no art, just brute force and ignorance.'

It was growing late, but experience had taught us not to succumb to the temptation of an early return to camp. We capitalised on the afternoon's momentum. John smashed his way a rope-length forward. I joined him, and we both sat astride the ridge, chatting happily. Honour was restored.

The sun hung low in the sky, a great star whose light was caught by thousands of tiny icy particles suspended in the air around us. The arm of the West Ridge pointed back to the sun, and we followed it. Beyond, a tiny figure was silhouetted on the tip of Neuschwanstein.

This ridge was a cutting edge between light and shade. A mighty barrier, it divided winds and snowstorms, cultures and countries.

Also, it was our only delicate support between earth and sky. A full moon illuminated the final ropelengths of our return to the tents.

Early the next morning, Tim shot off along the ropes whilst everyone else was dozily preparing their equipment and loads for the day. His sense of urgency was infectious.

'If you wait here any longer, Guy,' John taunted, 'it'll be three in the afternoon and time to come back.' The gibe worked, for Guy soon left in hot pursuit of Tim:

> A strong wind blows from the North, and it is bitterly cold. But when I am below the crest on the south side, it is quite warm. I join Tim at the end of the ropes, and he lets me lead the first pitch. The cornices are enormous and lean from side to side. I crawl along until I can put in an ice screw as a belay. We alternate the leads. 'Stick to the ridge,' I advise Tim. A lot of chopping is necessary. It is hard work and our progress is slow. All of a sudden I am faced with a series of three towers of ice and snow. I tell myself that this time … however, nothing collapses.

For three hours John and I sat on the rocks of the sunny side of the Red Tower, exchanging thoughts. We watched Tim and Guy, gazed at the mountain and scanned the great distances for signs of changing weather.

'I hope they find a camp-site somewhere around that rock tower. Trouble is, it'll be no higher than the last one, I mean, look across at the American route. Heightwise, we've hardly got anywhere, we're just traversing around the headwall of the valley – doing the Tseringma Horseshoe! We're really going to have to be careful on the descent, whatever happens, I don't fancy teetering down here all dizzy and dehydrated.'

'Do you think we're being too cautious? Perhaps we should go for it.'

'No, not on this route, not with this team. We're getting tired enough as it is; I mean, we're out on a limb and really committed already.'

'You mean you don't trust us?'

'Or myself. I just don't want to take that much risk. There are too many unknowns. I've got this nagging feeling that we're constantly overstepping ourselves. And you've got to admit, it's been erratic displays of pride, anger, competitiveness, and ambition that have got us all this far.'

'You hypocrite! You could say that about any climb.'

John was our sounding board. Always charitable in his opinions, he had the ability to put the most delicate of problems into the most tolerant words with a disarming humility. The armed forces had taught him to accept the foibles of others when there was no other choice, and to recognise and rise above the problems of close living. He never complained or excused himself, and seldom asked for help.

He was ashamed to mention difficulties, and believed that our little team was sacred, whatever its weaknesses. John was the least selfish of us all.

Pemba arrived after a morning's snow-melting at the camp, and the three of us moved on together. Meanwhile, Guy and Tim had reached the larger rock tower that marked the end of the horizontal section and the start of a steep 1,500-foot step in the ridge.

The sixty-foot-high rock tower blocks our way. After some discussion, Tim leads halfway up it and belays to a rock spike. The security of solid granite at last. There is a lovely, simple key to the problem – a beautiful little rock ledge down on the south side of the tower (in fact we now see it is a group of towers) which leads to a col on their far side, at the point where the ridge stands upwards again. The others arrive and we dump loads. If we do a lot of cutting, we shall be able to put a camp here; 20,000 feet – only 200 feet gained in many days. It is dark when we arrive back at Neuschwanstein.

The next day, 3 November, John and I returned to the 1,500-foot step. John was exuberant. 'This is the sort of climbing I really like,' he said.

We had no equipment left for a leader to protect himself. This meant that if the leader fell at the top of 150-foot ropelength, he would fall 300 feet. However, John was irrepressible, seemingly unconcerned. His spirit was unleashed upwards and he soared after it. I just paid out the rope, grinning encouragement at his comments.

'Look at that front-pointing,' he said, lurching over an ice bulge, 'the grace of a thousand startled gazelles.'

'Hardest bit of climbing so far,' he gasped, panting for breath above an overhang. 'Quite hairy, this,' he yelled, teetering across a cornice higher up. We quickly climbed ropelength after ropelength, until there was no more. 'Terrific,' he concluded. 'All that sideways scuttling on the horizontal was getting me down.'

Brim-full of joy, we swooped back down the ropes. It seemed that in two days the scales had been tipped in our favour.

Whilst we had been climbing, Guy, Pemba and Tim had spent four hours excavating a magnificent platform on the ridge that was just big enough for two tents. The cornice was carefully left intact, so as to protect the tents from the northerly and westerly winds. This shield, and the proximity of rock, helped us quickly feel at home there. Although the new camp-site was in an equally improbable position, it lacked the frighteningly dramatic vulnerability of Neuschwanstein. John christened it 'Fawlty Towers', after the BBC TV comedy. Tim and Guy then returned all the way back along the ridge to spend the night at Neuschwanstein, to be in a position to pull in the ropes and rejoin us at Fawlty Towers the next day.

Pemba was a connoisseur of fixed-rope ridges. He often compared our behaviour, our route and our equipment to those of Japanese expeditions he had been on. 'On ridge like this,' he said, 'Japanese put in many many snow pickets and make hand-rail. Your ropes aren't safe. Japanese have many more members. On Ama Dablam climb, we were seven climbers and seven Sherpas.'

However, he was impressed at our care and effort in making our tent platforms. 'The Japanese they have very rough camps. They just dig in snow not ice and then tie round with ropes.'

Pemba rarely mentioned the religious significance of Gauri Sankar, but quietly he undertook a rearguard action of appeasement, to offset the possible damage of an insensitive climb. Daily, he sang, chanted prayers and lit incense, and did not hear our mutterings of 'What a cheap stink.' His supply of holy rice was nearly finished, and he did not know that John had left at Base Camp the polythene bagful he had given to him. He taught us not to turn our plastic cups upside down. 'It is the same with porters' baskets – they must always be open to the sky.'

When John burnt one of the sides of his cup against the stove, Pemba told him 'Now you will have bad luck!' Our rationally trained minds found it difficult to accept the explanation, and Pemba always smiled with embarrassment. Some of his superstitions seemed as divorced from their long-forgotten meanings as our own Western ones about horseshoes and spilling salt. Just as they had done on Kangchenjunga, two black yellow-billed choughs followed us up the mountain, swooping around us in the cross-currents and turbulence around the ridge, rarely settling.

'They're probably the same two,' said John.

Pemba did not eat much of the evening meal – fortunately for him. It was a bad night. The few teabags that were left were with Guy and Tim, on Neuschwanstein. We melted throat lozenges, then chocolate, with snow to make drinks. Then we made a mistake – we did not mix enough water into the mashed potato powder. We woke in the middle of the night, our mouths parched and stomachs swollen with dehydration. We melted snow for three hours, restlessly trying to calm the internal torture.

Morning clouds dispersed and the morning wind died. The night's frost melted as the sun touched the tent, and lay as ice on the groundsheet. Pemba left to pick up ropes from Tim and Guy as they moved along the ridge towards us, and John and I waited, to relay the ropes up the mountain. After the rough night, we were glad of the chance to melt and drink some more water.

The rest gave a chance to shed scales. It was warm. I looked at my bare feet for the first time in many days. I peeled my silk suit off, and dead skin fell around like a snowstorm. I ran my hands over my shoulders and my ribs, rediscovering my body. Where had all the muscle gone? I was more like a bedridden hospital patient than a mountaineer. I twisted and turned the little mirror to encompass my face and saw matted hair, blotched, purple scars, scabs and weary lines. I was underneath that, somewhere.

We counted our possessions. At a stretch, we had four to five days' food left. We had no ballast to throw out. Like Robinson Crusoe, we knew that commonplace, insignificant things suddenly become precious when they are all that you have between yourself and thirst, hunger and cold. Seldom would life be simpler, but such simplicity cost no less than everything.

We looked around. Below us, the South Face of the West Ridge plunged in a 3,000-foot sweep of ice to the Tongmarnang Gorge, a tributary of the high Rolwaling Valley. Far to the south west we could see the soft pencil lines of the Siwaliks. To the west the lines of three rivers cut their swathes through the Himalayas from their headwaters in the north – the old trading routes of the Trisuli, Sun Kosi and Tamba Kosi, all known locally by the name of Bhote Kosi. Beyond and between them stood proud mountains – the distant hulk of Himalchuli, the Langtang Peaks and, nearest of all, the aggressive spire of Choba Bhamare. Most arresting was the dominating height of a double-summited peak to the north west. This peak, the only mountain above 8,000 metres to lie completely inside Tibet, was called Shisha Pangma. The Sanskrit name was Gosainthan, meaning 'the place of the saint'.

The first European to explore the area around Shisha Pangma was Heinrich Harrer, who was to make the first ascent of the Carstensz Pyramid in New Guinea nearly twenty years later. At the outbreak of the Second World War, he and a climbing companion, Peter Aufschnaiter, were interned by the British at Dehra Dun, in India. In 1943 they escaped into Tibet.

From the upper waters of the Rongshar Gorge, where it threaded between the mountains of the Lapche Kang and the north side of Gauri Sankar, the other New Guinea explorer, A.F.R. Wollaston had, in 1921, taken the famous first photograph of Gauri Sankar, showing a mountain perfect in outline and proportion. Wollaston remarked on the contrast of this area with the barren Tibetan Plateau. Here, he found soft, fragrant air, and flowers and trees in profusion, and called it 'The Valley of Roses'. In June 1924, after the traumatic loss of Mallory and Irvine, Colonel Norton led his expedition's retreat from the monsoon on Everest to recuperate here for ten days. Gauri Sankar was revealed slowly to them, through a rent in a curtain of cloud, until they saw 15,000 feet of it, from top to bottom. The sight made them giddy, and they acclaimed the vision 'a dream mountain'.

Norton rested his team at a Tibetan village called Tropdo, at the base of the northern side of Gauri Sankar. Like the 1921 expedition, they went hungry for meat. Norton complained in his diary that there were no chickens to be eaten, for the locals believed that if animals were killed in the sacred precincts of the mountain, misfortune would befall the village. I wondered if this was the same village that John and I could see – its cultivated fields splashed a different shade on the slopes, and its buildings just visible to the naked eye. Don Whillans, when he contoured on to the northern, Tibetan side of the mountain in 1964, had said he could actually see people there, walking about. According to our porters, a Chinese bus now went to within a day's walk of that village. John and I weren't the first, or the last, climbers to attempt Gauri Sankar and think wouldn't life be simpler if it could be approached from the north. However, Tibet remained to us the mysterious land – its secrets could not be revealed. Whether we could respond to it or not, Tibet focused spiritual energies on the sacred mountain in a particularly conscious way.

At mid-day, Pemba had not returned with any ropes, so we decided it was too late to move. If we were to leave now, it would be mid-afternoon by the time we reached our previous day's high point. There was no point in tiring ourselves for such limited progress.

'We haven't stopped for eleven days,' I said.

'It is Sunday, after all,' said John.

Meanwhile, on Neuschwanstein, Tim and Guy had also had a bad night:

> Tim cooks. What a horrible catastrophe: he succeeds in putting two packets of Knorr soup in half a litre of water, pours in two tins of meat and then stirs it a little – absolutely revolting. Then, during the night, he vomits in the tent – over his sleeping bag, boots, groundsheet, me, everywhere. And the smell.
>
> In the morning, after cleaning what we can, we leave to take in the ropes along the horizontal arête. The method which I have devised is simple. The first goes along the fixed rope to the anchor and then belays the other who follows whilst coiling the rope at the same time. I am very angry with Tim who will not do what I want (!). Then later I apologise for having shouted at him. All is sorted out. Eventually Pemba arrives to help carry some rope.

When Pemba returned to Fawlty Towers, he told John and me that Tim had been ill. A few minutes later Tim arrived swathed in ropes – angered at our inactivity and accusing us of being lazy, of not coming to help. The sudden onslaught bit deeply and quickly. I didn't even try to explain why we had not moved, but was overwhelmed with a rage that I could not control. I longed to reply calmly, but could not. I was amazed at my over-reaction. Feelings had been building up, and Tim had triggered something in my unconscious.

Tim gave his sleeping bag to Pemba to air, and left to help Guy. I started to rationalise my anger to John, and then stopped. In our other lives, at lesser altitudes, a confrontation can help strike through complexities to clarify and reduce a problem to a hard solution. But the stakes were too high to take that risk again. The mountain had amplified our words, and they could not be revoked. I relied on John to soothe our wounds.

There was a gust of wind and a slithering sound. We watched aghast as the knot attaching Tim's sleeping bag slipped through and the bag slipped into the abyss of the South Face.

Pemba offered to go down and fetch it, but was understandably relieved when we did not insist.

Guy arrived. 'It was full of vomit anyway,' he said. Like Tim, he was upset that we had not come to help them.

This time, however, I had my answer ready. 'Well why don't you have a rest day tomorrow?' I suggested.

When Tim arrived, he accepted his loss without comment. We all donated extra clothing to keep him warm, and he slept between John and myself. It was all we could do.

John relieved the tension. 'Well, it's probably keeping some surprised peasant down there cosy,' he said, looking into Nepal.

During the night a loud curse and clatter awoke us. John had stretched his arm out through the air vent so as to empty a pee-bottle, but had been unable to get his hand and the pee-bottle back in, so he had dropped it.

'It was a monkey's-hand-in-a-bottle-situation,' he explained. 'There was nothing I could do about it but let go.'

19   CLIFFS OF FALL

5 November 1979

The sunlight moved on to the mountain like the hand of a great clock – a constant reminder with long fingers that pointed at our mood. Today it was a reminder not to nestle down into the seductive cosiness of our sleeping bags until the day warmed up, but to light the stove and to stir ourselves out into the daunting cold.

'It'll be worth it, it'll soon be over, today's our big day, a big push is in the air.'

John and I left the tents, racing the steady creep of the sunlight along the ridge. We thought the end was in sight, and our optimism was born again. Scepticism dissolved and fell away like the wisps of morning mist in the valleys below.

'I feel great,' said John. 'Ready for the charge, Sir.'

John was prepared to tear upwards without protection, and revelled in the risk and daring of hanging tenuously in high places above the void. John's confidence and ability were irrepressible – if he climbed into danger there were surely untapped reserves to help him climb back. A day following him was fun.

A dead heat. We arrived at the top of the ropes at the same time as the sun. Pemba was following us, carrying a rucksack full of ropes. It was 10 a.m.

Like occasional monstrous waves escaping from a far-off storm, expanding their pent up energy unexpectedly across a calm lapping sea, the winds of approaching winter were beginning to whip across the West Ridge of Gauri Sankar. I looped a sling of nylon tape around a small rock spike, fastened myself to it. There was no ledge to stand on and the sling supported my weight as I leant out to watch John's progress. Our tiny figures were silhouetted far away on the West Face of the mountain. I paid the ropes out – an eleven-millimetre climbing rope and an eight-millimetre terylene non-stretch rope for fixing – as John gripped the ice ridge above me. After he had climbed 150 feet, the eleven-millimetre rope ran out and he called for me to release it and to continue to belay him with the eight-millimetre. Then he went out of sight on the north side of the ridge.

I did not see him fall. The wind carried the tune of pitons sinking into rock – and then, nothing. He made no sound of warning or alarm. Suddenly, the climbing rope he was trailing snaked wildly into the sky and disappeared, and the fixed rope scythed down the ridge towards me.

'He's fallen. The rope'll never hold.' I braced myself and then the shock came, jerking me upwards. The rope tore through my gloved hands and I let it slide as it whipped and snagged on the ridge. Accelerating thoughts slowed down time: 'He's pulling me off the anchor, the rope'll snap, I'll go too.' And then the force stopped. The rope had cut deep into the ridge forty feet above me. The rope was loose. 'He's gone.' I pulled it, hard, and it resisted. It had become caught – or John was on the end, unconscious, horribly injured, dead.

'John! John!' The wind snatched my shouts away, and there was no answer. A coldness inside suppressed my welling feelings of dread. I tied the rope off to the one beneath, uncoiled another one and, belaying myself, climbed out into the shadow of the North Face. I saw him.

His diary reveals what had happened.

> First new pitch of the day – feeling strong and happy – no man has ever been here before. The wind is strong but crampons and axes bite hard on the arête. Ropes tangle beneath Pete and I am preparing to wait while he sorts them out when a hideous shriek sounds above, followed by an incredible blast of

wind that nearly plucks me off the arête. I cling on tight on either side – it only lasts a few seconds. I consider going back down to Pete to try to find a less exposed alternative but decide to carry on. See rock belay above, but can't reach it on the climbing rope, so tell Pete to untie and hold me on fixed rope only – he extends it by knotting it to the end of the one below. Reach belay, put in pegs and am just about to tie on when another hellish shriek and blast of wind unbalances me. It is a good stance so I do not worry over-much until I find myself out in space. A frantic grab at the rock does no good, and down the North Face I go – tumbling over and over, hitting rocks and snow and falling forever in slow motion. I am dead, I am sure of it. Soon the rope will snap. There's thousands of feet to the ground and I hope that I am knocked unconscious before I get there. I think of Kath and little Joseph. Puzzled. No Panic. No Fear. Thoughts clear and rational. No effort under the sun can help. Really blown it this time.

Then I stop. The rope has held. I am alive and little J. has a dad. I seem to have broken my left wrist and twisted my left knee, but I am alive. I behave irrationally, shouting 'I will not die, I will not die.' I grab my jumar and start climbing like a madman up the fixed rope which has held me by snagging on the arête. I have fallen about 200 feet. I shout to Pete whom I cannot see that I am O.K. – more or less. At last he sticks his head round to see me below him. He throws a rope across and I swing to him. I am a wild sight, having lost my hat and bleeding from the head. He is wonderfully calm as I reach him and he holds me as I burst into tears at the relief of being alive.

I looked into his eyes, trying to gauge the extent of his concussion. Had the blood come from his ear or nose? Was he sure, in his shocked state, there were no other injuries? John was apologising, insistently. He said he could abseil, and started down, protected by a top rope. He reached a knot in the rope and fingered it, confused. I realised that someone would have to abseil with him and, after a flurry of knots, followed him on another rope, yelling to Pemba: 'Leave your sack, John's hurt. Go down and tell the other two to come up.' The turbulence had carried the noise of our shouts down the mountain. I could see Tim and Guy struggling to put their boots on and packing for the emergency. By the time they reached us we had descended two ropelengths.

Tim and Guy were cool and reassuring.

'Well, Guy, this is what Swiss Guides' Courses train you for,' I said.

We knew we could help John to the camp. Soon the ridge was criss-crossed with ropes, descendeurs, karabiners, slings and willing pairs of hands. For the first time on the expedition we worked smoothly and efficiently together, united as a team. After three hours of descent John was lying down in the security of a tent.

'I'll never forget the noise that wind made,' he said, shaking his head. 'It was the scream of an animal.'

'This'll make a good end to the story,' said Tim.

20 FINAL CHOICE

5–8 November 1979

'I feel as if I've just gone fifteen rounds with Rocky Marciano,' said John. His head was clearing, he said, but his speech was slurred and his face was cut and puffy. His knee was badly swollen, his wrist crooked and his hand unusable. His wind suit was torn and scraped.

'Even Marciano couldn't have done that much damage,' I said. 'You look as if you've been through a combine harvester. How come you didn't shout when you fell off? You didn't make a sound. I'm sure I'd have screamed my head off.'

'My dad once told me that if you're going to die, to die quietly,' he said.

Guy bandaged him and we all watched carefully for signs of head injury. Crammed together in one tent through the rest of the afternoon and early evening, there was no privacy for the patient, as he lay back listening to the objective discussion of his doctors over his body, occasionally interjecting a comment.

Could we tie all the ropes together and descend the North Face? The ridge was too insecure, too risky to descend. He would have to rest at least two days, for the concussion and shock to resolve themselves. 'I don't want to be the reason you give up,' he said. 'I'm heartbroken I won't be able to continue the climb, but you're right, I've a lot to be thankful for; I'm alive.'

We wanted to succeed. No one wanted to abandon the route. But we were a family – or, at worst, a marriage of convenience. Survival and success went together, never the last without the other. Guy mooted an idea. Pemba could stay at the camp with John, and he and Tim and I could go along the ridge for a day or two, and have a look at the final difficulties. On one thing we were all agreed. There would be no splitting up for the descent, we would stick together.

I could not sleep. A bright moon filled the tent with flat light and a cold wind shook the walls. Although he had taken painkillers, John twisted and turned, unable to drift into a sleep that would relieve him of his wrist's nagging ache. Tim, without his sleeping bag, was struggling to keep his feet warm. Neither of them complained. The day had been, as John said, 'a seminal experience'. It had shocked us into focusing together, all other squabbles transcended and forgotten.

On the morning of 6 November we ate the last breakfast – two fistfuls of muesli each. That is, all of us except John:

> I don't eat since I can hardly justify it, lying on my
> butt all day. Pete and Guy are off early at 6.30 a.m.,
> followed by Tim with ropes at 9.00 a.m. Pemba is
> left behind to look after me! Wrist hurts like hell,
> but leg not too bad – walkable at least. Watch with
> increasing envy the progress of Pete and Guy along
> ridge. We have to be quick – there's only about three
> or four days of food left, and that's skimping.

The loneliest moments for a climber are felt during a long lead without protection. I inched my way up the pitch which John had fallen down the previous day, my eyes darting circumspectly around, suspecting lurking treachery. But there were no vicious blasts, no hideous shrieks, for today the mountain was tranquil. I saw John's rucksack, stashed carefully on a rock shelf by him before he fixed the anchor. I clipped into the two pitons.

Above me was a leaning rock tower, capped by a jauntily tilted, pointed cone of snow. I traversed beneath it, my crampons and picks biting into hard ice as I moved between jutting rocks. These rocks were just big enough to stand on, and served as harbours of security where I could breathe deeply and recover. I laughed at myself. I had styled myself an anchor man and escort, not chief risk taker on this expedition, but now there was too much risk and too few people, so the risk had to be shared. And now it was my turn to lead, I was enjoying myself. Voices filled my head of old friends, veteran Alpine Club members, male and female, that I had met over the previous year. I told them what was happening. They understood and we appreciated the setting together. My mind detached itself and soared upwards, beaming back images of our tenuous hold on the mountain. My nose brushed against the rock tower. I scraped away snow and ice with the adze of my ice axe until I uncovered a crack. A piton rang home. I belayed Guy and looked up at the snow cone. 'And now for the Archbishop's Hat.'

I always laughed at Guy for his 'ski instructor's smile'. Whatever the situation, it was always impossible to distinguish a grimace from a grin. But when I looked down on his smile as he held my rope, remarks that were on the tip of my tongue wavered in a rush of transmitted kinetic energy. As far as I was concerned, it was a smile of encouragement.

I kicked up the airy crest of snow. The ropes looped down through space to Guy, with the purposeful sweep of a suspension bridge. Their graceful arc added to my confusion. Rope, cornices and slopes all tilted crazily away from one another. So how was I supported here? I hacked away four footsteps in front of me at a time before moving up. The steep angle confined the swings of my axe. Like a skier learning the improbable discipline of leaning out, I stood out in balance as much as I dared, keeping my weight over my feet. One little mistake ... if I should fall off here? I concentrated.

'Can you send up a deadman, Guy?'

I planted the device firmly in the ridge and clipped in the rope. Now only two were left. We would need this one higher up, Guy would have to take it out when he followed – but my mind insisted on it now.

We had reached the top of the 1,500-foot step in the ridge. The chaos of undulating whipped cream cakes and hidden steps blocked our upwards plans, and each ropelength was a revelation, alternately cheering, and then disheartening. We all led dangerous sections of the ridge, and longed for more equipment to make the climbing safer.

Tim arrived. 'I don't trust these deadmen,' he said. He and Guy took it in turns to hold my ropes. A huge unfurled sail of snow shadowed the northern side and I hung below it for an hour, cutting deep into the ridge, looking for rocks and cracks. I had only two large angle pitons, and I placed one sideways in an icy crack, tapping it gently so it did not split. It seemed to grip for an inch of its length. Tim and Guy joined me and clipped in. There were no footholds to relax on to. We balanced sideways along the inside edges of our crampons.

The clear line drawings in books on mountaineering techniques portray the safe traversing of corniced ridges as a simple matter. The climber assesses the width of the cornice, and estimates where its potential fracture line would be were it to collapse, and then walks beneath this fracture line. However, the West Ridge was not so clear-cut, because usually the snow overhung on both sides. We were balanced at a point between an icicle-skirted overhang on the south side, and the enormous cornice leaning over the north side. There was no alternative but to follow the tell-tale crack lines where the two opposing forces were beginning to part company.

Vivid, nightmare pictures of terrible precision rose in my mind, of the thunderous collapse of towers of snow in earthquake proportions. Occainally, a step collapsed and a hole appeared, enabling me to see through to Tibet on the other side. It was a journey surrounded by creaks and whispers. Slowly, the rock shelf on the other side drew nearer. There were more yards to cross than years in my life. At the end, I clutched the solid rock mooring with fervour – not elation. It was three in the afternoon.

I relinquished the lead to Tim, after peering over the next obstacle. More serried ranks of towers and cornices rose into view. The spectacle rubbed salt into my scarred nerves. This ridge was endless. I was drained of mental energy.

'I'm too tired to do it,' I said, and turned, to leave the next problem to the other two.

I retraced our steps. The soft evening light and my fatigue dulled my mind to the risk and exposure. I resigned myself to a complete, unquestioning trust in the ropes we had strung below us. It seemed that the mist would soften any fall.

Back at the camp, John, Pemba and I watched the tiny red figures of Tim and Guy returning across the snow turrets, which were now golden in the sunset. Even at this distance, it was possible to identify an individual from his shape and the way he moved.

My reports were pessimistic, but the other two had seen more ground. 'Tim forged across two appalling pitches,' said Guy when they returned, adding – ever-optimistically – 'I think another day's climbing should put us in reach of the top.'

'The fixed rope had got caught under the icicles on that last pitch you led,' said Tim. 'We had to solo it and a step collapsed on me.'

We tried to assess our progress from the photographs we had brought of the ridge. Doubts ebbed and flowed about the route, until the conversation turned to another obsession we shared – food. We had been spinning out our meagre supplies for a long time and were constantly hungry. We wriggled and groaned in masochistic ecstasy as we tantalised each other with imaginary menus.

'Be careful when you get in the tent, Guy. Don't knock anything over, Pemba's got turkey, roast potatoes, sprouts and gravy on simmer.'

'Followed by fresh air and snowballs and nowt warmed up.'

On 7 November, breakfast was a piece of chocolate and two cups of tea each. When we had finished there were only three teabags left. Tim and Guy were first to leave for the front line. There were only a few ropes to carry in support; I decided to wait at the camp until late morning, before following them – logistically it would be a waste of effort, but I wanted to be there.

John was feeling much better, and was beginning to contemplate joining us for the final push.

'I hope that if my hand is less painful I can jumar to end of fixed ropes and then plod easy snow slopes to summit. Not sure whether this is realistic – hand is useless and getting down from here could be an epic in itself. Still, I can give it a try and come back here if it doesn't work.'

Pemba was still on ward duty, keeping an eye on John, and singing to himself. It was evident from the way he was quick to suggest a retreat for more supplies, and by the way he looked towards Base Camp, that Pemba longed for the opportunity to chat for a few hours with his friends in his own language. This morning he spotted three figures near the Notch. They had come to look for us. We signalled by flashing a spade in the sunlight, but there was no reply. We had been away many days, and I wanted to tell them 'Don't worry, we're all right, we'll soon be back.' Pemba continued to gaze for a long time after the figures had gone.

We could only guess how near we were to the summit – or whether it was possible at all. However, I roughed out a telex message, announcing our success:

> Base Camp 10 November. Expedition successful and all safe and well. First ascent of Tseringma, 7,010 metres. Southern Summit of Gauri Sankar made by Boardman, Leach, Neithardt and Pemba Lama at 1500 hours on 8 November after prolonged struggle up very difficult West Ridge. Send love to all and longing for home. Will inform further on arrival Kathmandu approx. 18 November.

There was no way the message could be sent, it did not commit us, but it was a reassuring if rash projection into the future. I doubted that I would have the energy and confidence to write it when we returned. I signed off my diary: 'To be continued when recovered!'

Tim had been reluctant to give up the idea of following a line he had spotted beneath the ridge, traversing across the South Face. Most of his alpine climbing had been up steep north faces, and ridge climbing was new to him. Today, however, he understood what was needed. His perseverance brought a fresh momentum to the climb, and helped shed all thoughts that we should abandon it. By the time I reached the end of the ropes, he had crossed more of the ridge than I had dared to hope possible. Tracks threaded below, above and between leaning snow towers and enormous, madly waving cornices. The wind plucked the ropes as they hung through the air between the towers. Guy was pleased when I joined him.

'I thought you weren't coming,' he said. 'Tim's climbing like there's no tomorrow. He's done some crazy leads. Incredible. A bit back there he said, "Bloody hell, Guy, you'll never believe how happy I am." He had stood on a cornice, then stepped off it and hit it with his axe. The whole thing collapsed and fell down the North Side.'

Guy's voice was tired and droopy. He had missed his rest day. 'I'm going down after the next pitch,' he said. 'I have no strength left in my legs.'

Tim had just traversed a cornice on its south side, but had now noticed a safer way following a band of rocks beneath the overhanging snow on the north side. Guy tiptoed across this to join him. The holds were tiny and the climbing delicate. The ridge was beginning to declare its attachment to the West Face of the mountain. The impending sweep of this leaning rock wall gave a new dimension to the abyss. Occasionally, ice flaked off from the séracs on the edge of the plateau of the South Summit, to plunge down it without hitting anything for 2,000 feet.

All day I had been assessing the feasibility of John coming up the climb. We all agreed now that he would not be able to do it with one usable hand. I was relieved that Guy would return first and break the news – it was two-thirty in the afternoon when he went down.

When at rest, Tim was trembling with the vast expenditure of nervous energy that the ridge demanded. Once in the lead, however, he climbed coolly. The cornice was now too narrow and fragile, so he climbed steadily and calmly across the sixty-five-degree wall on the South Side. Occasional ice bulges forced him to hug the mountain, so as to keep his balance over his crampons. I belayed him astride the ridge with my left foot in the sunshine of Tibet, and my right foot in a Nepali snowstorm. The weather was sharply divided by a wall of turbulence that stretched hundreds of feet above me. The scene had a haunting unreality, as if I were witnessing a vision of schizophrenia.

Tim appeared and disappeared through flurries of snow. After I had paid out 120 feet of rope, I heard the ring of a piton and a shout: 'Come on, Pete, there's no stance but the peg seems O.K.'

There was no room to change over belays, so I led through, hand traversing around some rocks towards the end of the cornice. I tapped in our last piton and peered around the corner.

It was a depressing sight. There was a gap thirty feet wide and fifty feet deep in the ridge, with a little col at the bottom of it. An overhanging rock wall between my airy perch and the col barred progress. I had come the wrong way. We would have to cross the cornice. I flailed at the piton with my hammer but it refused to budge. 'I'll have to leave this till tomorrow,' I said. Time pressed us to return down the line to the camp. The next day we would return for the summit.

That evening John was quiet and monosyllabic with disappointment. It was awkward to discuss the route tactfully in front of him. We studied photographs showing how the ridge joined the West Face. There would be some difficult climbing, but it was not easy to calculate how much. However, there was not much packing to do. After some disagreement, we decided not to take sleeping bags but to take a stove and pan. We would try to be up and back within a day – if necessary completing the climb in moonlight. Tim and I would leave first, followed after two hours by Pemba and Guy.

As long as we felt our intimate way up the mountain, accidents could be averted. Yet, within, fear built up unashamedly. When controlled, fear can bring strength. But unleashed fear made us cling to the mountain in a tight panic. In some ancient cultures 'to clutch the mountain' was a euphemism for 'to die'.

When I reached the big cornice that I had led across two days before, the fixed rope was once again snagged around icicles.

Tim had evidently been unable to release it, for he was now moving amid the snow towers higher up, having soloed across the pitch. I tried flicking it around, then pulling it – without success. 'He could have waited,' I thought. 'We might have sorted something out together; now I'll have to solo it.'

I made two moves up the ice and stopped. An internal warning bell was ringing urgently in my head. It was as important a statement as had ever been made to me and I knew it had to be obeyed. The sun was stifling me in my down suit, and I felt hot and clumsy. The memory of the cornice was etched too deeply. I was hanging on too hard. I could not control the dread inside me sufficiently to force myself up wards; I could not summon a hard, brittle shell of will to protect me from the mountain, and it threatened to overwhelm me. Death was too near for me to resign myself to the risk. It was an absolute necessity that I should survive and return. He had been prepared to solo it, but I was not. To hell with my pride and the waste of time. I yelled up to Tim for him to come down and help. A distant curse, and the figure descended. The older gunfighter had backed out of the final shoot-out. He said nothing and I did not explain.

At the end of the ropes Tim retrieved the piton I had placed the previous day, and climbed over the crest. He slipped around and beneath the cornice on the north side, turning the frozen wave by the same route a surfer would have used on its fluid, rolling counterparts in the Pacific. The rope bit a deep notch through the eaves of the cornice, and I lowered him into the gap.

The ridge now rose up in a 400-foot arrowhead of ice and rock that leant against the wall beneath the South Summit's ice cliffs. Tim started working his way methodically up the lower and steepest section. His crampons and picks splintered the friable ice, and chunks clattered down into the abyss, leaving thousands of smaller particles suspended around his rope through the air.

Pemba joined me at the gap. 'Best to take cornices on the left side, like chortens, for good luck,' I said.

He grinned. He was impressed with the ridge and the distance from the camp. It was the most difficult climb he had ever done, he said. Then he pointed at the South Summit. Five eagles were circling around it, their wings golden brown in the sunshine. I tried to take a picture, but the film in the camera was finished. I fumbled to insert another. But the eagles were gone.

Guy slid into the gap. We all looked up the dangling rope at the soles of Tim's cramponed boots, a hundred feet above our heads. Tim was fixing a belay.

'You could count the number of pitches with runners on this route on the fingers of one hand,' I said. 'Will you follow him, Guy?'

We followed Tim up the rope. Pemba was ever eager to gain height and he hung close on my heels, unnerving me, as if he were trying to read over my shoulder. The blade of the Arrowhead leant back to fifty-five-degree snow that dripped in great icicles over a thirty-foot overhang below our feet. This rock overhang blocked our view downwards of the main South Face of the South Summit. There was nothing between us and the glacier 5,000 feet below. For a while our talk was bold.

'Not long to top, Sir, what do you think?' said Pemba.

'There's no way I'm going to spend the night on the plateau,' said Tim.

After three unprotected pitches, Tim was tired and Guy took over the lead. There were no more concealed gaps, and for the first time the way was clear. A 150-foot knife-edge of snow stopped abruptly in the rock and ice wall of the South Summit Plateau. The western flying buttress of Gauri Sankar sank into the mountain without trace.

'I'm not stopping here,' shouted Guy when he reached the meeting point. 'I've put an ice screw in but it's no good. Can you tie another rope on?'

A narrow diagonal ramp of rock thinly coated in ice leant back above him at sixty-five degrees. As soon as he stepped leftwards off the ridge, Guy was balanced above the West Face, the top 500 feet of which cut away in an overhanging wall beneath him.

Guy's long body stalked sideways across the wall with the patient stealth of a hunting spider. He devised a cunning protection by threading thin nylon slings through linked bubbles in the ice.

No one uttered the thought that he should hurry, for we all knew it was a long and difficult lead. Talk of the summit died, for the day was ending. We had only one rope left. I tried to memorise the ground above him, as he moved up a groove and attached himself and the rope to a rock spike. High on the left was a gap in the sérac wall. Two huge, grotesque horns of ice signposted a gateway to the plateau.

I tied off the rope to the ice threads as I followed him. If one of them should break, I would swing, perhaps irretrievably, like a pendulum into the darkening abyss. The thought obstructed a job to be done, and I chased it from my mind. I was heady with altitude and the exposure, and the risk was not painful. The irregularities of the earth below were lost beneath a gently undulating swell of fluffy grey-blue clouds. The last rays of sun picked out the thin white line of rope looping above the last crest of the ridge and the little red figure of Tim, clinging to the ice. I hid my emotion behind the detached eye of my camera. Firelight glowed across rock and ice, and then faded. Soon the cold would arrive.

'Looks like it's my turn,' I said to Guy. He nodded, smiling. The effort was to be shared.

I kicked my crampons into the frozen snow, climbing as quickly as possible in the twilight. I was soon panting in the thin air. Ribs of snow concealed dead ground; the ice horns were farther away than I had thought. Night was rushing in, filling me with the fresh energy and balance of urgency. The front points of my crampons skittered. I had reached the ice of the sérac wall; it was brittle and, as I turned in an ice screw, large dinner-plates flaked off. Eventually one sank in and I tied off the rope for the others to follow.

Like a blind man learning Braille, I felt my way across the ice, feeling the surface for a more forgiving texture. I smashed with my ice picks and ice tinkled away down the slope and into the darkness. It took three or four blows to clear the debris and implant the serrated edges enough for confidence. In the blackness gravity lost meaning, and angles were indecipherable. There were no guidelines for balance. Two ice-screw running belays helped me relax. I squeezed around a bulge of ice and saw the outline of the col between the two horns against the night sky. 'It's not far now!' I shouted.

Four on one rope move slowly, and it was a long, cold wait, hanging from an ice screw in the darkness. When Guy arrived he belayed Pemba. We imagined the possibility of the sérac wall toppling over and down the South Face and made facetious comments.

'It would be a long ride,' said Guy.

'Might make our descent easier if it falls over whilst we're above it,' I said.

I took advantage of the security of the anchor and extricated my head torch from my rucksack. The light flooded the ice around us, but beyond it cut a feeble stroke until it was lost in the night. As soon as some slack rope became available, I raced eighty feet to the col, scrambling over the lip on my knees.

'Hey, lads. I'm there!'

21 TSERINGMA

8–9 November 1979

It was a strange, new, horizontal world, a world of white spacious-
ness, of level snow crusts and wind-curved slabs and distant cliffs, all
expressionless in the flat light of the now rising moon. I walked away
from the edge, towing the rope behind me, staggering drunkenly
through the snow crust and breathing deeply with relief. It was 9.00
p.m. The night was clear. Far away to the south west, beyond dark
ridges, were the flickering lights of a town. But here, in the fringe
of the plateau, there was not a glimpse of rock or living thing.

The wind cut into us, and we were tired. We would have to stay
here for the night. If only we had brought our sleeping bags! We
were standing on a shelf 200 feet long and 100 feet wide just
beneath the edge of the plateau. We wandered around beneath a
small ice cliff, looking for a sheltered hollow, but the wind eddied
relentlessly around every corner. We started to dig in, but the
snow was hard and progress difficult. The altitude turned our
movements into slow motion in the flat moonlight. Fortunately,
where it was level it was possible to quarry with our axes large
flakes of snow two inches thick to use for walls. As soon as the
niche was big enough to fit him, Pemba slotted in and hunched
around the stove to melt some snow. We had no food, and warm
water was the only sustenance we could hope for. At this altitude,
in this cold, without nourishment, we would soon weaken.

Tim wriggled into the trench, his head near Pemba's feet.
Meanwhile, Guy had discovered a narrow crack in the ice wall
thirty feet away, and was excavating a tiny personal hole.

'I thought we were going to dig a big hole and all cram in to keep each other warm!' I protested. I started lengthening Tim's and Pemba's trench for myself. Soon Tim had turned it into a semi-detached. Self-sufficiency had capped the day and that night we could not be together. We hunched down in our separate, coffin-shaped prisons. Although Pemba, Tim and I were lying head to toe, we could have been miles apart. We were no team now – each of us was imprisoned with his own discomfort, his own thoughts and his own will to survive.

My socks were wet with condensation from my foam inner boots, and I had no spare pair. My feet were soon cold, and I reached down to warm them, whilst trying not to knock down the protective wall of snow behind which I was wedged. The cold spread through my body until my muscles were bound up in a senseless ache. I forced myself to shiver. Outside, spindrift scurried along the shelf, opening up crannies and sifting around me in an icy blast. By three in the morning I knew that I should not stay there.

I retrieved the stove and pan from beside Pemba and built a windbreak of snow around it. Once lit, the flame sputtered ineffectually – but I could not wait. I stumped around, trying to warm up my feet.

Guy appeared. 'I haven't dared fall asleep too deeply,' he said. 'I've been enlarging my hole and dozing a bit.'

'Any room for me? My trench is bloody useless.'

Guy had excavated a narrow cave. I squeezed in after him with the stove, my back blocking the entrance. We sipped the little water that had melted, and my feet began to tingle with life again, next to the warmth of his limbs. Our heads nodded drowsily until dawn.

'Well, Monsieur Guide, you go first, I'll go at the back – I'm only here as escort anyway.' We roused Pemba and Tim from their trenches, and handed them the pan of water.

We all tied on to the rope, and were ready – eager to move out of the freezing shadow of the mountain's threshold, and into the sun.

There were no shadows on the plateau. It opened out into a great, white, unfolded hand offering its snows to sun and wind.

No man had touched this vast whiteness since the mountain was born and now, after a long and dangerous journey, we had reached it. Tseringma – the musical name for the white goddess circled in my mind. Pemba had reported some lamas as saying she had already fled to southern Nepal. Or was she still the mountain? And were we fit to tread here?

The wind gusted across the plateau, plucking up thousands of ice particles in its path, scouring our faces. We held up our gloved hands in front of our eyes and faces as shields against the painful blast. The sun could not chase away the numbing cold. The snow surface was wind-crusted in a slabby pavement that occasionally collapsed under our weight. The angle permitted us to walk, crouching against the wind. Guy selected a cautious, dogleg line of ascent to the summit. It was a weary, trance-like effort with frequent pauses in a long line.

Four of us on the rope caused a chain reaction – whenever one slumped, hands on knees, to gasp for breath, the rope jerked and everyone was quick to snatch the chance of doing the same.

I smelt the fragrance of juniper in the wind. No, it was not an offering from Pemba – but now he was throwing rice into the air. Noises and buzzings filled my sleepless head. The ascetic fasts until his body chemistry produces visions. Hunger, thirst and exhaustion, cold and altitude have strange effects. But sciences and physiology were not all. Only a bold and senseless man would approach a sacred summit with a sneer at superstition.

The mountain was still a deep, serene, purposeful unknown and our last steps were awed and hesitating. The ridge that bounded the edge of the plateau arched upwards and then curved down, without a dramatic declaration of its highest point. We were sated by days of constant tension on ice towers and cornices, and the safety of this gentle summit was a relief. We could stand without fear. We arrived on the ridge a few feet below the top, smiling. We had agreed not to touch the highest snows a long time before. Pemba attached a small Nepali flag to his ice axe. For want of many words, we shook hands, our defences down.

'Thanks Pete, better than staying in Leysin,' said Guy. For a few seconds, his voice was thick with emotion and tears were in his eyes. 'Je suis à 7,000 metres, sur un sommet inviolé!'

The perfect, clear view was a tangible prize that we had won. Peaks rose to greet us on the summit, rotating sentinels in a vast and cloudless panorama. For many days Tseringma had screened this sight from us. The Northern Summit of Gauri Sankar, seen from the side, loomed up as a leaning spire. It was beyond our power to reach it and return. Cho Oyo, Gyachung Kang, Menlungtse, Everest, Lhotse, Makalu were all higher than us, but Menlungtse was the nearest and the loveliest vision of all. A mighty white obelisk of snow and pale pink granite, whose shape matched that of the Matterhorn from the east, Menlungtse harbours the yeti in the wild valleys of its feet, still unclimbed, isolated in the middle of its glacier-filled basin, and guarded by the Tibetan frontier.

The cold dark blue of the sky over the mountains spoke of winter, but to the south west the sky was pale and warm. We stayed on the ridge for fifteen minutes before the wind drove us down.

Surely Tseringma would not let us get away with this? I looked down, from snow to brown rocks, to green forests, to cultivation, to unseen distance. Now we had to descend without an accident. Our line down and across the plateau was straighter than that of the ascent, for now the wind was behind us and we were more confident of the snow conditions. We reached the bivouac site at ten-fifteen, just as the sun was touching the rucksacks we had left there over three and a half hours before.

The ice pitches of the previous night were unrecognisable. The angle had slackened, but the edge of the drop was a near-reality, rather than a dark thought. I went down first, and Tim climbed down at the back with the unprotected task of recovering a rope.

We steeled ourselves against the dizziness of hunger and fatigue. For four and a half hours we descended the ridge, grimly holding on to the idea of safety at the camp, and through this discipline, transcending time, space, fear and suffering. We strung out along the ropes like beads on a broken necklace. The previous day we had pulled up some of the ropes above the camp, and now we gathered together to safeguard each other down the final section.

John congratulated us. He had some soup ready.

'It's the best soup I've had in my life,' said Guy.

John had been on the verge of losing hope – we had been out of sight for so long, and the night had been so cold and windy. He had decided that something must have gone wrong. In despair he had written a note to say he was soloing down to try and find help. Then he had seen us, and counted us, coming down.

We had been away two days, and some unknown event was locked up in the heart of that slice of time.

'There was only one thing wrong, John.'

'What was that, mate?'

'You weren't there with us.'

He could not reply.

10–20 November 1979

The ordeal was beginning. We had pulled up the ladder and had left it above us. We had not the time or energy to recover it, and to lower it again. A mile of ground lay below, between us and safety, and there was no fixed rope to guide us down. However, 10 November was clear. Some of our earlier tracks remained. The storms of approaching winter had stayed away. Our bodies cried out for safety, food and rest. We were worn-out cars running on 'empty'.

John recorded:

> I don't want to see another ridge like this in my life. We set off at 9.00 a.m. after oversleeping and eating a freeze-dried meal for breakfast (first for a long time, and the last). A long way to descend – we will need all the daylight. Pete and Guy and I move on one rope, with Tim and Pemba behind. I soon realise we are in for an epic. We totter back along the knife-edges of the ridge – if one had slipped he would have taken the other two. Had to concentrate as never before and I kept having waves of nausea. I nearly faint every time my hand touches anything and my knee keeps collapsing on me. Agony for me – I have never been in such pain.

Our lives depended on no one slipping. Guy and I kept on glancing at John, pulling in and letting out coils of rope as we moved;

calculating if we could thrust in an emergency ice-axe belay, or if we could jump to the other side of the ridge, should he fall. We acted with unspoken suspicion, as if we were policemen chained to an epileptic on the steep roof of a skyscraper.

'It will be safer if we rope up more closely,' said Guy.

'But then all our weight will come on to the cornice at once,' I said. 'We must spread apart.'

Occasionally I slumped to my knees and rested my head upon my ice axe, summoning all my powers of concentration, trying to recover some strength. When we were halfway along the ridge I felt dizzy, and asked Guy to take over in front. There was little room for John and Guy to manoeuvre past.

'Don't you worry,' said John. 'I won't do anything stupid, I want to give little Joseph a cuddle again.'

We strove towards those we had left behind. It was a universal impulse.

We reached Neuschwanstein at mid-day. Guy and Tim had left a half tin of butter, half a pot of marmalade and a small carton of peanut butter. Within a few minutes, we had eaten the lot – neat. The food revived us a little, and we continued the descent.

We had three ropes between five of us, and there were long waits at the anchors. As the afternoon drew on, our initially optimistic sights for the day's end reduced from Base Camp to Advance Camp, and then to the Nid d'Aigle. I went down first, to find the slings I had left in place ten days before. Guy had the nerve-wracking task of climbing down last. The steep ice below the Vire Neithardt was too difficult to climb down, so we lowered two ropes for an abseil. As I slid down, I was preoccupied with finding the next anchor. Without realising, I went past it. I felt the end of the ropes run through my hands. Instinctively, I clenched my grip. The rope ends were within three inches of slipping through the friction device, and I was within a second of falling 3,000 feet to the glacier. My mind shrugged off the near miss – nothing had happened. I spotted the nylon sling of the anchor a few feet above me, peeping out of fresh snow, and climbed back up the rope to it.

It grew dark when we were 300 feet above the fourth rock tower.

The wind increased with the night, chilling us until we ached with cold. Myself, Tim, Pemba and John descended a ropelength, down a rock slab.

'I'm going to abseil,' shouted Guy. 'It's too dangerous to climb down in the dark.'

I became angry. 'You'll waste too much time,' I yelled. I put my rucksack on a ledge and climbed back towards him. 'It's easy,' I said. Then I felt ashamed. Guy had been taking risks for all of us for many hours. When I joined him he sensed that I had understood his point of view.

'I can't concentrate any more,' he said.

'O.K., I've come to relieve you.'

As I climbed down, I knocked my ice hammer from its holster. It bounced down into the darkness, clattering and sparking against rocks. The others had descended another ropelength. The wind snatched our shouts, playing with them in its eddies.

'Can I come? Are you ready? Are you all tied off?'

Pemba seemed nearest. 'No, O.K.' he shouted.

'What? No, or O.K.?'

Shivering with cold and impatience I detached the rope and started down, shouting 'Abseil down a double rope.' The messages were confused by the wind, and the others had missed an anchor, and only had one rope with them. This they had doubled, dropped over the fourth tower and Tim was abseiling down it.

'But it won't be long enough, Tim. Stop!'

Tim halted on a small ledge, a few feet before he abseiled off the end of the rope. We lowered another one down to him, and he continued to the foot of the tower.

'Pemba, you go first with Tim and start putting the tents up at the camp.'

John was next to disappear down the ropes. A few seconds later there was a terrible scream – and then a long silence filled with the dread of our imaginations.

'Oh God – he's fallen, Guy.'

Then he replied to our shouts. He had pendulumed, smashing his wrist and yelling with pain.

The darkness was total – the moon was behind the mountain and our head torch batteries had all died. We crawled the last 300 feet to the camp on our hands and knees. The rope became snagged, and Guy had to untie and solo along the ridge. 'I've just aged two years in twenty minutes,' he said when he arrived. It was 9.15 p.m.

Inside the tents, we warmed our frozen feet and sipped water. 'He who sleeps, dines,' someone said as we closed our eyes.

The next morning, safety was tantalisingly near. We were tempted to abandon caution and to move quickly. However, the mistakes of the previous evening reminded us to descend in a slow, safe routine. At the col in the first gap that had so confused our earlier forages, we were still undecided as to which was the best way to Advance Camp. Pemba soloed over the ridge, to start melting water at the camp. We chose the bottom, longer and easier way.

Ski sticks marked the top of the snow slope, where we had left them two and a half weeks before. Beside them were flags on two marker poles, still wafting prayers to Tseringma for our safety. We had little strength left, and this last slope stretched before us, an agonising eternity. Guy reached the flags first, and detached one of them, to keep it with him.

John arrived at the Vango tent of Advance Camp before I did. He dumped his rucksack and came down the slope towards me, offering to carry mine.

'Do you mean it?' I asked.

'No,' he said.

We walked the last few yards to the tent together. Pemba had left Advance Camp before we arrived – yearning for the company of his friends of Base Camp. However, he had left some water and an open can of beer. 'Heldenbrau – fit for heroes' – it was solid with ice, and we held it over the stove until it started fizzing. We lay in the tent for four hours, drinking tea and devouring baked beans and Spam. By late afternoon, we had regained enough strength to continue.

The snow was soft and collapsed under our weight, dragging at our feet. The 300-foot plod up to the Notch was, by common assent, the last piece of climbing we wanted to do for a while. Behind us, the massive backcloth of Gauri Sankar glowed in the sunset. Tim was first over the Notch, and descended to Base Camp alone. I shouted to him, but he only paused, hearing just the noise, not the words.

'He could have waited,' I said. 'After all that time up there it would have been good to go down together.'

'I just don't understand him,' said John. 'When I was his age this sunset would have moved me to tears.'

'Oh laissez-faire,' said Guy. 'It will come, in time.'

As we moved over the ridge, the snow yielded beneath the gravity of our downwards steps, no longer hindering us. We strolled down the glacier, breathing deeply and looking around. Now Gauri Sankar was hidden, a remembered presence behind our backs. Our impassive observer for many weeks, the great spire of Choba Bhamare stood black against the dark sky. And then the slope curved away below us, and we saw the tents and prayer flags, copper in the last light, as if burning with inner flames. We paused. These were last moments, tinged with regret — never to be forgotten or taken away. The evening's shadows grew dark and cool.

The Base Camp team came to the toe of the glacier, to greet us wreathed in smiles. John's right hand at least could join in the flurry of shaking.

'Ang Rinzi, me old codger – a face of a thousand stories! Fantastic, a brew. I'll never forget your cups of tea, Ang Rinzi. Good evening, Lieutenant; Dawa, you old drunkard. How about a nosh, been munching painkillers for days – distinctly lacking in calories. Pemba Sherpa, say some prayers of thanks for us; Jetha, you winged messenger – where's the letters?'

We were enveloped in warmth and affection. It was an overwhelming evening, a hectic relocation into a world of food, people, and safety, and the first opening of the door to the life we had left behind. Over the previous days our stomachs had shrunk and we were soon bloated with food and cups of tea. Nevertheless, it felt as if we had more to eat and drink that night than during the whole of the previous week. We had climbed the mountain in a single attempt, and there had been no chance of recovery in between tries, as there had been on Kangchenjunga. We had become worn out gradually. Food, initially planned for four people for fifteen to eighteen days, had eventually been stretched to feed five people for twenty-three days.

Harbouring private thoughts, we hunched around a guttering candle, quickly scanning our letters for news – good or bad. A tel-ex message in a sealed envelope made my heart jump – no, it was all right, it was a greeting from a friend. At first view, my news was reassuring – but of the time-lapse since the letters were last sent I knew nothing. Early in the morning Jetha would leave with news of our success, and Pemba Sherpa would descend to recruit por-ters from Lamobagar.

'I must write a report now to the Ministry,' said Sankar. 'What are the heights of your camps and the dates you reached them? How high is the South Summit?'

The Scheider map had disappeared in the darkness and confusion, so we guessed the answers. It was 1.00 a.m. when I finished writing letters, and much later when my thoughts stopped spinning.

Sleep had carried me elsewhere when at dawn a gust of wind shook the tent, touching my feet like moving ground. I woke with a start, thinking the camp-site was collapsing and we were being blown off the ridge – and then relaxed. The tense, rigorous safety code of high camps, of belays, tie-offs, insulation and measured movements could be forgotten. No, that was not a cornice creaking – Ang Rinzi was making tea, cups of tea unlimited! It was marvellous to be waited on and to get up late. My swollen lips and my eyelids were stuck to-gether. Numb toes – the bivouac; scratched hands – the night-time ice pitch; my body reminded me where I had been. Smelly body, lank hair, piles, dirty clothing, the dank taste of unwashed teeth, all re-emerged after a long exile in the sterility and singlemindedness of high altitude. Body and mind were different up there.

'This is the best Monday morning of my life,' said Guy.

Porridge for breakfast, jam and chapattis for lunch, noodles and sauces for supper, hunks of cheese, fruit cake – the food slid down and we remembered the sensation of taste.

'We must have been really dehydrated up there,' I said. 'I've drunk about twelve pints of tea since we came down, but I've only peed three or four times.

'Where's the wumpum?' asked John.

'Dawa says it's evaporated.'

'Sure, probably in his breath.'

Pemba was humming with happiness. He and Dawa finished the cigarettes and made little wooden pipes to smoke Guy's tobacco. He washed John's hair for him, and cleaned his boots. 'Now your shoe is smiling too,' he said when he had finished.

We had returned to music, and the cassette player was turned on all day. The breeze wafted snatches of music and song around the camp, filling our heads with associated thoughts of home and drawing us into ourselves. We were vulnerable.

Alone in my tent, I read and re-read the letters, slowly.

The struggle on the mountain, although it had affected me profoundly, was self-indulgent and superficial compared to my father's illness, and its effect on him. He had written to me from hospital:

> I suppose everyone reacts differently to a sudden onslaught of illness. I have become sharply aware of the stupidity of previous preoccupations with petty and trivial aspects of life. I am trying to relax and put myself completely into God's hands, as he works through the skill of the people who are looking after me here, and who are praying for me in the most wonderful and loving way.

I wrote in my diary, carefully:

> Human beings can adjust to almost any conditions. Or from a distance, they can appear to have quickly adjusted. The threat or realisation of death guides the mind away from minor concerns to the clarity of religion, strengthening what has always been there.

The recuperative pause was short-lived. The sudden squalls, restrained by the stability of the late summer, at last broke completely free. During the night the wind changed to a hollow, monotone, roaring ceaselessly with the confidence of a newly designed express train. In the early hours Ang Rinzi abandoned the cooking shelter as it collapsed. The Nepali flag was torn away, never to be seen again. 'That was the Base Camp Closing Ceremony,' said Sankar.

The porters trickled in and out of Base Camp with their loads after mid-day on 15 November. Below the rocks we walked on to the cushioning grass, our eyes watering after long exposure to the throb of sunlight on snow. Had it, I wondered, been a year's exposure, and this the only true return?

The noise of the wind that we had left, plucking the mountain high above us, stayed in our heads for many hours, emphasising the contrasting peace and patience of the forest. Slowly, the forest grew in our senses. We stopped for the night, stretching luxuriantly beside a warm fire, smelling the vegetation and the woodsmoke and watching the light flicker on dark, still clumps.

The night's coating of ice on the ground soon melted in the warm morning air. On the mountain we had wound ourselves up beyond minor aches and pains, but now that we were below the itch contour, the jolting of the descent re-aroused them to their restless work. Slipping and sliding from tree to tree, our weak, sticklike frames tottered down, to a polyphony of insects.

The ancient route of trade along the Rongshar was, after the jungle and untracked mountain, like the broad swathe of a Sunday afternoon path through an English wood.

We arrived at Lamobagar at the same time as the fresh early light spread across the flat level ground of the village. Children and old people glanced at us briefly.

Sankar strayed behind us, to change and groom himself in the bushes before the arrival at the police post. His high spirits mirrored those of Mohan after Kangchenjunga.

'You look a bit less glossy than when we were at the last party here, John.'

'You don't look exactly unwrinkled yourself, mate.'

We drank rakshi, relieved to hear that the news of our success had been radioed out five days before. We changed our porters to the lightly-clad Tamangs of the lower hills.

Baskets of oranges coming up the trail were signposts to the fertile south. We rolled the fruit around our mouths. A Tibetan girl accompanied us on the trail. For her, the long trek from the bleak plateau of her homeland to this abundance was a journey to paradise.

In the evening we sipped bowls of fizzy, fruity chang, and ate yams – the first sweet potatoes I had tasted since New Guinea. We soon chewed up a tough old chicken. However, John wished it had not developed its muscles by running to us from Kathmandu first. The joke was too much for Dawa, who was already wobbly with chang and he tripped over the fire. Ang Rinzi fielded him, explaining loyally, 'Too much oxygen for Dawa down here, Captain.'

The sun never became hot in those golden autumn days. In the morning it moved up in a slant and in the afternoon it declined, always low in the sky, reaching us only for a while, even as the valley widened. The river was lower and the leeches had shrivelled away into hiding. A white shrouded corpse was carried down to the water, for the ritual cleaning before cremation. Goats and buffalo passed us on the trail. An occasional light breeze filled the air with flying leaves. Fields whispered drily. Everywhere people were at work, goitred women and little children, harvesting the winter's grain with sickles and storing it high on platforms in trees and on poles.

Next day Jetha rushed along the path towards us with mail from Kathmandu. It was good to hear his squeaky, funny voice – to shake him by the hand. He had been so reliable on this trip when communications had mattered so much. We sat in a sunlit spot beside harvested fields, and read our letters – my last one was Hilary's, posted on 9 November, our summit day. She had spent spring and autumn, the two most beautiful seasons, alone, and described them to me.

One minute at a time, the days grew shorter. We camped at Pikhutu, a beautiful site remembered for a warm swim, and a dying, scalded baby in a primitive world. But the baby had not died, said the people of the hamlet. The family had passed through the village on their way back to their home. We had just missed them. Their departure and return had coincided with ours, to the very day. The baby was healed.

We had come the full circle. Our thoughts warmed to the baby. For the cost of eight pounds we had saved his life. We glowed with self-righteousness, for here was palpable evidence that our expedition was justified. But beneath that glow was awe and humility. It was the baby that had done the surviving – he had found the capacity to cling to life through a long, rough journey, and to struggle back to health from the edge of death.

The following day we climbed out of the valley, leaving the river, a thread of blue below us, stretching into the foothills. At the village Charikot, the syncopated rhythm of drums throbbed in the evening air.

'Is it another festival, Pemba?'

'No, Sir, the bank is having a party. Oh yes – and one thing, the people here, they say, we are not Gauri Sankar expedition, we are too small, we are trekking group.' Climbers and Sherpas all chuckled at the joke.

Gauri Sankar hovered, burnished by the sunset, above the grey twilight struts of its foundations. A cloud drifted between its two summits.

23 WINTER

20-30 November 1979

The aeroplane banked towards the west. In the space of a single eyespan, I saw them, from Dhaulagiri to Kangchenjunga – the snows of the Himalayas, the silvery line that dances on the edge of the world. Six times in seven years I had arrived, climbed in this range and departed. Now the geography was becoming clear, my knowledge becoming connected and I was seeing the relation of these mountains to each other. During those seven years, my eyes had seen east and west, from the stepping-stones of summits, for 1,500 miles. With each new view, the pattern had grown inside me. Now the framework was there, and I would spend a lifetime filling in the gaps. These mountains would always be part of my life.

There was a Buddhist saying: 'Fashion your life from a chain of deeds, like a garland is fashioned from a chain of flowers.' And here was a chain of sunlit mountains above a sea of cloud.

We folded up the white scarves, and ate the oranges that the Sherpas had given to us as parting good-luck gifts at the airport. The expedition was under control. We had paid the wages and debts, the journey home was organised, thank-you postcards sent, the expedition report written, and I had even had a haircut. The surface of my mind could become calm, and something far deeper could rise up. I brooded quietly, away from the others.

Will he die? Will he die whilst I am away? Should I go? I now knew the answer to the first question. Beneath my seat was a sheaf of letters. Before they had known I was safe and returning, brave letters from my mother and Hilary had been open to an optimistic interpretation, they had told me to get on with climbing the mountain, not to worry. On the mountain I had tried to bury uncomfortable, distracting truths.

Then, in Kathmandu, I had opened a recent letter from Hilary, telling me to stay in England on my return, to help my mother shoulder the fearful responsibility of caring for someone so ill, after she had been alone so long. My mother was worried that I would not be prepared to see the deterioration in my father's condition. The realisation that he would die became suddenly conscious. I re-read early letters,, seeing clearly what was guarded, how much they had hidden from me, and how much I had chosen to ignore.

In England, it rained for four days. The trees had long since let go their leaves to the winter. Each evening my mother and I drove through the wet, lamplit streets to the hospital in Manchester.

His face was thin and pointed and his teeth bared in craving for life, yet he was quiet and detached, as if halfway to the quietness that awaited him. He smiled often, reassuringly. Only his eyes were sad, but there was no fear of death in them, only a sadness at seeing his future no longer projected in a world with us – a world he knew he would miss. Fear was a terrible journey, but with sorrow he had at least arrived. We talked of little things, his car, the weather. I looked into his eyes, happy to have survived, to be there. Many things went unsaid, except in our eyes. I tried to think like the mountain, like the earth, and they helped me to balance and stand, fortifying me with their peace. I was supported by the steady weight of the whole journey behind me. The night before he died I showed him a colour poster of Kangchenjunga. 'That's lovely, beautiful,' he said.

Some words are worn down by time to their simplest sense. 'At one with the world.' 'In loving memory.' My mother, brother and I soon found out that though the loss was personal, it was not private. Our emotions were shared, and my mother had not been and would not be alone. My father had known this when he wrote in his last letter: 'It really has been wonderful to receive such a sustained love and concern ... this love is what will endure and be everlasting.'

I flew to Switzerland for the weekend, to see Hilary and to collect my things for a stay in England. There was fog at Geneva and
the take-off was delayed. I had time to think, to come to terms
with my father's death. Why him? Why us? I needed to have
known him better. Grief would persist, an old wound that would
never heal, that would always re-open. But then, why not him?
Everyone, at some time, would have to endure the finality of pain
and suffering – starting with those around you, and then with
those nearest you, and ending with yourself. At first, my father's
death had seemed so special, uniquely affecting my family and
those around. Yet bereavement and death were common experiences which everyone must go through. Life could not be trusted
unless peace was made with death; until life's impermanence and
imperfection was accepted, and that acceptance allowed to heal.

The aeroplane took off, climbing steadily through a barrier of
turbulent cloud.

I, a mountaineer, in the Dionysian fervour of my high youth,
intoxicated with my talents, had climbed mountain after mountain,
pushing the limits of my skill, vanquishing death in a series of
false victories. However, although I had seen death before, I now
saw it as a personal fact, for the first time. I realised there was no
sense in rushing. There was no hurry. There was no mathematical
progression in always climbing harder routes and higher summits.
There was no need to try to fight death off, by shrinking from the
fact and acting as if it did not exist, did not affect me. I had learnt
about motion, but now had much to learn about stillness. I would
find a trusting pace that suited my life and the mountains. I was
calm.

The pilot had a sense of humour: 'Ladies and gentlemen, as I
have explained to you before, there are problems in Geneva owing to ground fog. I have now heard from the control there, that
we cannot land. We have been diverted to Zurich. I apologise for
this. Arrangements are being made to carry you onwards from
there to your destinations. However, we have a consolation in
that the Alps are above the cloud. Now our journey is a little
longer, you will see more of them.'

I was already looking out of the window. Mont Blanc, the Grandes Jorasses, the Dru, the Aiguille de Tour and, yes, the distant Matterhorn, were tranquil in the winter sunshine. I loved them, but not with the trembling shock of first love – that could only recur in echoes and finer shades. But I knew them better. I respected them deeply, understood them a little, and loved them more tenderly. It was the last day of November.

ACKNOWLEDGEMENTS

Eunice Tietjens' poem, *The Most-Sacred Mountain*, appeared in *New Voices* edited by Marguerite Wilkinson for the Macmillan Publishing Company.

ABOUT THE AUTHOR

Peter Boardman was born on Christmas Day in 1950 and became one of Britain's most-respected high altitude mountaineers. He was a mountaineering instructor at Glenmore Lodge in the Cairngorms, and National Officer of the British Mountaineering Council before being appointed Director of the International School of Mountaineering in Leysin, Switzerland.

He was part of Chris Bonington's 1975 Everest expedition, made an almost impossibly difficult ascent of Changabang with Joe Tasker in 1976 and went on to climb Kangchenjunga and to attempt to summit K2, being beaten back by poor weather and exhaustion.

Mount Kongur followed in 1981 and, in March 1982, in a small expedition with Chris Bonington, Joe Tasker and Dick Renshaw, he attempted the previously unclimbed and highly difficult North East Ridge of Everest, where he and Joe Tasker tragically lost their lives.

Peter and Joe left two legacies. One was their great endeavour, their climbs on high peaks with bold, lightweight, innovative methods; the second and more lasting achievement is the books they wrote and left behind. Peter's talent for writing emerged through his climbing career. The success of his first book, *The Shining Mountain,* was immediate in the climbing world and won him wider acclaim with the John Llewelyn Rhys Memorial Prize for literature in 1979. *Sacred Summits*, published shortly after his death, described the climbing year of 1979, the trips to New Guinea, Kangchenjunga and Gaurisankar.